Bob Burns'
Monster Kid
Memories
THE REVISED EDITION

Bob Burns
AS TOLD TO
TOM WEAVER

About the Author

BOB BURNS has been a collector, actor, makeup artist and science fiction activist since he was a boy in the 1940s. He starred as Tracy the Gorilla on television's *The Ghost Busters,* and was involved in the production of the genre classics *It Conquered the World, Invasion of the Saucer Men* and *Aliens,* among others.

Published in the USA by:
BearManor Media
PO Box 1129
Duncan, Oklahoma 73534-1129
www.bearmanormedia.com

ISBN 978-1-59393-223-7

Printed in the United States of America.
Cover design by Kerry Gammill.
Book design by Brian Pearce | Red Jacket Press.

Table of Contents

This book is dedicated to all of the wonderful guys and gals who I write about in its chapters, and especially to my wife Kathy, who has been so supportive of all my endeavors.

Bob Burns

Foreword

by Leonard Maltin

I've spent much of my life around film buffs and collectors, and I've observed that there are two specific breeds: the hoarders and the sharers.

The hoarders may be just as interested in a given subject as anyone else, but their real goal is to be able to say they've got something, even though they have no intention of showing it to you — or anyone else.

The sharers can't wait to show off their goodies. In fact, they feel incomplete unless they're sharing their enthusiasm with like-minded people.

As you can probably guess by now, Bob Burns is one of the latter group. He is unfailingly generous with his time, his knowledge, and especially his world-famous collection of movie memorabilia. I felt as if I'd made a friend the first time I spoke with him (and got to sit in George Pal's Time Machine!) and I'm sure I'm not the only person who's had that feeling of immediate rapport.

Bob represents the very best of fandom, and this has earned him the respect and friendship of many people in the Hollywood community…including fellow fans who've gone on to build substantial careers behind the camera.

I'm so glad that so many descriptions of Bob's wonderful experiences have come together in this book. Now even people who haven't met him in person, but share his love of movies, may come to feel as if they, too, are part of Bob Burns' remarkable circle of friends.

Leonard Maltin is best known as the editor of the annual movie paperback reference Leonard Maltin's Movie Guide. *He appeared for thirty years on* Entertainment Tonight, *and currently hosts the weekly show* Maltin on Movies *for* Reelz. *He has written numerous books and articles about film history, and holds court at* www.leonardmaltin.com. *He also teaches at the USC School of Cinematic Arts.*

Introduction

by Joe Dante

Ever meet someone who reminds you of a particular book or movie, but you're never sure why? Bob Burns makes me think of *Fahrenheit 451*.

Wait a minute, you mutter. Bob Burns, the guy who owns the actual Time Machine and the original King Kong armature and, yes, the simian space helmet from *Robot Monster*? Who met or worked with everyone from Elsa Lanchester to Larry Storch? He reminds you of *Fahrenheit 451*?

Yes. I mean that Bob Burns.

You'll recall that, in the future world of Ray Bradbury's *Fahrenheit 451*, books have been outlawed and a small handful of true believers have dedicated their lives to memorizing the great works of literature. There is a beautiful moment at the end of Francois Truffaut's 1966 movie version where these "living books" pace back and forth in the snow to the strains of one of Bernard Herrmann's most evocative scores, memorizing…becoming a book. That's Bob.

Bob Burns is the first Monster Kid — those perpetual moppets-at-heart who grow up obsessed with monsters and never seem to grow completely out of it. (While this phenomenon seems to have peaked in the early '60s, there are still a lot of us around — some, like Bob and me, lucky enough to get to turn our hobby into a livelihood.)

Bob has been collecting fantasy film artifacts for more than 50 years, and he has shared all of this remarkable stuff with other Monster Kids around the world. He's the big brother of Monster Kids everywhere.

Best of all, Bob has collected memories over a lifetime of knowing and even working with the greats and near-greats of fantastic films. Bob walked with dinosaurs on an Unknown Island, journeyed to the Moon with George Pal, wired theater seats for a Percepto-packed screening of *The Tingler* alongside master showman William Castle (just like the teenage hero of *Matinee*), received the only surviving example of Jack Pierce monster makeup from the great man himself, and became a surrogate son to craggy Western actor Glenn Strange, last of the Universal Frankensteins.

He can tell you about the sweaty ins and outs of working inside a 60-pound gorilla costume (as taught to him by Charles Gemora, King of the Hollywood Apes), or about the time he touched Lon Chaney Jr., with memories of past performances warm enough to elicit a hug from the big man himself.

For those not lucky enough to meet Bob and hear these yarns directly, we have *Monster Kid Memories*, his story as told to fellow movie maniac Tom Weaver. We no longer have to fret about Bob's treasure trove of anecdotes being lost to time; they're captured here in this book, in the same amiably folksy language that Bob uses in person.

Bob Burns. *Fahrenheit 451*. Makes sense to me. Have fun…

Joe Dante is the director of such films as Gremlins, The Howling, Small Soldiers *and* Innerspace.

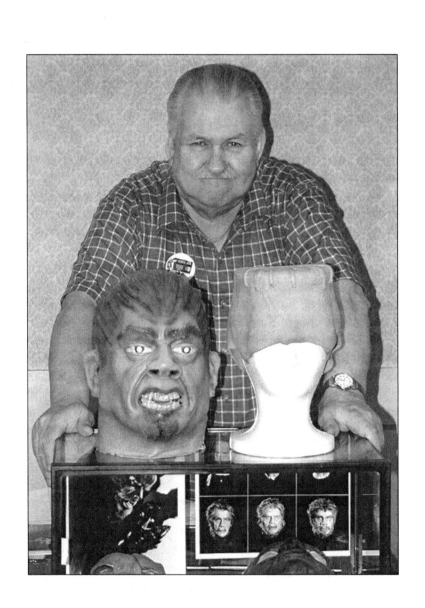

One Lucky Fella

I've been one of the luckiest guys on the planet. The expression "Being at the right place at the right time" really applies to me. As you read the stories in this book, you'll see just how lucky I've been.

First, just a bit of background (I'll keep it short!). My folks moved from Oklahoma out to Burbank, California, when I was six, and I grew up in the shadows of the studios. I met my wonderful wife Kathy in 1953 and we were married in 1956. I worked for CBS for 42 years, first at their KNX radio facilities and then at their TV station KNXT (later KCBS). While working in radio, I ushered shows like Jack Benny and Amos'n'Andy. When television came in, I wound up in the film department.

One of my best-ever "right place at the right time" moments was when Kathy and I met Paul and Jackie Blaisdell at a talk that Ray Bradbury was giving on writing the screenplay for *Moby Dick*. Paul was one of the great movie monster creators of the 1950s. We became best friends and I ended up working as his assistant on films like *Invasion of the Saucer Men*.

I eventually worked my way around to the other side of the camera, playing gorillas (including my favorite, Kogar), mummies, Major Mars and other far-out roles.

But that's not what this book is about. I covered all that in another book I did, *It Came from Bob's Basement*. I mention it only because it's background you'll need for some of the stories that follow.

This book is a collection of the articles that I did with my good friend Tom Weaver for the magazines *Monsters from the Vault*, *Fangoria*, *Chiller Theatre*, *Films of the Golden Age*, *Classic Images*, *Cinefantastique* and *Scary Monsters*. I wanted to pay tribute to a few of the great actors, producers, makeup artists, stuntmen and special effects people that I had the privilege of knowing. Compiling all these articles into *Monster Kid Memories* is our way of having them all together in one volume.

Here are just a few of the people who are represented in this book:

GEORGE PAL, the visionary producer-director who made the incredible science fiction films *The War of the Worlds*, *Destination Moon*, *The Time Machine* and more. ROY BARCROFT, a heavy in hundreds of B films and serials. But he was actually a sweetheart of a guy, and took me to my very first movie set when I was ten years old. How cool is that? CHARLES GEMORA, the best gorilla impersonator in the business. He taught me how to play a gorilla, and eventually that helped to get me a series on television. JACK PIERCE: This incredible makeup artist created the Frankenstein Monster, the Mummy, the Wolf Man and many others. DAVE SHARPE, one of the very best stunt guys in the business. He performed every kind of stunt you could imagine. He doubled for Tom Tyler (in *Adventures of Captain Marvel)* and many other serial heroes. HOWARD LYDECKER. He and his brother Theodore did some of the best live special effects ever put on film. WILLIAM CASTLE, King of the Gimmick Movies — *House on Haunted Hill*, *The Tingler* and many more. What a showman. And, dearest of all, GLENN STRANGE. He was one of the bad guys in countless Westerns but he's probably better known for playing the Frankenstein Monster three times. He became like a father to me.

I'm very happy to have this opportunity to let the world know what wonderful people these folks were.

Yep. I'm a lucky fella.

Bob Burns
Burbank CA

The Republic Thrill Factory

From the time I was five years old, I loved Republic serials. Republic simply had a "feel" for that type of action stuff and they did the top serials around, much better than Universal's or Columbia's or anybody else's. They were the serial kings. All their people and all the different departments worked together so well, it was like a well-oiled machine. Republic had the best production staffs, the best music people and (by far) the best directors — William Witney, John English and all those guys really knew the genre and knew what they were doing. The work they did was just great.

Good guy Dennis Moore gets the drop on malevolent Martian Roy Barcroft in *The Purple Monster Strikes.*

No serial hero, superpowered or otherwise, ever had foes who were more formidable than the Republic heavies. And very few productions — serials or features, for that matter — had better stuntmen and special effects teams. It was my privilege, as a kid (and later a young man) living in Burbank, to get to know Republic's top people in those professions: The top villain, Roy Barcroft; the top effects man, Howard Lydecker; and the top stuntman, Dave Sharpe. As a ten-year-old, I even got to visit the set of a Republic serial.

The Bad Guy

"Bad" guy — ha! Roy Barcroft was one of the sweetest men who ever lived.

It was 1945 and I was out playing in the yard of my parents' house on Brighton Street in Burbank one morning when a guy drove up in a camper truck, parked in front of the house to the right of ours and got out. I immediately recognized him, because even at age ten, I was an old serial and Western buff and I'd seen him 100 times. In those days, I didn't know the name Roy Barcroft, but I certainly knew that strong "character face"!

Roy went up to the door of that house, knocked and was admitted. I was absolutely thrilled. I rushed inside my house and told my mom, "I just saw the guy from the serials! The Western bad guy!" From the window of our living room I watched for him to leave and, as soon as he did, I ran next door to find out why he had been there. Joyce was the name of the daughter of the people who lived there, a beautiful gal in her mid-20s, and it turned out that she was Roy's secretary at Republic; he was popular enough that he needed someone to take care of his fan mail, send out photographs and so on. Joyce and her family had been living by us for years, but I didn't know this about her. "Oh my God," I said, "I think he's the greatest guy...!" Joyce said, "Well, he's gonna be back over in about an hour, to pick up a script. If you want to meet him, I'll bring him over."

In my homemade Spy Smasher costume in the early 1940s.

An hour or so later, I was again looking out the window of my living room, a little scared to go outside, when I saw Roy's camper pull up again. And, sure enough, about ten minutes later there was a knock at the door from Joyce, who said, "Bob, I'd like you to meet Roy Barcroft." Roy was just so nice, right off the bat — "Hey, Bob, glad to meetcha..." and so on — really a good guy. There I was, talking to Roy Barcroft in my own living room! "You know, Bob," he said, "I'm workin' on a thing right now called *The Purple Monster Strikes*." Of course, my ears perked up immediately at *Monster* — I thought, naturally, that it was a monster film. "Would you like to come over on the set and see us shoot? If you'd like to go, I —"

"I'd love to!" I blurted out, not even letting him finish the sentence!

Roy invited me to come visit the set on a weekday, so with my parents' permission I played hooky from school. About seven in the morning, Roy came by and picked me up and took me over to Republic in Studio City for my first-ever day in a movie studio. I was wrong about *The Purple Monster Strikes* being a monster movie, of course; it was about a man from Mars (Roy) arriving on our planet by rocket and, with the help of a gang of Earth criminals, making preparations for the Martian army's planned invasion. It was kind of a forerunner of the "space alien" invasion pictures that would come along in the 1950s.

The first thing Roy did was go in the makeup room, where Bob Mark started making him up as the Purple Monster. I'll never forget one thing Bob did: He glued a rubber band to a half-inch square of fishskin and then glued the fishskin to the outer corner of Roy's left eye, just above his cheekbone. He then repeated the procedure with a second piece of fishskin and a second rubber band on the other eye, and stretched the two rubber bands and tied them off behind Roy's head. (The Purple Monster cowl that Roy wore hid the rubber bands.) The tension on the pieces of fishskin pulled at the edges of Roy's eyes and gave him a slight "Oriental" look. Looking at the serial now, you can see that half the time they forgot to do that, so Roy's appearance changes from scene to scene: Sometimes his eyes are slits, sometimes they're not.

After Roy was made up, they brought his Purple Monster costume out and he put it on. You'd think the Purple Monster's costume would be purple but mostly it was black. The tunic and cowl were made of a gold, metallic-looking material.

Makeup artist Bob Mark used rubber bands to give the eyes of Roy's Purple Monster a slightly "Oriental" look (top). When he *didn't* do it, audiences saw a more recognizable Roy (bottom).

The first of my misconceptions about the way movies were made was about to be shattered: All of a sudden, I saw another Purple Monster come walking by! I was shocked. "Oh," Roy laughed, "that's Fred Graham. My stuntman." I had to ask what a stuntman was. Roy explained, "Why, he's the guy who does all the fights for me." My heart sank a little. This meant that John Wayne, Roy Rogers, none of those guys did their own fights — that's what jumped into my head right away! Roy continued, "Fred does all the hard stuff. It's not that the actors couldn't do it, it's just that the studio doesn't want us to. 'Cause if we get hurt, we could hold up the whole film. We've got the best stunt men in the business over here."

Roy, of course, introduced me to Fred Graham, who was very nice. Since I was just a ten-year-old kid, I think Roy took pleasure in walking me around — I bet it was fun for him too. Then I met Dennis Moore, the hero in the picture. I'd seen him in movies, but I never realized how short he was. At ten years old, I was almost as tall as he was — it was kind of weird! But he was a nice fellow too, and he had the greatest voice in the world. It's a shame he didn't go farther than he did. I next met Dale Van Sickel, who was Dennis' stunt double even though he was quite a bit taller than Dennis was. (But then, look at the great Davey Sharpe. In *Adventures of Captain Marvel*, Davey stunt-doubled Tom Tyler, who was over six feet while Davey was about five-seven. But, unless an audience was looking for it, they would never notice. That's how good the intercutting between actors and stuntmen was in these serials.)

Roy said, "The stuntmen are about to shoot the master shot of a fight scene that Dennis and I are gonna be doing later. Come on, we'll watch it." Following Roy, I walked over to an office set where two cameras were set up. (Republic was the first studio that I know of, that would sometimes use two cameras for a fight scene.) I don't remember who the stunt coordinator was that day, but it could have been Tom Steele; he and Dale Van Sickel alternated. Costumed to look like Dennis Moore and Roy, Dale and Fred Graham did a run-through of the fight. They went through the motions, but without (say) breaking a chair or knocking over the table.*

---

* It's called "choreographing" a fight, and it's something that Republic's greatest director Bill Witney had come up with. In the early, "pre-Witney" days, a fight scene's stuntmen used to just mix it up and wreck the set, and the audience would see lots of cuts that didn't match, But, following a visit to Warner Brothers where he happened to observe Busby Berkeley choreographing one of his big, kaleidoscopic dance sequences, Witney came up with that idea of also "choreographing" serial fights.

Dale and Fred did their run-through, and (by watching them) the camera operators now knew how the fight was going to go. Finally everything was all set, the cameras rolled and the fight began. Dale and Fred went as far as they could go, and then the director called cut. Everything they had broken or knocked onto the floor — chair, papers, file cabinets, etc. — was left right where it fell. Then they started up again and busted the place up some more. Shooting the whole fight took about two and a half hours.

Around midday the company broke for lunch, and Roy and I ate together at the commissary. When we got back to the office set, I could see that it had been cleaned up and

Murderous Martian Roy and henchman Bud Geary have the upper hand over Kenne Duncan in this *Purple Monster Strikes* shot.

redressed; duplicates of the props that had been broken were now in place. The stunt coordinator worked with Roy and Dennis ("Okay, on this shot, Roy swings a chair at you, Dennis…"), and the two of them recreated, in medium shots, a little bit of the action that Dale and Fred had done in long shot that morning. Roy and Dennis did little "pieces" of the fight, but none of the flying-up-onto-file-cabinets or rolling-over-tables, because they might have gotten hurt. It took, I'd say, another couple hours to shoot all the footage of Roy and Dennis, the half-dozen or so inserts of them that would be cut into the master shot of the stuntmen's fight. A couple of retakes were necessary, I recall — maybe there was a punch or two that didn't look quite right to the stunt coordinator, who stood right by the camera and watched everything. Or maybe one of the guys didn't react fast enough. (In a fight scene, the whole thing is the reaction, not the punch. The reaction is what "sells" it.) It was a full day by the time they got done, and everybody was tired…except me. I went home and probably didn't sleep for three nights, I was so excited! It was the kind of wonderful, incredible day where you keep thinking you're going to wake up and it was all a dream — but it wasn't.

When *The Purple Monster Strikes* finally came out, it played down at the Magnolia Theater, nine blocks from my house. I didn't know which chapter that fight was in, so I had to go see the whole serial, week after week. (And it was a 15-chapter one, too!) All my buddies would go with me, and I kept telling them, "It's gonna come up, it's gonna come up" — and it never did. After eight weeks in a row and no fight, I was so disappointed, I was starting to think the scene wouldn't be in it. Then of course Chapter Nine ("The Living Dead") came along and, boom, there it was! I yelled, "There it is! That's it! I was there, I was there!" — and my buddies yelled back, "Shut up! Shut up!" Not only was it one of the best fights in the whole show, but it was also neat knowing which parts were the stuntmen and which parts were Roy and Dennis, and seeing how it was blended.

Another thing that really struck me about that day at Republic was how nice all the people there were to me. Everybody came over and treated me so well that I almost felt like royalty.

Hero Dennis Moore locks horns with Roy at the beginning of the *Purple Monster Strikes* fistfight that I witnessed in person.

I later realized why that had happened: Because I was a friend of Roy's, and everybody loved Roy. *Every*body. Years later, Roy would tell me that the camaraderie at Republic was what he loved so much about the place. "That's why I *stayed*," he said. "I didn't make any money. I was gettin' maybe 400 bucks a week. But I *loved* workin' for that studio." He said he'd worked at other studios all over town, but if he had to pick a studio for his "home," it would have been Republic: "That was the best place and the nicest people."

Needless to say, since I was ten years old when I met Roy, we lost touch afterwards. But we hooked up again when I was grown: In 1960, when I was 25 years old, Glenn Strange and I were at a Western cookout when Roy showed up and remembered me, and we just seemed to take up where we left off years before. Roy and I were friends from that day forward. From then on, he would come over to my place pretty regularly, every other month or so, and we'd talk about the serials and the movies. (Somebody came up with the nickname "Bearclaw" for him, and he'd use it himself: He would knock on the door of my house and growl, "This is Bearclaw! Open up! Open the door!") Kathy had a special tuna recipe that she'd made up, and we served it one day while he was visiting. It became Roy's favorite dish: Every time he came over, Kathy would say, "I got your favorite," and he'd go, "Tuna sandwich!" We always had those for him when he was here, because he just loved 'em.

Roy drove an old camper truck with a weird horn. I'd hear that horn go off and I'd know he was coming even before he walked up to the door and did his "This is Bearclaw!" bit. I still remember a lot of the things he told me about the people he worked with. He had done a lot of Roy Rogers films and he said what a nice guy Rogers was and that he loved working with him. He thought Gene Autry was an ass, that Gene was stuck on himself, but Roy Rogers, he said, "remembered his roots" and thought of himself as the luckiest guy in the world just to be in the business. Rocky Lane was another guy he couldn't stand — he didn't even want to talk about him. According to Roy, Lane was not a nice guy at all.

Later, through Roy, I met another great Republic bad man, Kenne Duncan. Roy and Kenne used to hang out together all the time, they were buddies on-screen and off. They did an amazing number of films together — mostly Westerns, but also a lot of serials where they were both on the wrong side of the law: *King of the Texas Rangers, Haunted Harbor, Manhunt of Mystery Island* and so on. Kenne was a great guy too. Kenne, a Canadian, was brought down to Hollywood by Republic, who planned to groom him and make him a Hopalong Cassidy type. (Kenne was then a good-looking guy who looked a little like William Boyd, and he already had gray hair like Boyd did.) But it never worked out…maybe because Kenne just wasn't that good an actor. Well, Boyd wasn't that good either, but Boyd had a great voice, which helped him out. Kenne wasn't the least bit bitter about it, though; he told me, "I got some mileage and a career in the business out of it, so I didn't care!" Like Roy, he was a sweet man.

Candid shot of Roy Barcroft and the camper he owned for years.

Kenne soon became part of the get-togethers at my place. On one occasion, I borrowed a friend's 16mm print of *The Purple Monster Strikes* and showed it to Roy and Kenne. (Kenne

On the day I showed *The Purple Monster Strikes* to Kenne and Roy, they also perused my copy of the script.

was in it too, playing a scientist in the first chapter.) By then I had come to realize that, back in the days when they were making serials, these guys never had the opportunity to see them. "Some of the movies we'd go and see," Roy told me, "but we weren't about to go 12 weeks or 15 weeks to kiddie matinees for the serials!" These guys had never seen these serials — not one of 'em! We watched the entire *Purple Monster* that night, all three and a half hours worth, Roy, Kenne, Kathy and I, and Roy loved it. His nickname for himself as the Purple Monster was "The Thing in Tights from Boyle Heights," because they shot a lot of it down in that industrial-warehouse area.

Roy and Kenne Duncan in their villainous prime, laying evil plans in the serial *Manhunt of Mystery Island*…

…and years later, during their first joint visit to my home (that's me in the middle).

One of my favorite memories of Roy is the day he gave me the Purple Monster suit. We were in my house talking when *Purple Monster Strikes* came up and I said, "You know, I really loved that outfit. That was cool." He said, "Oh, I got that thing. You want it? I'll give it to you," And he just brought it over the next time he visited! There was no ceremony, nothing at all, just, "Okay. Here it is. I don't know what you're gonna do with it…!" That was the kind of casual guy he was. As usual during the making of a serial, there had been "multiples" of that suit, maybe as many as five or six, and Roy had taken one home one night and never brought it back. Roy was a real smoker, so one of the neat things about the costume is that he'd had them give him a secret pouch on the inside of the belt, to hold his cigarettes. "I gotta have my cigarettes with me, that's all there is to it," he told the costumers, and so they made that little pouch for him. Then, funnily enough, a short time after Roy gave me the costume, he was over by my house and we were talking about the cigarette pouch when he said, "I just remembered, I have the boots for the costume in my camper," and he went out and brought them in and gave them to me. And when he was leaving that day, he told me to come out to his camper, he opened the back door and there was the great original painting of himself as the pirate Captain Mephisto from *Manhunt of Mystery Island*. He was taking it over to give to his son. It looked like he had tons of his stuff in his camper — God only knows what else was in there!

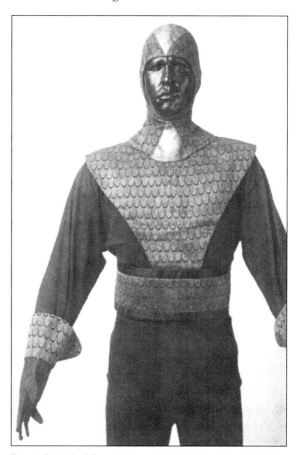

Roy's Purple Monster costume, today part of my memorabilia collection.

I got another great "souvenir" one time when Roy brought over Kirk Alyn, another Republic alumnus (and, of course, Superman in the Columbia serials as well). Kirk was another good guy not stuck on himself, not like the new breed of actors today, just a cool guy. I'd borrowed a 16mm print of the serial *Federal Agents vs. Underworld, Inc.* (Kirk as the hero, Roy as the baddie) and invited the two of them over, and also Glenn Strange. It was another three-hour marathon; we started in the afternoon and went into the evening. Of course, these three guys were also swapping stories back and forth, and it was the greatest thing just to sit back and listen. The stories I remember the best were about the Westerns. The way Republic got the riders to go all-out in their posse chases was, they'd have a bottle of bourbon at the end of it, and the guy who rode the hardest and got there first won the bottle. That's why the posse chases in Republic always looked like these guys were in a mad rush: because they *were*! Then Glenn got onto the subject of one of the Westerns that he and Roy had done. Just before one fast-riding scene, Glenn and Roy had, unbeknownst to each other, loosened the cinch on the other's saddle. (In those days, they used to play practical jokes like that. You can't do it any more at all, because time is money.) Each of them had thought of it and done it independently, and now they were doing the scene, riding beside each other, and looking over at each other and grinning. But of course, neither of them could figure out why the other guy was grinning! The first one to go off was Roy — down he went, crashing to the ground. Glenn was laughing his head off when all of a sudden, *he* went off, and right into a cactus bed! He said he was pulling cactus thorns out of his butt for weeks. And that's when I got my souvenir of the occasion: As Glenn was telling this story, and the three of them were laughing like crazy, I shot a Polaroid picture of them. I still have it today, a shot of these three guys who I admired and loved so much, sitting in my living room, rocking with laughter. The date on the back of the photo: April 21, 1966. Almost 50 years later, it's still one of my favorite pictures in the world and one of my fondest memories.

That's generally how it was when we would get together, the serial guys telling stories and me just sitting there listening to all this crazy stuff. They'd get the greatest kick out of reminiscing about the old days. Today I think, "Why didn't I record all that? Wouldn't that have been the greatest thing, to have them on tape, rambling and talking on?" But I always thought that pulling out a tape recorder and putting a microphone under their noses might wreck it.

Baddie Barcroft and government agent Kirk Alyn duke it out in *Federal Agents vs. Underworld, Inc....*

Kathy got Roy the very last job he ever got. He was at our place one day, saying, "I can't find any work any more. I'm an old geezer…" Kathy was working at the Mirisch Corporation at that time (1969), and they were making the comedy *Gaily, Gaily*. She knew they needed an actor to play a doctor, so she asked Roy, "Do you happen to have a picture of yourself today?" He gave her one, she took it in to work — and they cast him. Kathy and I got to go to the *Gaily, Gaily* wrap party, and Roy and his wife Vera were there too. Roy was like a big kid that night, because everybody who knew him came over to talk to him. I remember George Kennedy coming up to our table and telling Roy how good it was to see him again. It was neat that so many people who knew Roy, or who simply knew *of* Roy, went out of their way to say hello — actors, technicians, whoever. Even the director, Norman Jewison, who told Roy that he was "the best doctor I've ever had" and said he wished the part had been a lot bigger than it was. About three weeks later, when Roy was starting to get pretty ill with bone cancer of the leg, I was talking to Vera when she said, "Roy was so 'down' about not working much any more. You and Kathy did more for him that night than you'll ever know." Kathy always felt very good about that, that she actually helped him out by getting him that part.

Kathy and I knew Roy clear up to the day he died, November 28, 1969. He even donated his body to UCLA — donated it to science. That's the kind of guy he was.

The Special Effects Guy

When it comes to special effects, nobody did it better than Howard and Theodore Lydecker, the brothers who worked their magic on scores of Republic serials. From crashing cars, trains and planes to exploding houses and flying superheroes, they were the best in the business, devising techniques that are used to this day.

The opportunity to meet Howard Lydecker came out of the blue almost as unexpectedly as

...and, 17 years later (joined by Glenn Strange, left), saw this serial for the first time, in my living room.

my first sighting of Roy Barcroft did. In the '60s, my friend Art Ronnie was a publicity man at 20th Century-Fox; Art had already arranged for me to visit the sets of the Irwin Allen TV series *Voyage to the Bottom of the Sea* and now (1966) he was one of the publicity people on Irwin's *Lost in Space*. I loved the show and very much wanted to get a behind-the-scenes look — especially after Art told me that Howard Lydecker was the special effects supervisor on it. "Oh, God," I told Art, "I'd give anything in the world to meet that guy." "Well," Art said, "come on over."

I went out to Fox, where Howard was shooting on the insert stage. Sitting off to one side of the stage was the miniature of the Chariot, the tank-like vehicle seen on *Lost in Space*; it was about three feet long, a good size for a miniature, and it had little rubber figures of the characters in it. It was pretty cool, but even cooler was the miniature of the *Jupiter 2*, the spaceship on the show, which Howard and his crew were working with that day. The *Jupiter 2* was probably almost four feet across and it had batteries in it for the spinning light at the bottom. It was suspended by wires against a black background and they were preparing to shoot a scene where it was in the process of taking off from an exploding planet. During the course of the day, I'd get to see it buffeted around by the puppeteers up above as little off-camera fire bombs and smoke pots were set off below it. Howard had set it up and he was directing the scenes, which I could tell were going to look terrific.

During a break, Art introduced us. For my money, Howard was one of the top effects guys in the world...and, to my delight, he turned out also to be a real sweet man. Tall and gray-haired and quite thin, he was excited that I even knew who he was — he was one of these typical "unsung hero" guys who just "did his thing." At that first meeting, of course, I wanted to talk mostly about the serials. I was interested in the way he flew the Commando Cody spaceships and the dummies of Captain Marvel and Rocket Man, I wanted to know about the miniatures and the explosions and, well, *every*thing. Once he realized what a keen interest I had in this stuff, he was just great about answering every question.

For scenes of aircraft (and people) in flight, he said, don't have wires hanging down. Everybody sees vertical wires. Have 'em horizontal, because people never look for a wire that's

horizontal. That's what he and Theodore did with their planes, the Cody spaceship and all that stuff — horizontal wires. As for the Captain Marvel flying dummy, it was about six and a half feet long, made out of papier-mâché. They created a costume for it, including a cape that was made out of China silk, which is so light that it flutters in the wind a lot easier than anything else. The reason the Captain Marvel dummy was configured like it was (the hands out in front, the slight arch in the body), was because they had little pulley wheels inside the hands and inside the backs of the heels of the feet. A wire went in through the hand and out the heel on the left side; the same on the right; and the dummy could run down those wires like a track. Crew members would get one set of wire ends up to some high point, fasten the other ends somewhere down below and let gravity do the rest.

A detailed Lydecker scale model of a warehouse, before and during its demolition in the serial *The Black Widow*.

For *King of the Rocket Men*, Howard said, they did something that was totally illegal: They climbed up onto one of the big power line towers, tied the wires off up there and then sent the Rocket Man dummy down head first at a 45-degree angle. Also, of course, they could turn the camera different ways, put it on its side, anything they wanted to do with it, and make the dummy look like he was going up when it was actually going down. As long as they had the sky behind the dummy, no one could tell. So in every scene you saw of Rocket Man flying up into the sky, in reality he was going down — but by shooting it with the sky behind him, and by turning the camera at an angle, they made him look like he was going up. It was a wonderful idea. They did the same thing with the airplanes in the classic World War II movie *Flying Tigers* with John Wayne and probably dozens of other pictures.

The Lydeckers always made certain to shoot outside, using sunlight, because you just can't simulate sunlight with miniatures, it never looks right. For scenes of the Commando Cody rocket in *Radar Men from the Moon* and the *Jupiter 2* in *Lost in Space*, they even went on location, out to Red Rock Canyon. That Cody rocket was close to seven feet long — a very big model. But that was another one of the secrets of their success: They knew that, the bigger your model, the better it looks, and the easier time you have with scenes involving water or fire.

When I asked, "How did you get those big mushroom explosions, those big fireballs?," Howard said it was easy. They took weather balloons, filled them with gasoline and then put them inside whatever it was they were going to blow up. The best one they ever did, I think, was a miniature of a warehouse blowing up (seen at the end of Chapter Eight of *The Black Widow*, for one place). That miniature warehouse was pretty big, he told me — about 12 feet long by eight or nine feet high. They took a weather balloon filled with gasoline, put it inside the miniature and set it off, and that's how they got that big. mushrooming ball of fire.

Incidentally, if he were alive, Howard wouldn't appreciate me using the word "miniature" to describe these things he and Theodore and their department made. I remember that I said "miniature" to him and he immediately corrected me: "No, no. Wait a minute. These are not miniatures. These are *scale models*. A scale model is anything that's one inch less than the real object," In other words, if you've got a real ship that's 40 feet long, your scale model can be 39 feet long, or three feet long — it doesn't matter. That used to bug him — he said, "Miniatures are things you have sitting on your desk," and he was right.

Howard and Theodore Lydecker with the Flying Wing scale model from the 1937 serial *Dick Tracy*.

The Lydeckers did the same thing with the scale model cars they blew up, using smaller gas-filled balloons of course. (These were usually pretty good-sized models, maybe two and a half, three feet long.) In those days, they didn't have electronic trigger devices like they do today, so they had to use fuses. Howard said, "We had to determine how long the fuse should be, how many seconds before it would go off." They'd put the balloon in the car, the fuse would be lit, the car would go over the cliff, and by the time it got right to where it was supposed to blow up…it blew up. Howard and Theodore Lydecker were geniuses, to be able to figure all this stuff out on their own.

I was at Fox for most of the day — I went out there about ten o'clock in the morning and stayed 'til about five. Howard must have enjoyed talking with me because he took my phone number, and then a couple weeks later he phoned and invited me to his house. On a weekend I went over to see him at his home in Studio City, right by the old Republic studios. My main memory of his house is not of the two *Flying Tigers* airplanes he had hanging up

The Lydeckers examine the remains of the scale model truck they just demolished.

in his garage, but of what he had in his backyard. Remember the dam they had in a number of features and serials, *King of the Texas Rangers* for one, and the truck that went crashing off the top of it and exploded in mid-air? He had that dam in his backyard. His wife always wanted a waterfall, so that dam was set up in his backyard, as a waterfall. And he had a scale model truck rigged up on top of it, on a pulley wire, "driving" across, backing up and then "driving" across again. It was a cool-looking thing.

I only went to Howard's house once but I talked to him on the phone a few times afterwards. He told me anything and everything about the work they did, not only in the

A Lydecker-designed rocketship comes in for a landing. Notice the arrow pointing to a match on the foreground miniature landscape set.

In the foreground, Cody's rocketship lands on one of the Lydeckers' fantastic miniature sets. The cabin is a scale model. The man walking at the far left (see arrow) is actually hundreds of feet away.

serials but in features like *Flying Tigers, San Francisco* (the MGM movie that recreated the 1906 earthquake), *The Underwater City* and others; he had no secrets at all. He was a great guy, and so appreciative of the fact that *I* was appreciative. Down through the years, he and Theodore (who I never met) just did their work and didn't think much about it. That's why there's really not a whole lot of stills of their work around — Howard said they never even thought about that. They went in, did their jobs and, when they were finished, went on to the next job. I believe the last thing Howard worked on was *Tora! Tora! Tora!*, and then he had a stroke after that — or maybe during. He died a short time afterwards, in September 1969.

On location, a crew member carries the seven-foot Cody rocketship (already attached to its wires) as another man holds the wires on a rod.

You look at some of the stuff the Lydeckers did, and it measures up to anything being done today. Their work was just incredible. I didn't get to know Howard Lydecker as well as I did Roy Barcroft or Dave Sharpe or some of the other serial veterans, but in retrospect that seems to make the time I did spend with the man even more precious.

The Stunt Guy

Davey Sharpe always had to have his cigar. From the day I met him on the set of TV's *The Red Skelton Show* to the last time I saw him, hospitalized at the Motion Picture Home, the cigar was there. It was a habit he picked up in "self-defense" at some point in his legendary stunt career. In the early days, the directors would film his rehearsals — and the footage of those "rehearsal" stunts would sometimes wind up in other movies, movies he wasn't paid for! Friends would tell him, "I saw you get punched and fall off a building in such-and-such a picture," and he'd think they were crazy because it was a film he hadn't worked on. But, sure enough, one or more of his "rehearsal" stunts would be in that movie. He got ticked at that, understandably so. And from that point on, he kept the cigar in his mouth during the rehearsals so that no one would shoot and use that footage. Finally, when it came time to actually perform, he'd hand the cigar to somebody, do the stunt and then get his cigar back. That was how he put a stop to that.

Davey was the king of the Hollywood stuntmen, nobody else could touch him. The way he threw a punch, the way he took a punch, his incredible leaps and dives — there was no mistaking a Dave Sharpe stunt, once you'd seen a few of his movies and marveled at his technique. He began his stunt career at age seven, being tossed in the air in a Douglas Fairbanks silent. By 1952, *Life* magazine reported, he had already filled in for heroes in more than 3000 films without a major injury. (At that point, no insurance company had ever given him a policy.) He was known as the Crown Prince of Daredevils but he was more than a stuntman — he also played leads in serials, shorts and features, including the Range Busters Westerns, and worked as a stunt coordinator and second unit director. He did some of his most amazing work in the Republic serials, stunt-doubling for the heroes in *Mysterious Doctor*

Davey doubled for Gene Kelly's D'Artagnan in the 1948 MGM version of *The Three Musketeers.*

Satan, Drums of Fu Manchu, Spy Smasher, Adventures of Red Ryder — even standing in for the hero *and heroine* in *Jungle Girl* and *Perils of Nyoka.* And the most amazing of the bunch, *Adventures of Captain Marvel.*

The first time I met him was on the *Red Skelton* set in 1967 or '68. He did that show for five or six years, playing the recurring character of an old man (and sometimes lady) in a wheelchair who'd always be taking a tumble or falling out of a second story window. Every time you saw a frail old person come on that show, you knew the whole building was gonna fall on him or something like that! One day Charlie Dugdale, the announcer at KNXT-TV where I worked, asked me, "You want to go over to Television City for the 'Skelton Dirty Hour'?" (That's what they called the rehearsals for the Skelton show — Red could get very blue!) It sounded like a lot of fun so I went over with him. On the set, Charlie asked me, "Would you like to meet Dave Sharpe?" (Turns out Charlie knew Dave from a dog club they both belonged to.) I almost fell out of my chair. I blurted out, "Dave Sharpe…?! He's my idol!," which Charlie took as a yes.

During a break, I got to meet Davey — that day, he was made-up as the old lady, with the wig and all. Of course I mentioned that I knew Roy Barcroft and Glenn Strange, and he responded just the way I knew he would: "Those are two of my favorite guys." We had about a half-hour talk there on the *Red Skelton* set, and as it wrapped up, I said I'd love to get together with him again. When I told him I lived in Burbank, he said, "I do too. On Rose Street." I said, "I live a block away!" He gave me his phone number and said, "Give me a call."

I did call and invited him over, and one afternoon he walked to my place. I was now seeing him out of the old lady get-up and he looked almost exactly the same as he did in the serials I grew up with; outside of his hair being gray, he simply hadn't changed. Of course we got to talking about his career, and I kind of put my foot in my mouth when I told him that, whenever he did a stunt in a movie or serial, I was always able to pick him out. All of a sudden he got a little standoffish — he almost got mad. He said, "Well, I must not be doing my job right then, if you can always tell when it's me, and not John Wayne, or whoever."

"No, no, no — that's not it at all," I said, trying to get out of the hole I'd dug for myself. "It's just that I'm such a diehard fan of this stuff that I started studying your techniques. You have a way you punch and so on, and I think it's the best I've ever seen. So I started paying close attention and 'still-framing' stuff, and I finally could see who it was. Because I just had

THE REPUBLIC THRILL FACTORY   27

to know who it was that was doing all those incredible stunts and leaps and things." Once I explained that to him, then he was totally cool about it. But for a minute there, I think I'd actually made Hollywood's #1 stuntman think he wasn't doing his job!

We talked about *Captain Marvel* and *King of the Rocket Man*, two of my favorites. He doubled Tristram Coffin as Rocket Man in the takeoff and landing scenes, and also in most of the fights. (Tom Steele did some of it, but Dave said he did the majority.) He said, "Of course, the reason I did Captain Marvel and Rocket Man is because I was a gymnast." In fact, it was Davey who came up with the first miniature trampoline and used it when he

Tom Tyler as Captain Marvel gets ready for takeoff as Davey watches from behind a reflector.

Dave Sharpe, stunt double for Tom Tyler in *Adventures of Captain Marvel*, with his everpresent cigar.

did those great takeoffs in *Captain Marvel* and *Rocket Man*, running toward the camera and then leaping up and out of sight. They've since started making them for home use, you can get 'em all over the place now, but he actually cooked up the idea because he needed to jump high enough to get over the camera. "I'd bounce off of it, go over the camera and grab a horizontal bar that we'd have set up over the camera. I'd grab it, pull my legs up, swing over the camera and then drop down on the other side."

He also mentioned that he'd recently done a Western called *Day of the Evil Gun* with Glenn Ford, and it was playing at the nearby Magnolia Theater. "I'm gonna go up and see it tonight — you wanna come with me?" Sure! The inside story on that picture was, the director Jerry Thorpe had called Davey and said, "I don't have much of a budget, but I have a lot of stunts with Indians and cavalry guys getting shot. Can you stunt-coordinate and do the stunts?" Davey said he would. And, sure enough, every time you see a nondescript character get killed in that picture, whether it's an Indian or a cavalryman or whoever it is, it's Davey.

Once you know that and can recognize him, it becomes hilarious. They also gave him a walk-on as a cavalryman — he blurts out one line, then immediately gets shot with an arrow and crashes through a window into a building! It was a lot of fun watching that picture at the Magnolia and knowing, every time anybody fell off a building, or a horse, or *any*thing, that it was the guy sitting next to me. After a couple of death scenes, he cracked me up by saying, "You'll notice my scenes are short. Very short!"

At some point he told me, "You know, I've never seen one of my serials." Here again, he simply didn't have time to go to the theater every Saturday. I said, "Well, I can get a-hold of one of the Dick Tracys." "A Dick Tracy? Y'know, I reeeally liked the Dick Tracys for some reason." That was all I needed to hear. I borrowed a 16mm print of *Dick Tracy vs. Crime, Inc.* from a friend and, one afternoon three or four weeks after *Day of the Evil Gun*, he came over to my house again, this time bringing along his niece and nephew, who were eight or nine years old. "You're gonna see some of Uncle Dave's work here," he told the kids.

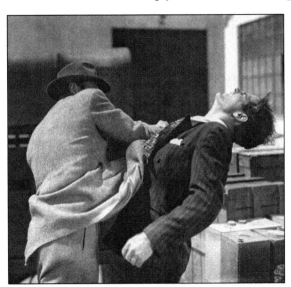

I ran the whole thing for them just like I'd run *Federal Agents vs. Underworld, Inc.* for Roy and Kirk: We started in the early afternoon, took a break for lunch and then watched the rest. He pointed out to me all his stunt stuff ("Okay, I'm gonna do this leap off here…," "That's me as the bad guy in this fight scene…"), and he told me that this was the only time he was injured. In one scene, he had to dive into a harbor — and he got an ear infection because it was so polluted! He said. "That was my one injury, and not even from doing the stunt!" He enjoyed seeing the serial, a long 15-chapter one, and after it was over he said, "Well, now I know why we put so much work into these things [the serials]. I couldn't figure it out before." He thought they were like features, and so he couldn't understand why they worked on 'em so much longer!

Davey and I kept in touch after that. talking on the phone and bumping into each other all the time at Foodcart, a little grocery store down at the end of Magnolia. Then in 1975, I had him over one more time and showed him *Spy Smasher*, and he loved it. He said that was a fun serial to do, and that Kane Richmond was a sweetheart of a guy. "Of all the hero guys I ever worked with," Davey said, "*he's* the guy that *I* actually looked up to. He was a good-looking guy, he was good at what he did, and he made a perfect hero. A couple of the other guys I've worked with, big stars, big 'hero' guys…Naaah. I won't even *tell* you about 'em." He wouldn't tell me the names, because he obviously wasn't happy with them! "But Kane was great," he said.

Davey's exaggerated reactions to movie punches make him a cinch for serial devotees to spot even in the thick of the action, as in these two shots from *King of the Rocket Men.*

By 1975, Davey Sharpe was already living with Lou Gehrig's Disease; he'd first noticed the symptoms a few years earlier, during the making of *The Life and Times of Judge Roy Bean* with Paul Newman. By the late '70s, it had gotten so bad that he was living at the Motion Picture Home. I went out one time to see him in the Home, and it was heartbreaking. It'd be heartbreaking to see *any* friend in that condition, but especially a guy like Davey, who all his life was such a strapping, physical man. It's a shame that a heart attack couldn't have killed him; with Lou Gehrig's Disease, his body just rotted away, literally, with that great, indomitable spirit still trapped inside it. Once I saw him out there, I knew I couldn't come back a second time. He could barely talk, and he couldn't move…but he was still smoking his cigar. He had a guy there with him who put the cigar in his mouth. He finally passed away on March 30, 1980.

I went to Davey's funeral, which was held at a mortuary in Burbank. Most of the old stunt guys who were still alive were in attendance, some in wheelchairs. Tony Curtis, who was doubled by Dave in most of his action films, gave a wonderful eulogy. Dave wasn't actually there, but they had a big photo of him in his best Western finery, in a frame with his gun

Executing one of his "patented" acrobatic leaps, Davey (doubling for Clayton Moore) takes out an Arab heavy in *Perils of Nyoka*.

Davey Sharpe, dressed at Rocket Man, bouncing off of his miniature trampoline and reaching out for the horizontal bar to make sure that he clears the camera.

My serial stunt hero Davey Sharpe and I in a June 1975 photo.

belt hanging around it. It was a very bittersweet event. It was easy to tell how much he would be missed.

An image of Davey Sharpe, incapacitated at the Motion Picture Home — that wasn't the image I wanted to have "stay" with me. The lasting image I have of Davey is the way he looked on June 29, 1975, the day he came over to my place and we watched *Spy Smasher*. We had just finished running it and we were now standing in my living room when he took the cigar out of his mouth and, with a "Here, hold this," handed it to me. I took his cigar from him and, to my delight (and amazement!), he did a back flip — the exact same, marvelous back flip he did doubling Tom Tyler in Chapter One of *Adventures of Captain Marvel*. And he was well into his sixties by then! "Here, hold this," a back flip, and then he reached out to take his cigar back. "God," I gasped, "you can still do that?"

"I do at least five of those a day," he grinned casually. "Keeps me in shape."

That's the lasting memory I have of Dave Sharpe.

As usual with me, it was the dumb luck of being at the right place at the right time that enabled me to strike up friendships with the great old Republic serial guys. There I was, a ten-year-old kid, and Roy Barcroft shows up next door…what were the chances? Or of being invited to a Red Skelton rehearsal where Davey Sharpe was on hand, or having a fondness for *Lost in Space* that led to a meeting with Howard Lydecker? It certainly was not talent or hard work that got me those opportunities — I just happened to be there. And, luckily for me, they were all really swell guys, every one of 'em.

Davey doubling Kane Richmond as Spy Smasher dives in pursuit of a baddie fleeing in a motorboat.

Above: Doubling for Jack Mulhall, Davey makes a flying leap at bad guy Duke Taylor in *Dick Tracy vs. Crime, Inc.*

Left: Davey springs into action as Rocket Men. (Note the soft mesh face plate.) Right: The miniature trampoline helps Commando Cody stunt double Dave soar high enough to grasp the horizontal bar.

My Visit to *Unknown Island*

Ellis Burman, the man who helped me begin my photo and prop collections, in his amazing workshop.

Watching the making of *Unknown Island* was the second time I was ever on a movie set. The first time was on *The Purple Monster Strikes* in 1945, then *Unknown Island* in 1948 and George Pal's *Destination Moon* in '49. Wow, how lucky a kid was I, to be in all those right places at the right times? Imagine being 13 years old and being invited out into the desert to watch dinosaurs fight. It was like dying and going to Heaven.

In 1948, I was going to Edison Elementary School with "Sonny" Burman, the son of Ellis Burman, a Hollywood prop maker. Ellis had two sons, "Sonny" and Tom Burman, who are now both makeup artists. I was 13 in 1948 and "Sonny" was about the same age, maybe a year or two younger. As I got to know him, I found out that his dad made props and that his studio was only about five or six blocks from my folks' house. I lived on Brighton Street in Burbank and Ellis Burman's studio was on Orchard. "Sonny" would talk about his dad once in a while, and one day he said his dad was doing dinosaurs. I said, "Oooh, that sounds cool. I'd love to see it," and he asked, "Well, do you want to come over to Dad's shop?"

One day after school, "Sonny" took me over to his dad's studio. Ellis' studio wasn't a Quonset hut but design-wise it sort of looked like one. It was a big building just off of an alley. And the first time I went over there, Ellis Burman and his crew were working on the dinosaurs from *Unknown Island*.

After that, I started going over to Ellis' by myself. Ellis was a big, robust guy — not heavy-set, but a big man. Wore glasses. And, oh, he was just so nice to me. I know I bugged him to death, I *had* to — I asked him a million and one questions. As soon as I saw all this stuff, I wanted to know all about it, beginning with the *Unknown Island* dinosaurs. On my second or third visit, Ellis gave me the first movie still I ever owned: He had made the Monster's rubber headpieces for *The Ghost of Frankenstein* and he had a handful of photographs, including an 8x10 proof picture of Lon Chaney as the Monster that he gave me. A little later, the very first prop in my collection, the wolf's head cane from *The Wolf Man*, came from Ellis. I used to see it sitting on a shelf in his studio — it didn't have the stick attached any more. I'd always pick it up and look at it, because I loved *The Wolf Man* even as a kid. One day Ellis said, "You really like that," and I said, " 'Like it'? I *love* this thing." And he said, "Ahhh, it's yours. Take it." It was that simple. I was dumbfounded — completely speechless. I knew the movie so well, and of course that's a pretty prominent prop. That "planted" something in me, I guess, because later on I began collecting movie props and artifacts like that.

It wasn't until recently that I began to fully realize how instrumental Ellis Burman was

"Dinosaurs" converge on a fallen native sailor during the Palmdale location shooting of *Unknown Island*.

in getting me started, how important that man was in my life. There were a lot of "firsts" with Ellis: He allowed me in to see the great *Unknown Island* dinosaur suits, he started my still collection and he started my prop collection. It was quite an education. Plus, as I said, he was just a delightful man. I think he got a kick out of the fact that I was that interested. "Sonny" at the time really wasn't. That's just how kids are: When your dad's in the business, sometimes the kids don't care. But for an outside kid like me, it was like, "Oh, wow! If only my dad was doin' this…!" I hung around as much as he'd let me. And he always let me. I could go over any time I wanted.

All throughout these early visits, Ellis and his crew were building the *Unknown Island* dinosaur suits. Of course, liking dinosaurs as a kid, I thought those suits were the coolest things ever. For that project, he had seven or eight people working at his studio. I think they were just there for the one movie, because I was over there a couple of times when Ellis was working on other projects, and on those occasions he only had a couple of guys in there. The molds for the dinosaur heads were gigantic because they had to be about half-again bigger than the dinosaur heads themselves. In other words, if the dinosaur head was four feet long, the mold would be around six feet long. They were pretty incredible to me — I'd never seen molds before, and I didn't even really know what they were.

The dinosaurs suits were already built by the time I saw them, so I don't know exactly how they were made. Seems to me there were five of them. The suits were made of canvas, or a canvas-type material, and then rubber "dinosaur skin" was glued on top of it. Ellis had the suits hanging up in his shop: Cables came down from the ceiling and looped around the necks of the dinosaur suits, holding them up. They looked like dinosaurs hanging from the ceiling by their necks!

Ellis and his crew also made a mechanical fin-back lizard that I saw in the shop. With the tail, it was probably close to eight feet long, about the size of an alligator. I never saw it

The *Unknown Island* actors, in front of the studio rear projection screen, react to the footage shot in Palmdale.

work until I saw the movie at my local theater. It had motors that made the legs move back and forth, but to make it actually move in the movie, it was pulled by a cable. (Without that cable, it wasn't going anywhere!)

One day Ellis said they were going to go out to Palmdale in about a week and shoot all the dinosaur scenes for *Unknown Island* — and he asked me if I wanted to go. "Oh, yeah!" I said instantly. I immediately remembered my experience with *The Purple Monster Strikes*, the thrill of being on that set — and now here was a chance to see monsters work! I had to ask my parents' permission, of course — for one thing, I'd be skipping school that day in order to go. I told them I had a chance to go out and see these dinosaur scenes, and they were pretty good about things like that. They could see how excited I was, so I was "sick" that day as far as school went.

It was probably about seven o'clock in the morning when we set out for Palmdale. (I hadn't slept the night before, I was so excited.) I went with Ellis and his crew — five or six cars convoyed out, and I rode in the car that Ellis was in. It was just so cool. Palmdale is 70 or 80 miles from L.A., out in the desert. Today that area is pretty much built-up, but back then, a desert is what it was. The camera crew must have gone out there in their trucks a couple hours earlier, because by the time we arrived, probably about eight, all the equipment was there already. Those guys had all the reflectors set up, and they put up a couple of tents so people could get out of the sun now and then if they needed to. The dinosaur suits were already out there, and so were the fake bones you see in one of the dinosaur scenes. I never got that close to them, but it looked like they were made out of plaster. And I think there were some real bones, too — I remember seeing a real cow skull sitting around.

They also had some extras out there to play natives and, of course, the fellows who were going to get into the dinosaur suits. They were just extras, not stuntmen — not as far as I know, anyway. The poor guys…! Those dinosaur suits had to be some of the most uncomfortable monster suits anyone ever had to wear. The whole back of each suit would open up and the guys got into them through that opening. Each guy would literally climb in, like getting inside of a sack. He would put his feet in there, and then get the rest of his body into the thing. I didn't try one on because I was too small, but they had to be really heavy — these things were eight, nine feet tall! Inside each suit was a padded brace that sat on the wearer's shoulders, to take care of that weight up above. Say an average guy is six feet — well, the suit still towered a couple, three feet over his head. And once they were in there, Ellis' crew then laced the suits shut. The suits didn't zip up, they tied up the back, along the spine. The dinosaurs' backs had spiny ridges going down, and those hid the laces. It took at least 20 minutes to get these guys in these suits — and then they would just stand there in them.

This was in the summer and, *oh!*, it was hot. I mean, it *is* the desert! And these fellows were in the suits for three or four hours at a time. It was rough, *really* rough on them. And you know they probably got paid diddly, too. I've got to say that they were troupers — I don't know if I could have taken it. But here I was, a kid, thinking, "God, I'd love to be in that suit."

The arms of the guys in the suits weren't in the dinosaur arms — the dinosaur arms and the head were up above their heads. So to work the little teeny arms of the dinosaurs, the guys inside would pull on some wires. The arms didn't do much, they'd just wiggle. The dinosaur mouths had springs in them; the guy inside would pull down on a cable and that would open the mouth. Then when they'd let go of the cable, the mouth would close. Almost like a ventriloquist's dummy-type of situation. But half the time, the mouth wouldn't go back exactly right, it would end up off-center. That looked a little weird!

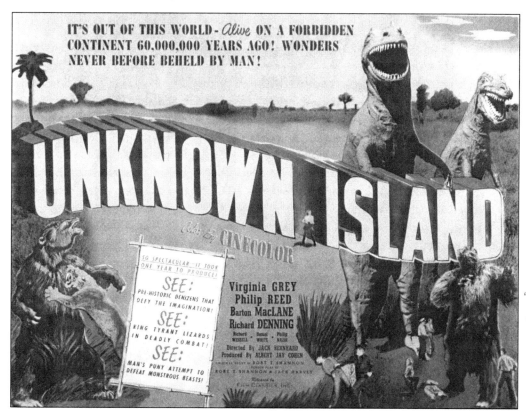

"See Man's Puny Attempt to Defeat Monstrous Beasts!" This hype-filled lobby card promised the prehistoric world.

What a cool experience for me: Here I was, watching dinosaurs walk around! But it was probably 100, 101 degrees that day, and the guys were dyin' in these suits — it was just like being a real hot tent, taped up inside of it, and you can't get out. Needless to say, they couldn't sit down in those suits between takes, so what each one of them did when they needed to rest was to just literally lean on one of the prop guys. Several of the crew members, grips and people like that, would walk out onto the desert "set" and bend over slightly and a dinosaur would lean on them. On this page you'll see a photo of a couple of those guys with dinosaurs leaning on them, and it looks like some weird mating ritual

The bizarre mating ritual of man and dinosaur? The Palmdale heat takes its toll on the men in the rubber suits.

between dinosaur and human! Very strange! But that was the only way these dinosaur guys could rest for a few minutes.

As these guys were getting in and out of the suits, they'd be bitching. They didn't have any ventilation in there whatsoever, and once they got in the suit, they were totally blind — they couldn't see anything. Whoever the director of this second unit was, I remember him saying to his "dinosaurs," "More action! More action! Move around more! More animation!" Well, the dinosaurs couldn't do *anything* — all they could do was stomp, make the mouth open and close, and wiggle those hands a little bit. Those suits were pretty much immobile.

When the camera crew had to do new set-ups, Ellis' crew would open the dinosaur suits up and give the guys inside some water. If they hadn't, those guys would have *died*, they really would have. People talk about animal cruelty — what about *human* cruelty?! Sometimes these directors tend to forget there's a guy in a suit there. They think it's some sort of animal, and then they don't think about it any more! They'll just leave you there for hours, unless you say something. That's one thing that Ellis Burman was great about: He was worried about his guys and he was real good about making sure they were okay. He'd say, "These guys are in big hot suits, man. We gotta hurry up. Those guys are suffering in there." They were extras, but they were in Ellis' suits and he wanted to take care of them. Ellis was just an incredibly nice man.

In a couple scenes, the dinosaurs were being shot at and having grenades thrown at them. The "bullet hits" on the ground around the dinosaurs were done with an air gun and clay pellets — the clay pellets "puffed up" when they hit. For the explosions, they had a "powder guy" (a pyrotechnician) who would bury the charges a little bit and then set them off, kicking up a lot of dust and dirt. Of course, the dinosaur guys couldn't see anything, so the powder guy and his assistant made sure that they (the dinosaur guys) weren't too close to the charges. Most of the charges go off in front of the dinosaurs, far enough in front that it looked good but there was no danger to the guys in the suits.

In the movie, some of the long-shot explosions are followed by a closeup of a dinosaur getting hit with a lot of dirt. To get that effect, they had a guy throwing dirt at them! It was either a sack or a bucket he was using and he was just slinging the dirt around. I remember

"I want a nice, clean fight": Giant sloth and dinosaur square off in the Palmdale desert.

seeing them doing that and not knowing what they were doing — seeing it live, I had no idea what was going on half the time. In fact, I thought maybe he was doing that to try to cool them down.

While they were shooting, while the camera was rolling, one of the dinosaur guys actually fainted. A couple of dinosaurs fall over in the movie, but you can tell which fall I mean if you can tell a "stage fall" from a real fall. In a stage fall, the guy kind of sllllowly goes down. In a real fall, the guy goes over, *plop* — very unceremonious! These guys were dehydrating all over the place, and that's why this one guy fainted — he had heat prostration, obviously, and just fell over. And they used the shot in the film anyway! It was just too hot, and he got overheated.

That happened to me when I played Tracy the Gorilla in the TV series *The Ghost Busters* — I fell over twice! It just happens. These guys on *Unknown Island* were fairly thin, gangly guys — a heavy man couldn't fit into one of those suits — so they probably weren't the strongest guys in the world. And, being extras, not stunt guys, they weren't prepared for that kind of activity. It was not an easy job; the more I thought about it later, the more I came to realize that. (And then when I started doing stuff in suits, I *really* had respect for those guys then!) After the "dinosaur" fainted, and after they got the take and the director yelled cut, two or three crew guys ran out onto the "set," opened up the back of the suit and got him out of it and put him in the tent. He was okay after that, but I don't think he worked any more that day.

They also had Ray "Crash" Corrigan, the cowboy actor from the 1930s, out there to play the giant sloth. He was a very big man, probably 6'5" at least, On top of being a cowboy actor, Corrigan owned his own gorilla suits and played gorillas in movies; he'd found that that was a good sideline occupation to have, when he wasn't doing a Western. He didn't make the suits himself, he had them made, and he owned four or five different ones. For Corrigan to play the prehistoric sloth, Ellis had taken one of Corrigan's gorilla heads and rebuilt it a little, adding some tufts of hair and some weird ears to make it look more "prehistoric." Ellis also gave him three-fingered hands instead of his gorilla hands. It was hot in that gorilla suit, so

Ray Corrigan's gorilla suit was modified to make him look like a prehistoric sloth.

Corrigan suffered greatly too. And the fact that he was drinking a bit didn't help matters. He had a thermos there, and you knew what it was full of! He didn't really complain that much, but he was having a lot of problems because of the heat. At least he could pop the head off, and that helped a little bit. The poor guys in the dinosaur suits had no ventilation at all because the heads didn't come off of those.

Corrigan didn't have too much to do in the picture outside of one scene at the end where a dinosaur attacks him and he bites at the dinosaur's neck. Ellis had a bloody red wound appliance, with bits of flesh dangling off of it, which was glued onto the dinosaur suit. Then they bloodied up the sloth's face a little. That was about it — Corrigan and the dinosaur didn't do a whole lot, there wasn't too much to the fight. I have to give a lot of credit to the editor, Harry Gerstad; in the cutting room, he made it look like something was really happening! He saved that whole fight sequence with the way that he cut it.

They shot until the sun went down, and we probably didn't get back to Burbank 'til eight or nine. Needless to say, I was jazzed. I went home and immediately told my folks everything — "Oh, it was the greatest thing! I saw these big dinosaurs!" And of course, the next day at school, that was "the buzz" with me — I told all the other kids about it. It was funny, "Sonny" Burman didn't seem to care that much about it — but, since he was around it all the time, evidently it wasn't any big thing for him. "Sonny" grew up to become a very good makeup artist, with credits like *Gargoyles*, *Outbreak* and *Star Trek: Deep Space Nine*.

As far as I know, *Unknown Island* was the only movie Ellis Burman ever got screen credit on even though he worked on literally hundreds, making props and different things. *Unknown Island* was, I'm sure, one of his biggest on-camera jobs, making those dinosaur suits and the fin-back lizard and everything else he did. At that point in time, not too many people had done any of that stuff. He was one of the first to make whole big, complete dinosaur suits. The 1940 *One Million B.C.* had a T. Rex that was a guy in a suit, but I have no idea who built it. That's the only earlier one I can think of.

Watching them shoot that day in Palmdale, I thought the dinosaurs looked neat. Not until I saw the movie at a theater in Burbank did I realize that they didn't look quite as good as I thought they did in person. In the film, in closeups, you can obviously see that the eyes aren't moving at all (which I never even noticed when they were shooting), you can sometimes see the mouth not quite going back in the same position and so on. Those things are in the film when you see it. But seeing them live, it looked totally different. These looked like dinosaurs walking around to me, and I just loved them. I still like the "look" of them, and think they're cool. To see them on the screen, and to know I was actually standing out there when they shot those scenes, is still very exciting.

I was there thanks to the kindness of Ellis Burman — such a sweet man. It was one of the big thrills of my life.

Ray Corrigan in his gorilla suit in a shot from the Western *Come On, Cowboys!* with Shirley Temple lookalike Anne Bennett.

A dinosaur cutout is perched atop a special display trailer—part of the *Unknown Island* promotional campaign.

A Giant Called "Pee Wee": Glenn Strange

For close to half my life now, fans have been asking me what Glenn Strange was really like, and I'm not sure I've yet been able to properly, adequately put it into words. This was a man I loved so dearly that he became, in my mind, a father figure — in fact, I actually was closer to Glenn than I was to my own dad. This book is a tribute to many of the genre greats who befriended me in my lifetime but if I could only have gotten to know *one* of them…that *one* would have to be Glenn Strange.

Being a B Western fan right from childhood, I saw Glenn on the screen every few weeks at the kiddie matinees, some in Oklahoma theaters but most of them at the Magnolia, the Major and the Loma in Burbank. At first, naturally, I didn't know Glenn's real name, or the real names of any of the other heavies who, week after week, tried to match guns with Hopalong Cassidy or Tex Ritter or the Durango Kid. But after a while I was finally able to start connecting names in the credits to the recurring faces in the films, and I figured out which one Glenn Strange was. Then too, of course, Glenn played the Monster in *House of Frankenstein* and *House of Dracula* and made a big impression on me in that role. I thought he was the strongest Monster, and he had that great, lined, craggy face that gave his Monster so much character. When Glenn "turned it on," he really looked angry — that great shot in *House of Frankenstein* when he goes after Daniel the hunchback, for instance. Plus, he was just so darn big and tall.

Glenn played the Monster a third time in *Abbott and Costello Meet Frankenstein*; like the *House* films, this one featured the Wolf Man (Lon Chaney Jr.) and Dracula (Bela Lugosi) along with the Monster. To help promote *Abbott and Costello Meet Frankenstein*, Glenn and Bela performed in a

Glenn "Pee Wee" Strange in the early 1930s, when he was a member of a singing group called The Arizona Wranglers.

midnight spook show at a few of the theaters that were playing the movie, appearing in a stage presentation with an illusionist called Dr. Silkini.* I had the great experience of seeing Glenn, Bela and Dr. Silkini do their spook show at the Orpheum, a very ornate theater in the heart of L.A., one summer night after the showing of the movie. This was the first time I saw Glenn in person.

The Orpheum played *A&C Meet Frankenstein* just once a night (they showed a different film the rest of the day, to make the *A&C Meet Frankenstein*-spook show package seem special). I'd already seen the movie about a month earlier, when it first came out; I think I saw it about five times during its original theatrical run. To my mind, the Monster looked even better in it than he had in the *House* films. I certainly don't mean to put down Jack Pierce, who did the Monster makeup in the *House* movies; it's just that makeup techniques had really advanced by 1948 with the introduction of foam rubber appliances, which were now being used for Glenn's Monster. As for Glenn's performance, I thought the comic touches he brought to the role were really funny as they fit so well in the context of the film. It was also nice that Glenn's Monster got to do more here than he did in both of the *House* films put together.

The spook show came after the movie in order to begin closer to midnight — "the witching hour." Wearing the traditional magician's attire, a tuxedo, Silkini came out first and did a number of his tricks, sawing a woman in half and so on. Silkini's real-life wife and another man and wife were his assistants in the act, bringing out props and so forth. Silkini wrapped up that part or the show by disappearing into a trunk. He then came back out on stage and introduced Bela, who made an entrance dressed in his traditional Dracula garb (evening clothes, cape, etc.). Bela proceeded to "hypnotize" the audience, using those wonderful hand movements of his. (This bit fell sort of

Three Strange Monsters: *House of Frankenstein, House of Dracula, Abbott and Costello Meet Frankenstein.*

* Dr. Silkini, whose real name was Jack Baker and who was in his mid-30s at the time, was the producer and star of what thought were some of the best and classiest spook shows of that era. I was a real spook show man — I loved 'em! My buddy Lionel Comport and I went to every one we could find. There were a lot of 'em in the late '40s and early '50s, especially out on the West Coast.

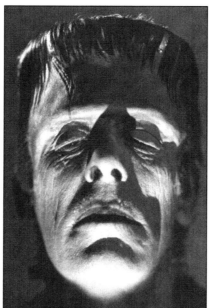
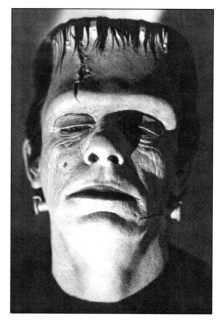

flat. It would have played better if there had been a "plant" in the audience, someone who was part of the show, for Bela to single out.) Then Bela said something along the lines of, "It's time to call the Frankenstein Monster to me. I need him," and, with the hand motions again, he began summoning the Monster. Suddenly the Monster (Glenn) appeared in the back of the auditorium and started lumbering down an aisle ramp toward the stage where Bela was standing.

The entire time he was making that long walk, the whole audience was yelling and screaming — they really got into the spirit of the thing. Glenn went up onto the stage and then

Glenn as the Monster staggers on stage to menace an Orpheum spook show audience.

pretended to attack Bela. Still grappling with each other, they moved offstage, at which time Silkini came out again and thanked everybody for coming. The whole show clocked in at a little over an hour, and the Bela-Glenn part was only around 15 or 20 minutes of it. But at least you got to see these great guys live on stage, which was really cool.

About six months later, Lionel Comport and I saw Glenn in yet another Orpheum spook show — in some ways, a much better one. I would later learn that, after the success of the *Abbott and Costello Meet Frankenstein* spook show, Wyman Baker, the brother of Jack Baker (Dr. Silkini), came to Glenn and offered to build a spook show around him, and Glenn said sure. (Glenn loved doing this stuff.) So Wyman came up with a show called "The Maniac" — and The Maniac was Glenn! The show began with Dr. Silkini (played in this show by Wyman Baker) doing some illusions and then introducing Glenn: "And now here's Glenn Strange, the Frankenstein Monster of the movies!" On a lab set that they had on stage, complete with a table crowded with bottles of chemicals, Silkini asked Glenn, "You've heard of Dr. Jekyll and Mr. Hyde?" Glenn said he had. "Well," Silkini announced, "I've come up with this chemical that can do the same thing as Dr. Jekyll's potion. Since you played monsters in movies, would you mind trying it out?" Glenn said, "Oh, sure!" Glenn drank the smoking potion and then, of course, did the gyrations and the "agony bit" and fell out of sight, behind the table. Under the table, unseen by the audience of course, were a werewolf mask and hands and a guy to help Glenn slip them on. Glenn slowly climbed back up to his feet, the hands coming up from behind the table first and then the werewolf face. He started running around, chased Silkini offstage and then ran down toward the audience. At that point, all the auditorium lights went out and the theater staff began projecting onto the ceiling and the walls images of flying ghosts and bats and so on. It was actually pretty impressive. They even had air hoses set up and, during the blackout, they fired little blasts of air toward the audience. You'd feel this small gust on your face, as if somebody was breathing down your neck or something was flying by you, very close — a pretty creepy feeling when it happens in the dark!

Soon the lights came back on and Glenn was gone. Silkini did another couple of tricks and then, right in the middle of one of them, Glenn came back out, now as the Monster. Silkini shouted, "Oh my God, the Frankenstein Monster!" and, of course, the crowd went wild. Glenn went out into the audience this time and grabbed a girl — obviously she was a "plant." Screaming and struggling, she was carried up onto the stage by Glenn and placed under the blade of a full-sized guillotine — and the blade fell and cut her head off! Then Silkini picked the head up out of the basket and threw it into the audience. What it really was, was a head of cabbage, but the audience didn't know that. There were people yelling and carrying on all over the place!

At the very end of the show, which ran about an hour, hour and a half, Silkini and Glenn came out (Glenn of course now had the mask off) and took their bows. Glenn even stuck around after that for an hour or so, signing autographs; I didn't get one, I was much too shy to approach him. But it was a terrific night and, I thought, one of the very best spook shows I'd ever seen, as it had a real "monster actor" changing into a monster on stage.

It was about three years later, around 1951, that I first met Glenn. I was in a cafe in Burbank, having lunch with an actor named Jack Ingram, another guy who played heavies in scores of Westerns and who owned a movie ranch where a lot of Westerns and many episodes of the *Lone Ranger* TV series were shot. Glenn just happened to walk in. Glenn saw Jack, who he'd known for years, and he made a beeline over to our table. Of course, I recognized him immediately too — "Oh my God, it's Glenn Strange," I said to myself.

Jack called Glenn "Pee Wee" — that was Glenn's nickname, believe it or not, even though he had to be at least six-foot-six — and he introduced him to me: "Pee Wee, I'd like you to meet a young friend of mine, Bob Burns." Right off the bat, Glenn was as nice as could be, a big friendly handshake and that great ear-to-ear smile and "Hi, Bob, how ya doin'?" and all of that.

Then, to my delight, Glenn sat down at the table with us and had his coffee while we were having our lunch, and he and I got to talk a bit. When I recognized him coming into the place, probably the first thing I thought of were the cowboy pictures, because I'd seen him in so doggone many of them,

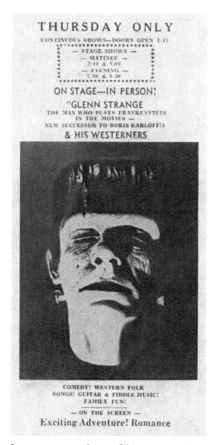

In one stage show, Glenn not only played the Monster, he sang and played fiddle with the singing group The Westerners.

but then as he got closer and I began to appreciate just how big he was, the Monster popped right in my head. I told him, "I've enjoyed you in so many Western things, but I really thought you made a great Frankenstein Monster," and he thanked me and said what a great time he had playing that role. And then he went right into thanking Boris Karloff for helping him. (Karloff played the Monster in the first three Frankensteins and then appeared as a mad scientist in *House of Frankenstein*, Glenn's first film as the Monster.) I would eventually notice that almost every time Glenn talked about the Monster, he made a point of mentioning that on *House of Frankenstein* Boris would stay over on his own time after he was finished for the day, even though he was suffering from back and leg problems, and tutor Glenn on how to play the Monster in scenes that were coming up. Glenn always used to say, "Look, if you liked me as the Frankenstein Monster, all the credit goes to Boris Karloff for helpin' me." That's the kind of guy Glenn was.

A great shot of Glenn taken during his heyday as a Western heavy.

I also asked about some of the Westerns, the Hoppys in particular, and I think he was pretty impressed with this snot-nosed 15- or 16-year-old kid who had seen so many of his movies. "Boy, you know a lot about me," he said — I think he was a little taken aback, but also flattered. "Well, I really enjoy this stuff," I told him.

Unfortunately, it was kind of a short conversation — when Glenn walked in, Jack and I were just finishing up our lunches and getting ready to head hack to my folks' place. Jack said, "We'll see you again!" or something like that, which made me think there'd be a chance to get together with him again soon — but that was the end of it. In those days, I was very shy. I'd have liked to get together with Glenn again and I could have pursued it right then and there, or through Jack Ingram later, hut I didn't. I'm just that way.

My second meeting came about ten years later, when I was the Official Photographer for *Famous Monsters of Filmland* magazine. Editor Forry Ackerman called me one day and asked, "Would you like to meet Glenn Strange?" I said, "I've met him one time but, yeah, I'd love to see him again. It's been a lot of years." Forry gave me the address over in Glendale where Glenn and his wife were living and he and I both went there in our own cars, And even though it had been at least ten years since our first get-together, Glenn recalled it: "Oh my God, I *do* remember that. With Jack Ingram. You guys were havin' lunch or something." The guy had a very good memory.

Forry did a little interview with Glenn (no tape recorder, he just took notes — I think that's the way he always did it) and I snapped some pictures that would be used to illustrate the *FM* article, including one of him holding two Frankenstein head cut-outs that I had brought over. Glenn's wife Min fixed lunch for us and we stayed a couple, three hours. I even got to meet the Stranges' daughter Janine, who happened to drop by that day while we were there. By that time, she was already married and the mother of a little boy, Glenn's

26-month-old grandson Mike. Like Glenn and Min, Janine was very pleasant. It was such a nice visit and I felt so welcome there that I did muster up the courage to tell Glenn, "I'd love to talk to you more about this stuff. I find this fascinating." He said, "Well, here's my phone number, just give me a call. You've already got my address…"

I came home and I told Kathy what a nice guy Glenn was, and that his daughter was very sweet too. About a week later I got up my nerve again and called Glenn and said, "I'd like to have my wife meet you," and without hesitation he said, "Well, why don't you guys just come on over for dinner?" He was so nice! When Kathy and I went over, Janine the daughter was there with her husband Nick and little Mike; Janine and Kathy were about the same age, and they became fast friends. It was really something: We all just kind of clicked, and not long after that, we began hanging around together, all the time. Kathy and I went everywhere with the Stranges, from then on — we saw Glenn on a regular basis from that night forward. Over the years, naturally, I asked Glenn probably a million and one questions about his life and his movies and the people he worked with. According to Glenn, he was a real-life cowboy who got into the picture business around 1929 as a result of competing in a bronco riding contest at the Hoot Gibson Rodeo in Texas. He didn't win, but Gibson, the Hollywood

The man who introduced me to Glenn Strange, veteran Western heavy Jack Ingram.

cowboy star who owned the rodeo, noticed how tall Glenn was. After the rodeo, Hoot asked Glenn if he would like to be in the movies and play a bad guy as he (Hoot) liked to beat up on big tall bad guys in his Westerns. (Hoot was around five-six.) Glenn had nothing else going on at the time and took the job and, as they say, the rest is history.

Elena Verdugo's birthday on the set of *House of Frankenstein.* Glenn credited Boris Karloff with helping him play the Monster effectively.

Another interesting thing Glenn told me was that, in the early '30s, he was in a Western group called The Arizona Wranglers, singing and playing his fiddle and guitar over the radio. To my amazement, Glenn also revealed to me that he provided the singing voice of John Wayne in some of Wayne's early Westerns, during the "singing cowboy" phase of Wayne's career — and that he'd written the songs as well! He got a dollar a song for writing them in those days. Needless to say, Glenn was much better known for playing B Western heavies than he was for songwriting and singing. The down side of being a baddie, of course, was that he was sometimes injured during the making of those movies — that's one of the hazards of

A photo I took at Glenn's house when I went with Forry Ackerman to do a *Famous Monsters* interview. The cut-out heads were used to promote *Abbott and Costello Meet Frankenstein.*

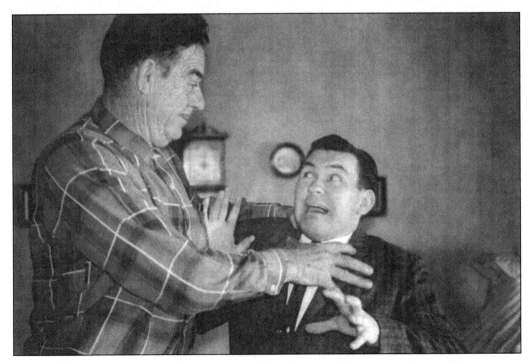

Gag shot of Glenn and me, taken by Glenn's wife Min.

that fast and furious trade. When you play the head bad guy, Glenn told me, you're always the leader of the pack when they're racing around on horseback — and he'd had horses fall under him and then had the whole pack run over him! The worst, though, was when he was doing a Durango Kid with Charles Starrett and the stagecoach horses bolted with Glenn in the coach — and nobody up top driving! The horses got to running just as fast as they could possibly run before the coach went crashing down a 55-foot embankment. The horses were killed and Glenn wound up in Cedars of Lebanon Hospital with a leg that was smashed all to pieces, including the knee joint. From that day on, Glenn walked with a slight limp.

Glenn's daughter Janine and her son Mike posing with Glenn at my house in the early '60s.

The way Glenn got the Frankenstein Monster role was interesting. He was playing a scar-faced pirate in a movie at Universal and makeup man Jack Pierce kept studying his face the whole time he was applying the scar. Glenn got a little nervous as he felt that Jack was looking at him a little too close! Finally one day Jack asked if he (Glenn) would stay late that night so he could do an experimental makeup on him that might get him a good part in a film. Also, Jack said, they'd pay him $25. Glenn agreed, called Min to tell her he'd be home a little late and, after the shoot that day, he came to Jack's makeup room. Jack had him sit in the makeup chair and then, after cleaning the scar off, started covering all the mirrors with sheets of newspaper. (Glenn had no idea why he was doing that, but it became obvious later that Jack simply didn't want Glenn to see what he was doing.) Jack then spent about an hour working mainly on Glenn's forehead and the top of his head. When he finished, he went to the phone and called Universal producer Paul Malvern: "Come over, I want to show you something." Glenn still had no idea what was going on, but he was making $25, so what the heck.

A few minutes later, in came Malvern — and Jack said, "Here is your Frankenstein Monster." Jack then pulled the paper from the mirrors and Glenn got his first look at him-self — and the first words out of his mouth when he saw his reflection were, "My God, I look just like Boris Karloff!" That's how Glenn got the job in *House of Frankenstein*: Jack had noticed that Glenn had the kind of craggy face that he always really wanted for the Monster, even when he was doing Boris for the original *Frankenstein.**

In addition to telling me about his experiences on the Frankenstein movies, Glenn also talked about his spook show days. He said that the show he did with Bela Lugosi, in connection with *Abbott and Costello Meet Frankenstein*, only played short runs in Los Angeles, San Diego and San Francisco — the reason for that, Glenn suspected, was that Bela may not have wanted to be on the road very long or go very far. (Bela was an old man at the time, and not in the best of health.) Glenn said he got the feeling that Bela wasn't real thrilled

Glenn in the "Maniac" mask and hands he wore in live stage shows.

about doing the show and, perhaps as a result of that, they did it only for a few weeks, about 15 performances altogether. Playing the Monster, Glenn wore the Monster outfit and built-up boots and a light gray Monster mask that Universal makeup man Jack Kevan had done up for him. It was a real neat mask (complete with hair) that he could put on over his head and zip up in the back. Because he had that mask, Glenn didn't have to get made-up for every appearance. Glenn later wore that same mask on TV in the *Colgate Comedy Hour* skit where he once again menaced Abbott and Costello.

For "The Maniac," Glenn went back to Jack Kevan and had him make him up a special werewolf-type mask. Jack used part of the Wolf Man mask from *Abbott and Costello Meet Frankenstein* and altered it a bit (bigger ears, weirder teeth), and he also gave Glenn some furry gloves. Unlike the spook show with Bela, "The Maniac" went on for quite a while — I think Glenn said almost three years. He went all over the country with that one, even to New York. Glenn got to be such a popular spook show star that other spook show presenters began using his name in connection with *their* shows but just dressing some big local guy in

---

* This goes with another story that Glenn told me: He said that when the original *Frankenstein* came out in 1931, he and his brother Virgil went to see it in El Paso. They thought the film was good and on the way home they were discussing the movie and the Monster. "Neither one of us knew a thing, of course, about makeup," Glenn told me. "But we knew that people couldn't just dig somebody up out of a grave, a piece here and there, and make a man out of it. Virgil said, 'You know that they can't build a guy up and make him breathe again. We know better than that. But,' he said, 'where the hell did they ever find a guy that looked like that??'" Little did Glenn know that in 1944, he would become "the guy that looked like that."

a Frankenstein mask. Glenn would get letters from friends all around the country saying that they went to see him at one of these shows and it turned out not to be him. Sometimes he would (supposedly) be in shows states apart on the same day!

Oh, and another great story about the *Abbott and Costello Meet Frankenstein* show: They were doing it at the Orpheum (not the night I was there), Bela beckoned and Glenn's Monster came down the aisle — and all of a sudden, this smart-ass teenager, 14 or 15, jumped out of his aisle seat and kicked Glenn in the knee. Right in the replaced kneecap of the leg Glenn had broken in that stagecoach accident. Glenn said that he could barely see out of the mask and so he wasn't even sure exactly what had happened, but he knew that he hadn't felt pain like that since the stagecoach wreck. When Glenn got kicked, he just threw his fist out and felt it connect with something, he wasn't sure what. Then he did his best to keep on walking and go on with the show. Well, at the end of the night, when the house lights came back up and people were exiting, they found this kid out cold, crumpled over the back of a seat. Glenn had broken his jaw! Glenn hadn't meant to hit him but, he said, the shot to his knee hurt so much that he just lashed out. Nobody pressed charges because the kid really asked for it — even the kid's own buddies later said he had it coming to him and claimed that they'd told him not to do it. Glenn felt awful about it, of course, and he even talked to the parents of the kid he had socked. And even they had the attitude of, "That's fine. It was his own fault!"

By retelling all these stories that Glenn told me, I'm probably giving the impression that all I did was talk to him about movies, but that wasn't the case. We did do quite a bit of that, of course, but I got over the fan business pretty quick, actually. He loved to talk about the movies but

A shot of Glenn taken in 1931 or '32 when he was with the Hoot Gibson Rodeo.

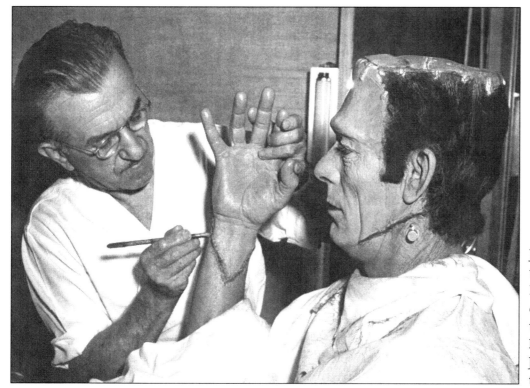

Jack Pierce making up Glenn as the Monster in *House of Dracula*. Notice the size of Glenn's hands compared to Jack's. (Glenn called them "ham hocks.")

there were lots of times when we didn't talk about any movies at all. We just talked about stuff…nothing in particular. It wasn't an actor-fan relationship, it was an honest-to-goodness friendship, Glenn and Min and Janine and her family and Kathy and I. Glenn would frequently drop by our house when he was in the neighborhood — there'd be a knock at the door and there was Glenn. "I thought I'd just drop in for a while. Got any coffee?" (Glenn was a big coffee drinker. Kathy and I don't drink it much, so we had to have a big pot sitting around all the time for him, because we never knew when he was dropping in.) As I mentioned before, after a while I was actually closer to Glenn than I was to my own dad. I

Glenn teamed with Bela Lugosi in live stage shows at the Orpheum Theater. Here they take a break while filming *Abbott and Costello Meet Frankenstein.*

certainly saw Glenn more than I saw my dad — *much* more. He became a father figure to me and, to him, perhaps *I* sort of became the son he never had. "Pappy" was a nickname I had for him. Everybody called him Pee Wee, I called him Pappy, I don't even know why. Maybe because I wanted him to *be* my dad — a subconscious thing. Glenn and I were buddies and we did stuff together all the time, and Kathy and Janine were really good friends who would go everywhere together. Kathy and I were the Stranges' "second family" and they were ours.

One of Glenn's hobbies was repairing television sets. I can't imagine why, but he just loved to tinker with them! If any friends of Glenn's were having trouble with their TV, he'd try and fix it. I used to go with him on his rounds: He drove an old, beat-up Chevy station wagon and I'd tag along when he'd pick up these TV sets from people. We'd go to the homes of his friends and stay for half an hour or whatever, chitchatting, and then he'd take their TV out to his wagon to bring it home and work on it. Because it was Glenn, even doing stuff like that was fun.

There was a place in Burbank called Chili John's that used to have the best chili in the world, and we went there with Glenn all the time. They had two types of chili — one was regular, one was so hot you sweated when you ate it. (Glenn and I could eat that, but one time Kathy and I went there by ourselves and they mixed up the bowls. She got the hot one, and has never gotten over it!) But whenever Kathy and I went out to dinner with Glenn, we noticed that the poor guy never got to finish a meal. One person after another would recognize him, and of course they all wanted his autograph. Glenn was most gracious about it. Some celebrities get bent about that when they're trying to eat a meal — and I don't blame 'em. But he was always so accommodating. He'd say, "Look, if they like me well enough to come up and talk to me and want my autograph, boy, that's just the least I can do. It's people like this who made me what I am today." That's the way he always looked at it.

My favorite shot of Glenn and me, taken at one of the annual Strange family picnics.

Every year or so, his family had what they called The Strange Picnic — it's a spooky-sounding name, but it was always a real nice get-together! Over at Verdugo Park in Glendale, the Stranges had a big annual picnic, the whole family, all the relatives who were in town or who could come into town for it. Kathy and I would always go, and one year Glenn's best friend in the world Eddie Dean the singing cowboy star came with his wife. Something else that Kathy and I would do every couple of months was go with Glenn's whole family out to Vasquez Rocks, a park near Agua Dulce Springs, and cook up a big breakfast. For five dollars a car, you could get in there; they had barbecue pits in the picnic area and we'd have big cookout breakfasts. Bacon, ham, eggs, toast, biscuits, fried potatoes, country gravy — and gallons of coffee. Glenn would sometimes sit and gaze around at all the great big, fabulous natural rock formations there in the park and say, "Oh, I shot so many Westerns up here…" God, those were fun times.

We even did a lot of silly stuff together. One night Glenn and the whole family were over to our place for dinner — that would be Glenn, Min, Glenn's mother Blanche (we

Glenn, his wife Min and me during a 1964 visit to their Glendale home. Non-drinker Glenn has a Coke in his left hand — and one of his "cancer sticks" in his right.

always called her Mom Thompson), Janine and Nick and their little boy Mike, who by now was five or six. At one point we were just sitting around, and I asked, "Would you guys like to do a radio show, just for fun?" Kathy's folks had an old Philco machine which you used to make your own records, and it came with these real corny scripts that you could enact. Glenn said the idea of doing a radio show sounded like fun, so we performed two or three of these things. To give you an idea what they were like, one was titled "Dastardly Deeds" and it featured the heroine who couldn't pay the mortgage and the typical old-fashioned villain with the mustache and the top hat who was going to run her through the buzzsaw. I

set up a microphone and my reel-to-reel tape recorder and I did the narration and all the sound effects, plus I played one of the characters. Glenn, naturally, was the villain in these things, and he really milked these roles — different accents and the hammy delivery and the "Heh-heh-heh-heh!" and the whole bit. He was genuinely funny! Most fans don't know this but Glenn had a great sense of humor and was an incredible comedian. He didn't get to show it much in films — the best opportunity he got to display his talent for comedy was probably the Abbott and Costello movie *Comin' Round the Mountain* where he played Devil Dan. He had a great sense of humor and he had so much fun with these radio shows and he really got into them. Well, *every*body got into 'em, even little Mike and old Mom Thompson, who was in her eighties by then but a very sweet lady, and game for anything.

The second time we did this, it was a disaster — and it was even more fun. It was one night a couple years later that we decided to try it again…but perhaps we weren't in any condition to try it again. Glenn had recently mentioned that he used to make his own margaritas, and even his own Triple Sec. "I never drank 'em, I never knew how they were," he told us, "but people said they were good…" Well, margaritas used to be one of my favorite drinks — I loved 'em, especially in the summertime. So the next time Glenn came over, he brought all the ingredients and started making margaritas. He didn't drink, but Min maybe had one or two, Kathy had one — and I think the only other people who drank were Janine and me. Well, these were some wild margaritas that Glenn mixed up: They were real strong but they didn't taste strong, and so Janine and I got blitzed! Later that same night, Glenn said, "Y'know, we oughta do those old radio shows over again. I had so much fun doin' that stuff…" I said, "Great!" and I got all the equipment set up and we did it but, oh, by then Janine and I were really smashed pretty bad. It was so funny: Everybody else was fine, but Janine and I were just "off" somewhere. We did the same scripts again and I was trying to do sound effects, but I

Frankenstein's Daughter: Janine Strange on Daddy's lap on the set of *Abbott and Costello Meet Frankenstein,* and then again in the 1960s.

was so drunk, I didn't know what I was doing half the time. Then we all got the giggles, too. So the second time around, the shows turned out very funny.

Another fun thing we did was put Glenn into a "movie." My friend Don Glut came over to our house one time to meet Glenn and, naturally, Don was very impressed with him. Later, when Don was getting ready to make one of his little amateur 16mm serials, *The Adventures of the Spirit,* he phoned me and asked, "Do you think you could talk

Glenn into maybe doing a cameo in it?" I passed the request along to Glenn, and of course he said, "Sure. Love to. No problem." It was a crazy little movie: Don played the Spirit, the comic book hero, and I played a lot of characters in the thing: Superman, a werewolf, Captain America and the Mad Mummy. In one chapter, Glenn played the Monster for maybe about a minute, minute and a half. His scene was shot at his place in Glendale, the same house where Forry Ackerman had interviewed and I'd photographed him for *Famous Monsters*. Wearing a Don Post Monster mask that I'd bought in 1948, he came out of a basement door, up a few stairs and grabbed and choked the Spirit (Don). That was the end of that chapter. Then in the next chapter, I played Clark Kent and I had a vision that the Spirit was in trouble. I quickly changed into Superman and flew to the scene and fought the Monster. Actually, the guy I was fighting was my buddy Lionel Comport, who was doubling Glenn. But Glenn did the majority of the thing — you can tell those big ol' hands of his when they're around Don's throat. Glenn thought it was fun, he had a great time doing it.

By the time we did *Adventures of the Spirit*, Glenn had started appearing on the TV Western series *Gunsmoke*, playing Sam Noonan, the big, leathery bartender at the Long Branch Saloon. Don Glut originally wanted me to do a Frankenstein Monster makeup on Glenn for *Adventures of the Spirit*, but Glenn of course had a mustache which would have made that tough. Glenn being Glenn, such a sweet man, he said, "If you want, I'll shave it off. The *Gunsmoke* makeup guys can glue one on me 'til it grows back." (Glenn did shave off his mustache to play the Monster in the *House* pictures and *Abbott and Costello Meet*

Glenn as the Frankenstein Monster and me as Superman in the amateur serial *The Adventures of the Spirit*. The rubber monster mask is the one I got from Don Post in 1948.

*Frankenste*in.) Don was all for it because he wanted to see me do a makeup on Glenn — and I would love to have done it. But I said, "No, we can't ask you to do that for a project like this" — I was sure that the *Gunsmoke* people wouldn't have appreciated it at all if he'd lost the mustache! I said, "I've got this Monster mask, it'll be fine," and that's what we ended up doing.

Speaking of Glenn's house in Glendale reminds me of a very sad story. Glenn and his father-in-law literally built that house from the ground up, by hand. Glenn built it to his specifications and he loved that place. For one thing, he had his own den in the basement,

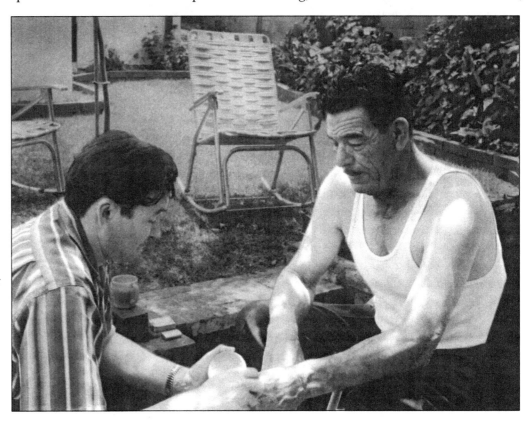

Me making up Glenn's hands for *The Adventures of the Spirit.* The Don Post mask Glenn wore in this amateur serial was the first ever made of the Monster, based on Glenn in *Abbott and Costello Meet Frankenstein.*

small but a really neat place, all fixed up Western style — there were Western blankets hung up and some steer horns and all sorts of Western-type furnishings. He had a great old easy chair and a TV set and a little refrigerator where he kept drinks, and that was his "sanctuary," Until…the city of Glendale took his house, and four other houses, because a new freeway was about to come through that area. Cities have the right to do things like that, and they did. They of course paid Glenn…but not what the house was worth. Leaving that house just broke his heart — it seemed almost to break his spirit a bit. He and Min moved into another house in Glendale, one on Valencia, closer to the Burbank line, but he was never really happy in that second house. And the horrible thing about it was, the five houses were torn down — and then the city planners changed the freeway route and never put the freeway through there! The site where Glenn's house and the others had stood sat there for years, as vacant lots. Oh, he was so upset about that.

It was at the Valencia house that Glenn made me a present of the boots he wore as the Monster in *Abbott and Costello Meet Frankenstein.* Universal had given them to him to wear in the midnight spook show, and when Universal never asked for them back, Glenn just kept them. We were in his garage one day when I happened to spot them and I gasped, "My God, those can't be what I think they are…!" He went, "Oh, yeah, those are the old boots I wore. I don't know why I kept those old things, but I just did…" When he realized how excited I was about it, he said I could have them if I wanted. They've been a proud part of my collection ever since; in 2001, I brought them with me to Monster Bash, a horror film fan convention in Butler, Pennsylvania, and it was fun to see scores of fans of Glenn Strange and *A&C Meet Frankenstein* have the same wide-eyed reaction to seeing those boots that I must have had that day in Glenn's garage! I had another *A&C Meet Frankenstein* souvenir at the Bash with me that year as well: A foam rubber Monster headpiece from the movie. Again, it was a gift from Glenn: I was visiting him at the first house one afternoon (this was before he gave me the boots), talking about the Frankenstein movies and asking about the makeup and appliances. He said that wearing Jack Kevan appliances in *A&C Meet Frankenstein* was a lot more comfortable than enduring the cotton and collodion and putty that Jack Pierce used to put on his face and head for the *House* pictures. (According to Glenn, the only down side to the foam rubber headpiece was that, wearing it all day, sweat would build up under the brow, and when he would pull it off at night, all the water that had collected would run down his face!) "Gosh," I said, "I wish I could have seen one of those headpieces."

"Oh? Well, I *got* one."

A shot I took of Glenn between takes on the *Gunsmoke* set.

I said, "*What??*" and I was still collecting myself as he went to a closet, rummaged around a bit and then came out with a paper sack. I looked in it and there it was — and in perfect condition! "Well, it wasn't actually used," Glenn explained. "It was an extra one, and I just *took* it...I don't know why. A souvenir or somethin'." He could tell I was fascinated and, Glenn being Glenn, he asked, "Ya *want* it?"

Did I want it? Did Galahad want the Holy Grail??

Glenn and me on the *Gunsmoke* set. I was there many times over the years.

The only time I was on a set with Glenn was on *Gunsmoke*, but what an experience that was. One day when *Gunsmoke* was on hiatus, Glenn was over at my place and we were talking, and he said that they were going to start shooting *Gunsmoke* again the following week.

"Hey, why don't you come on over with me?" he asked. "I'll pick you up some morning, take you over…" I thought that would be great. so I just put in for a week's vacation from my job at KCBS. I didn't know if I'd use it all, but I asked for a week off, and they said I could have it, and Glenn picked me up the first morning of my vacation and took me over to Studio Center where *Gunsmoke* was shot. And I did end up spending the whole week there, going in with

Glenn at the Old Western Days cookout near Hanson Dam in Sylmar, California. To Glenn's left is actor Victor French, who did a lot of episodes of *Gunsmoke*.

him every day and coming home with him at night, because it was so much fun. Milburn Stone (Doc) was a great guy, and so was Ken Curtis (Festus) — well, *all* the guys were great. Jim Arness (Marshal Dillon), the star of the series, was, I thought, somewhat of a loner, but he was a good guy, too. A few years later, I would find out *just* how good a guy he was.

Glenn, I could tell, was the "father figure" on that set — everybody came around to Glenn wanting to hear his stories. "Tell us about when you worked with Hoot Gibson," "Tell us about John Wayne," on and on. He had an old rocking chair that he would set out on the porch of the Long Branch Saloon (the whole Dodge City main street was a Studio Center sound stage) and everybody would gather around to hear Glenn spinning his yarns. One day during a break, to my delight, Jim Arness did come around and join me and all the rest of the folks who happened to be grouped around Glenn and his rocking chair there. In those days, Jim was kind of touchy about having played a monster in *The Thing* early in his career, and never talked about that picture too much. So there we were sitting on the Long Branch porch that day, and out of the blue Jim looked over at Glenn and he said, "I just thought of something."

Glenn said, "What's that'?"

"Y'know," Jim said, "we're just two old monsters sitting here."

"What do you mean?" Glenn asked.

"Well, a mad scientist tried to save *me* [in *The Thing*]…and a mad scientist created *you*." Glenn said, "By God, you're right. You're absolutely right!"

I thought that was just the greatest thing, hearing that statement come out of Jim's mouth, (Well, for one thing, it reminded me that here I was, sitting between the Frankenstein Monster and the Thing — how cool is that?) Then, since Jim himself had opened the door, I talked to him a little bit about *The Thing*, and he was just fine with it. He said, "Oh, I enjoyed the role. It's just that everybody seems to think that, prior to *Gunsmoke*, that was all I ever did. That kind of bugs me sometimes…" But he went on to say that he'd enjoyed it and that, even though he only worked a few days on the entire film, it had helped him get his start. Then Jim said to Glenn, "Tell me a little about that Frankenstein role," so we got into a big conversation about that, Glenn and Jim and me, with other people around us, too — Ken Curtis and some of the crew guys. Glenn talked for maybe 30 minutes about the monsters he had done, and even some of the Western stuff, and I got the impression that Jim was sort of a closet fan. It was really nice, a neat conversation.

On another occasion, Glenn finished up a day's work on *Gunsmoke* and dropped by my place together with a buddy of his, a musician-extra named Bud; they had just finishing shooting a barn dance scene for *Gunsmoke*, Glenn playing his fiddle and Bud his guitar. I can't remember now why Glenn stopped by but he did, around five or six o'clock, with Bud, and Glenn happened to mention that he'd played his fiddle on the show that day.

I took this shot of Glenn holding one of the Monster boots that he wore in *Abbott and Costello Meet Frankenstein* along with one of the foam rubber headpieces. He'd just come back from location shooting on *Gunsmoke* and looks a bit windblown.

Buck Taylor, Glenn, Kogar (me) and Eddie Dean at the Burbank on Parade event in 1968.

"You know, Glenn," I said, "someday I'd love to get a tape of you playing some of that stuff."

"Well," Glenn said, "I got my old fiddle out in the car, and Bud's got his guitar."

That was all I needed to hear. I set up the microphone while they got the fiddle and the guitar, and I recorded those guys right in my own living room. Glenn played a pretty mean Western fiddle and Bud was no slouch with the guitar. They played for about a half an hour, and it was really great. Another time Glenn was over by himself and we got to talking about the session I'd recorded, and all of a sudden he wanted to go out to his car and get that old fiddle again. (He must have always carried it in his car.) So this second session that I recorded was just him, sitting down playing the fiddle and singing a whole bunch of the songs that he had written, including "On the Banks of the Sunny San Juan" that had become a real big hit for Eddie Dean back in the '40s, and a really funny one called "The Tom Tom Boogie." He even gave a little history of each song ("This is a little song I did for…") before he would go into them.

A great group shot of the *Gunsmoke* cast: Glenn, Ken Curtis, James Arness, Amanda Blake, Buck Taylor and Milburn Stone.

I'm so glad now that I had the sense to record that stuff; it's really great to still be able to hear his voice and the way he talked and sang those two days. It was just like Glenn to go to the trouble of doing all for me — he just loved to extend himself for his friends and his fans.

Another memory: Every year at a big old park out by Hanson Dam in Sylmar, they had what they called an Old Western Days cookout, put on by some organization of Western fans I suppose. Western stars would show up at this thing and the public would have a chance to come and meet them. It also featured a big cookout, and Glenn, who absolutely loved to cook (he made the world's meanest batch of chili), was always the head cook. He would make up these big pots of chili and other stuff, and some of the other Western guys who could cook (Victor French, for instance) would help. Kathy and I went out there a couple, three times, and there'd be Glenn and Jack Ingram and Roy Barcroft and Lash LaRue — an awful lot of the old B Western actors were still around in those days. They would show up for this thing and mingle with the crowd and sign autographs and talk. The old Western fans just loved it — and so did Glenn. He loved being around people, especially the Western buffs, or — well, fans of *any* kind, really. He was by far one of the kindest men in terms of dealing with fans. He enjoyed talking to them, he was very friendly and he always, *always* had that wonderful ol' grin on his face at those occasions. Glenn would also do charity work — the guy did charity work all over the place. Any time anybody would call him, to appear at an auction, to be an emcee, whatever it was, the answer was yes. He would even go to hospitals and talk to sick children — kids with cancer or some other life-threatening disease. He was a genuine human being who simply loved doing it.

Another fun memory: In the late '60s, there used to be a local event called Burbank on Parade where there would be (naturally) a big parade and then, on a blocked-off street in Burbank proper, entertainers up on a platform doing musical numbers, in front of a store or something like that. One year they asked Glenn if he could get some of the other Western guys together and do a Western-themed show. Since Eddie Dean was his best friend, Glenn asked Eddie if he'd be part of it, and then he asked Buck Taylor, who played Newly, the gunsmith-deputy on *Gunsmoke*, if he would join them. (Glenn and Buck used to go out on tour for *Gunsmoke*, just the two of them, talking about the show and singing at Western events.) Once Glenn got the two of them, he asked me, "Would you mind coming in your gorilla suit? I think that'd be real fun."

Well, I just jumped at the chance: We did a skit where Glenn, Eddie and Buck were singing on stage when suddenly I came running out onto the stage in my Kogar gorilla suit. Glenn said, "Oh my God, somebody's monkey got loose!" — I was scampering all over the place, snorting and grunting and reaching down off the stage at people in the crowd. Eddie asked, "What's his name?" and Glenn said, "Somebody told me it was Kogar." Well, as soon as Glenn said "Kogar," I reacted right away. "Come here, Kogar," Glenn called out, and at that point I began acting almost like a dog — I went over to him and started looking up at him and the whole bit. But then, as they started to sing another number, I began running around and messing them up again. The audience was laughing like crazy and I had a blast. I was part of the show for about 20 minutes, the second half of the act, and I just loved it.

Glenn was never a heavy drinker. Many of the other actors of that generation used to really put it away, even on the set, but I personally never saw Glenn have a drink of anything stronger than a Coke or 7 Up even when we would go out to dinner. He just didn't care for it, and he didn't care for the way

A shot I took of Glenn on the *Gunsmoke* street.

guys would act after they'd been drinking. He never wanted any part of it. But, unfortunately, he smoked like a fiend and that's what killed him. He smoked Lucky Strikes, I don't know how many packs a day. That was the only vice he had, and that was the one which finally caught up with him.

Glenn between takes with a *Gunsmoke* extra.

Kathy and I were over at Glenn's one night, not long after Glenn had been in the hospital with pneumonia. I noticed — Kathy and I *both* noticed — that everybody was more sober than normal. Finally Glenn said, "I got somethin' to tell you guys. Please don't spread it around, but I just found out I got lung cancer."

I was just shocked, I had no idea what to say. He explained that when he was in the hospital for his pneumonia, they took x-rays and detected the cancer in his lungs. The doctors told him right from Day One that it was terminal — it was in both lungs, and there was no way they could do anything about it. But Glenn was philosophical about it: "Well, I smoked

Glenn and me at one of the last picnics (early 1973). Glenn had cancer by then and wasn't doing well.

all these dang cancer sticks," he said. "People warned me and everything, and I didn't listen. I'm one of those fools that didn't listen. Now I'm payin' the price." Cancer sticks — boy, he hit it right on the head all right. Smoking has ended the lives of so many wonderful people. Including my mom and dad.

Kathy and I of course honored Glenn's request and we kept the news to ourselves. And I've really got to hand it to Jim Arness: When Glenn got cancer, Jim and Ken Curtis and Milburn Stone were the only guys on *Gunsmoke* who knew about it, and Jim kept Glenn on the payroll until the day came that Glenn just couldn't work any longer. After a point, Glenn really couldn't deliver the dialogue any more, and so Sam the bartender became a silent extra: He would sit up on a stool that was hidden back behind the Long Branch bar, a stool so tall that it looked like he was standing even though he was not. And in the background of saloon scenes, you would see Glenn wiping off the bar or washing out a glass or something. Jim Arness told him, "Glenn, you can continue to work on the show just as long as you *want* to work. You just let me know. You just tell *me*." I thought that was pretty dang nice of Jim to do that.

It took about a year, I guess, for the cancer to kill Glenn. At one point, he became kind of desperate and started trying anything he could, even alternative medicine: He went down to Mexico and took a lot of weird shots which, of course, didn't do dump. It was heartbreaking to watch him getting weaker and weaker. Kathy and I would go over there to see him, and he'd sit with us in his living room for a little while, but then he'd have to go back to bed for a couple of hours. Then, if we were still there when he woke, he'd come back out and join us again for a while. He continued to do his little background "bits" on *Gunsmoke* until one day some time in the summer of 1973, when finally Min Strange had to call the production office and say. "Glenn can't come in any more."

It was so typical of a great person like Glenn that, even after he decided that he was too ill to continue with *Gunsmoke*, he still got up from his sickbed to pay tribute to a departed friend. When Lon Chaney Jr. died on July 12, 1973, the people in the news department at KCBS began calling around looking for one of Lon's veteran co-stars to talk on TV about his passing. But no one at all was willing to speak for Lon. He had burned all his bridges. The news department people now contacted me (they were aware that I knew Glenn) and told me what was happening, and asked if I thought Glenn would be willing to come to the studio and say a few words about Lon. (They had no idea that Glenn was gravely ill himself.) I went to see Glenn at his home, where by this time he was pretty much bedridden, and told him that the people CBS had contacted refused to speak about Lon.

"You mean, *nobody's* gonna speak up for Lon? *Nobody*?" Glenn asked with concern in his voice. "Glenn, they can't *find* anybody," I said.

Well, Glenn loved Lon — and Glenn was one of the very few guys that Lon loved — so I think I knew what Glenn was going to say next. Glenn told me to tell the folks at CBS that he would do the interview but that he had to have a place where he could sit down. (Our cover story to CBS was that Glenn had a severe case of the flu.) I got him out of bed — literally — and I took him in my car down to CBS, where he sat in the conference room and gave the most wonderful, heartfelt tribute to Lon. It ran on the local news that night. There's a real measure of a man, I think: Glenn got out of his sickbed, when he was dying himself, in order to do that. Here again, that shows you the kind of guy Glenn was.*

Finally, in September, Glenn's end came, very fast: He went into the hospital and didn't come out. The last time Kathy and I saw him was there at the hospital, St. Joseph's in Burbank. We were at his bedside along with Janine and Nick; he was hooked up to all kinds of bottles and doped up with morphine, because otherwise he would have been in

My very favorite shot of Glenn. This is how I'll always remember him.

an awful lot of pain at that point. (The four of us were the last to see him alive; Min had been there earlier in the day but she had gone home. The doctors had told her that this was probably the last day.) His eyes were closed and I thought he might be in a coma, but I talked to him anyway.

"Pappy?" I said. "Pappy, it's Bob. How ya doin'?" And after a moment or two, he opened his eyes a little and looked up at me and gave one of those big smiles…and then went right back to sleep again. But he knew we were there — that smile was to acknowledge that he knew we were there.

* After Glenn passed away, of course, I told the CBS news people, including Ruth Ashton Taylor, the gal who did the interview with him, the real story of what had gone on that day. Ruth said, "Oh my God, Bob. I would have never had him come down here if I'd known he was that ill." I said, "Ruth, once I told him nobody else would speak for Lon, no one could have stopped him."

Glenn Strange died that night, Thursday, September 20, 1973, at St. Joseph's. He was 74. Kathy and I had been there around seven-thirty, eight o'clock, and they say he died about midnight. Kathy and I got the sad news the next morning in a phone call from Janine.

There was no wake, just the funeral. In the slumber room at the mortuary at Forest Lawn, they had Glenn in an open casket over the weekend as friends came by and made their goodbyes, and then the funeral at Forest Lawn's Church of the Hills was at nine A.M. on Monday the 24th. I've never seen such a crowd at a funeral, before or since. So many people showed up — there must have been 900 there. And not just a bunch of Looky Lous — these were all Glenn's friends, including a lot of the old cowboy guys. Seemed like every oldtime Western actor or stuntman who was still around was there. Some were walking with walkers, others were in wheelchairs — they were pretty bad off themselves, but they all came to pay their last respects to Pee Wee. Glenn would have been so thrilled that all these people showed up that morning.

Eddie Dean, Glenn's best friend, was supposed to sing one of Glenn's favorite songs, but he pre-recorded it in the event that, when the time came, he was too distraught to perform it live. And that's what happened: He was so broken up that they did have to use the tape he'd made.

In Glenn's last wishes, he had specified who he wanted as his pallbearers and as his honorary pallbearers. Eddie Dean was going to be one of the pallbearers, and Jim Arness and I were to be honorary pallbearers. (Honorary pallbearers don't carry the coffin, they just walk alongside it in the procession.) If I'm remembering right, James Arness and I were the only two honorary pallbearers.

At first, I was doing fairly well — I was holding up much better than I thought I would. But then they closed Glenn's coffin and moved it into a little anteroom, in preparation for the pallbearers to carry it out to the burial plot. That was the moment at which I fell apart. I knew it was over then — somehow it just finally hit me. I became a blubbering idiot and came close to collapse. That was the moment when Jim Arness came over and put his arm around my shoulder, looked down at me and he said, "Bob, we're allll gonna miss him. But he's always alive in our minds and hearts. Always remember that. He's always with us, he's never really going to leave us. He just left us in body only, because we've got so many wonderful memories of that man."

That gave me strength — for some reason, that really helped me, and I was able to get through it after that. I will always have the utmost respect for James Arness, a very kind man. His words, the way he said them and the look in his eyes were so comforting, they spurred me on. And Jim stayed with me the whole rest of the funeral. The pallbearers wheeled the coffin on a church truck over to Glenn's burial plot, which was about 50 yards from the church itself, Jim and I accompanying them. Even after we got there, he stayed with me, standing right at my side. And every once in a while, he'd tap me on the shoulder, as if to ask, "You doin' okay?" It was a very sad experience, of course, but at the same time it was a very wonderful experience that I had with Jim. I'll be forever grateful to him for that. Jim Arness was one great human being.

Glenn's eulogy was given by John Mantley, the producer of *Gunsmoke.*

After the service, people were milling around and talking at the gravesite, including Dick Foran, the singing cowboy with whom Glenn had appeared in a number of Warner Brothers Western features and shorts in the '30s. (Sad to say, Dick had cancer also; in fact, he'd just lost his nose to it, and was wearing a prosthetic one there at the funeral.) "He was one of the best human beings on the face of this good earth," Dick said to me that morning, and that seemed to be the consensus of everybody there.

Glenn Strange was one of the best-loved guys in or out of the business. Truly a one-of-a-kind individual. I still miss him every day.

A GIANT CALLED "PEE WEE": GLENN STRANGE   63

Glenn played one of Emperor Ming's soldiers and battled Buster Crabbe in *Flash Gordon.*

Below: Glenn looks particularly fierce in pirate garb and as a tough Western hombre.

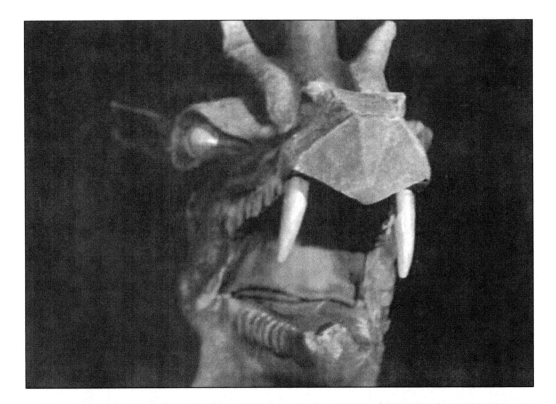

Wearing the same "smelly old" suit, Glenn played two different monsters in the 1936 *Flash Gordon* serial. In one chapter, he picks up Flash Gordon (actually a little boy suspended by a wire). For his appearance in another chapter, the costume was slightly changed and he became a fire-breather. Glenn said there was a gas nozzle inside the mouth and at one point the costume's head almost caught fire.

Werewolf Glenn accosts heroine Anne Nagel in *The Mad Monster.*

Glenn carries Karloff's double, Carey Loftin, into the "quicksand" in *House of Frankenstein.*

Two photos of Glenn as the monstrous Atlas in the Bowery Boys' *Master Minds.* In part of the picture, he swapped personalities with Huntz Hall. There were many retakes as cast and crew kept cracking up. Glenn loved doing comedy.

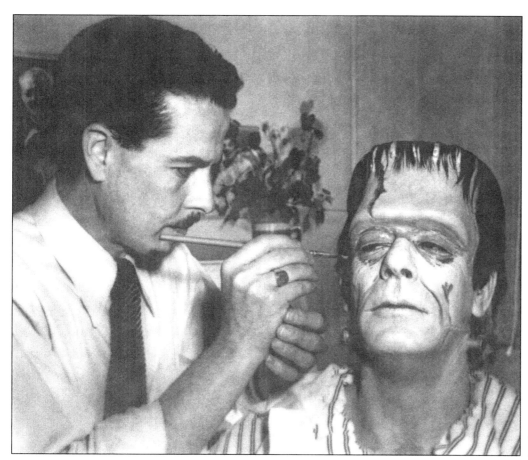

Makeup man Jack Kevan works on Glenn's Monster makeup for *Abbott and Costello Meet Frankenstein.*

Below: Glenn grabs a bite between scenes, and menaces a trio of bathing beauties on the set of *Mr. Peabody and the Mermaid.*

Monster and Wolf Man caught in an informal moment as Glenn shares a laugh with Lon Chaney Jr. on the set of *Abbott and Costello Meet Frankenstein*.

Glenn and *Abbott and Costello Meet Frankenstein* co-star Jane Randolph in a publicity shot.

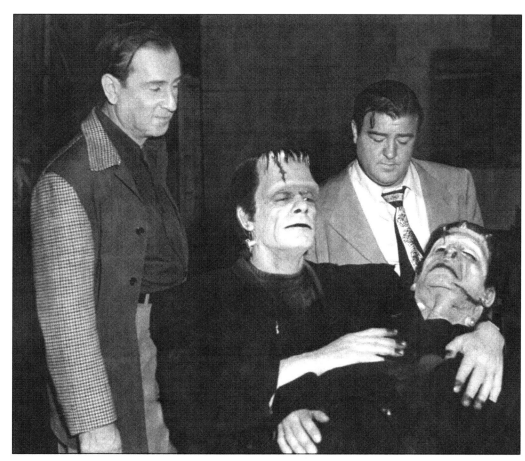

Left: A little person was made up as the Monster in publicity shots for *Abbott and Costello Meet Frankenstein.*

Right: In addition to his stage appearances as the Monster, Glenn also hit the radio airwaves. This is a gag shot from a radio appearance with a live audience.

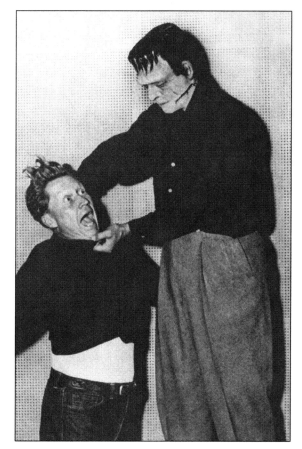

WHO IS KTLA'S "MYSTERY TOWER-SITTER"?

CHANNEL 5 viewers received a powerfully close view of The Mystery Tower Sitter with the aid of what is reputed to be the world's most powerful TV lens. It is a Raycote 10-60, 30 Power.

CHANNEL 5's "Mystery Tower Sitter" begins his daily ascent up a steel-rung ladder that takes him to his "home-away-from home" from 12 noon to 12 midnight through October 14. Public can enter mystery contest by sending a postcard to Mystery Tower-Sitter, Post Office Box 1, L.A. 51. First one to identify person wins a new automobile

GOLD RUSH at Channel 5's "Mystery Tower Sitter" waves to the television audience after his successful climb up the KTLA Tower.

Page 8

ACCOMPANIED BY one of Pinkerton Guards, Bill O'Hara, the Mystery Tower Sitter arrives at the entrance of one of Hollywood's finest hotels. Each night, the hooded mystery man descends the Channel 5 tower and is driven immediately to the hotel accompanied by a guard who is ready and able to protect the identity of the mystery man.

TOWER SITTER takes one last look at the hall to make sure he hasn't been followed by anyone other than his bodyguard, the armed Pinkerton man. After closing the door each night, the mystery man bolts himself in with a special bolt installed by the hotel.

October 2, 1957

In an October 1957 publicity stunt, Los Angeles TV station KTLA defied locals to guess the identity of their Mystery Tower Sitter; it turned out to be the Frankenstein Monster (Glenn).

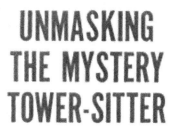

UNMASKING THE MYSTERY TOWER-SITTER

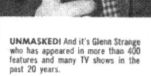

UNMASKED! And it's Glenn Strange who has appeared in more than 400 features and many TV shows in the past 20 years.

IN THE FIRST UNVEILING, the Sitter turns out to be the actor who played the Frankenstein Monster in three movies of the series. With him are his wife, Min, and daughter, Janine.

THE KTLA MYSTERY Tower Sitter approaches the elevator which is to take him to his room.

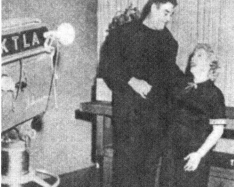

GLENN WITH MAE WILLIAMS who has her own show on "Breakthrough" on KTLA. Mae hosted this special telecast on final night of the contest, October 15.

KTLA's MYSTERY Tower Sitter towers over the Grand Prize winners. Winners were Earline Lofland, Thomas Wilson, Mrs. G. J. Bertonneau, Bob Evison, Sheldon and Doris Bennett, and Sam Schultz.

Page 8

November 2, 1

These pages are from different issues of *TV-Radio Life* — the first one ballyhooing the stunt, the second announcing the Tower Sitter's identity and the names of the contest winners.

My Pal George

I stood at the perimeter of the crater Harpalus, on the high northern latitude of the Moon. The view was breathtaking and completely enveloping. The "cracked mud" surface, dotted with mounds of rock, extended to the foot of the craggy hills in the far distance. Hundreds of stars shone fiercely in the velvety black expanse of space above; hanging over the mountains in the distance, I could see our own planet Earth. And there, situated in the middle of that barren lunar plain, was the atomic rocketship *Luna*. Its four-man crew, outfitted in their bulky red, yellow, blue and green spacesuits, had already exited the ship and made the first historic footprints on the Moon surface. Now, slowly, laboriously, they began to lumber in my direction…

I was 14 years old.

This was just part of my day on the set of *Destination Moon*, America's first "adult" space travel movie. Based on a novel by the celebrated Robert A. Heinlein, shot in Technicolor and graced by the astronomical art of Chesley Bonestell, this classic 1950 motion picture was not only a pioneering Hollywood space adventure, it was also as technically accurate as the

The *Destination Moon* scene that was shot the day I visited the set. The film is now listed in NASA's chronology of events leading to Neil Armstrong's 1969 Moon walk.

best scientific minds of the day could make it. The man behind this groundbreaking movie: the Oscar-winning creator of the popular Puppetoon series, a 41-year-old Hungarian-born producer named George Pal. A man I would later be honored to call my friend.

It was almost a fluke, the way I got invited onto that set. In school, I was always drawing pictures of spaceships and monsters and reading science fiction pulp novels. Those were the days when you could get in trouble in school for reading sci-fi — and get in trouble I did! But I couldn't get enough of it. One of my schoolmates there at Thomas Edison School in Burbank, Vern, knew I liked this sort of stuff, and he took an interest in me because of that.

Crew members bundle up against the cold on the refrigerated *Destination Moon* set.

Detail of the 13-foot-long small-scale Moonscape painting that Chesley Bonestell did for the film. The Earth is a painted ping pong ball.

One day in the fall of 1949, he came over to me in the cafeteria during our lunch break and said, "Hey, my dad's working on some picture about a trip to the Moon, and he's taking me over to the set today. Would you be interested in coming along?" And I said, "Y-y-y-yeah!" It turns out that Vern's dad was a grip who happened to be working on *Destination Moon.* At that age, I wasn't keeping up with what was going on in Hollywood news-wise and I hadn't heard anything about the picture.

I lived just a block and a half from school, so I ran home to ask my mom if it would be okay for me to go with Vern and his dad to the studio that afternoon, and she said, "Fine."

The bottom section of the *Destination Moon* ship was painted over and over with silver paint to hide the grain of the plywood.

It was great that the invitation and the visit to the set came on the same day; the fact that there was no lengthy advance notice made the experience even better. The anticipation, and the suspense, didn't have to build. It was just right there. Vern's dad picked us up in his car after school and we went over to General Service Studios in Hollywood. Outside of the visit I had made to Republic during the making of *The Purple Monster Strikes* a few years earlier, I had never before been on a studio lot.

Vern and I had passes and we were cleared to go onto the stage, which was something of a privilege: The *Destination Moon* set was pretty private, and didn't play host to a whole lot of "civilian" visitors. The visitors they had were dignitaries — representatives from the Air Force, Navy people and so on. A lot of important people were taking interest in this film.

I'm shy on sets — right to this day, I'm not the kind of guy who goes on a set and becomes very gregarious. I prefer to stay in the background because, frankly, I'm always afraid that I'm going to mess something up. In fact, the day of the *Destination Moon* set visit, once we were on the lot, Vern's dad had to prod us a bit to get us onto the sound stage. (Vern was a little shy too.)

My first surprise came as I stepped in through the sound stage door: The set was refriger-ated. Here I was, dressed in short sleeves for a typical 75-degree California day, and the cold hit me as soon as I entered. So now I was "double chilled" — I already had chills from being excited, and now chills from being cold. But what I saw quickly put all thoughts about the temperature out of my head: There on this largest stage on the General Service lot was that giant, now-familiar Moon set, with sand and rocks on the floor, the partial spaceship and the starry cyclorama. It was nothing like the sterile blue-screen stages used today, where the actors have to imagine what's going on around them, and their surroundings are added in post-production; on *Destination Moon*, everything was right there. To a 14-year-old kid, especially one who loved space stuff, it was an unbelievable experience. "My God…I'm on the Moon!" I told myself, because it really felt like I was.

The reason the set was so cold, I soon learned, was because the poor actors playing the space travelers (John Archer, Warner Anderson, Tom Powers, Dick Wesson) were suffering from the heat that built up inside their suits. To make their spacesuits look inflated with oxygen, they were stuffed with kapok, the silky fibers most commonly used to stuff sleeping bags, pillows and mattresses. It was the insulating material that Hollywood's greatest "gorilla man" Charlie Gemora used to use in his gorilla suits — and which Charlie later told me never to use ("Don't use kapok, whatever you do. It'll kill you!"). But back in those days, the late 1940s, I guess that's

Technicians work with the spacesuited little people on the *Destination Moon* set.

all there was, so these *Destination Moon* actors were dressed in spacesuits packed with it. Of course, the suits were also heavy, they had helmets on and, if all this wasn't tough enough on the actors, the sound stage rafters were loaded almost past the safety point with great banks of "Brute" arc lights, the hottest and most intense on the market, to simulate the effect

Little people in spacesuits (visible in the distance) were used to make the *Destination Moon* lunar set look even bigger.

of raw sunlight. That's why it became necessary to refrigerate the place to the extent that it was actually cold on the periphery of the set, and crew members were walking around in overcoats.

The ship was also really interesting. I thought it was metal, but it wasn't. Vern's dad showed Vern and me what it was: It was actually made out of plywood which had umpteen coats of paint on it, so that the wood grain wouldn't show through. Years later, Paul Blaisdell did just the same thing when he made the saucer for *Invasion of the Saucer Men*: He made it out of white pine and put coat after coat of paint on it, to hide the wood grain. It was kind of amazing to me to realize that those "two minds," Paul's and the *Destination Moon* people's, worked exactly alike.

George Pal shows off one of the *War of the Worlds* Martian machines to Janet Leigh and Tony Curtis, stars of his film *Houdini.*

John Archer, who played one of the spacemen, complained in an interview that the cracked Moon surface made the actors' footing insecure and that they had to look down a lot to avoid tripping and falling. He wasn't exaggerating. The surface was made up of scores of irregularly shaped slabs of plaster, six or seven inches thick, put together like a giant jigsaw puzzle. And the gaps between some of these slabs was six inches or more. If you weren't careful, you could slip your foot down into one of those gaps and snap an ankle pretty darn easy. And the spacemen, with helmets on their heads, couldn't see where they were walking — they could only see straight ahead unless they bent down. Practically the entire stage floor was covered with those jigsaw puzzle plaster slabs; in fact, they had to put the camera on a big crane so it could go in and out. They couldn't have a camera on the floor the conventional way, not with all those spaces between the slabs, and with some slabs higher than others.

Needless to say, between the starry cyclorama and the lunar surface and the spaceship itself, I was completely blown away by that set. And, to make the day complete, a little later on, maybe about an hour into our visit, they actually shot a scene with the actors — the scene where Archer stops his fellow spacemen from carrying the big telescopic camera back onto the spaceship and tells them that the ship is too heavy for lift-off. It was fun to watch them shoot that, but I must admit that I would have rather been there one day sooner: The day before, they did a forced perspective shot of Archer coming down the ship's ladder and three "little people" in spacesuits visible in the distance, carrying a smaller version of the telescopic camera. Using little people made it look like the set was that much bigger, and the three spacemen that much farther away.

During one break, Vern's father took me over and introduced me to George Pal, which very much surprised me — I didn't hold out any hope that he would do that. (I knew who George Pal was, from the Puppetoons. The only picture he did before *Destination Moon* was *The Great Rupert*, and I don't know if I'd even seen it at that point.) George seemed to be quite taken with me because I was a 14-year-old kid who had such a love for this stuff. I guess at that time not too many kids did — or, if they did, George wasn't aware of it. Vern's dad said, "This kid, all he does is draw spaceships all the time," and George seemed to be very impressed with that. He said in his very heavy Hungarian accent, "I'm glad you like this stuff," "How nice that you're interested in it," and "We should have *more* people interested in space, because someday we're gonna go to the Moon." George knew that was going to happen one day, he simply *knew* it (and, of course, it did, exactly 20 years later). So we had a conversation but not a real big one, because I was so in awe — and so scared to death I was messing up something!

I didn't talk to George after that for a few years. Then I met him again at a convention, a sci-fi con if I'm not mistaken, where he was giving a talk. When he was finished, I mustered my courage and went up to him and reintroduced myself. And, to my amazement he remembered me! "You were the young chap who came over to see the *Destination Moon* set," he said. "I was very impressed to meet a young kid who was so interested in science fiction and science stuff."

The sleigh-like look of the Time Machine was the result of George's creative input.

George (on ladder) observes as Byron Haskin directs a *War of the Worlds* scene.

By this time, he had finished *When Worlds Collide* at Paramount and was getting ready to make *The War of the Worlds* there. He mentioned that the Martian ships in his movie were going to be saucers, not the tripod-legged ships in the H.G. Wells story, but he didn't elaborate on it at all — he was keeping it quiet. When I asked, "Are the Martians gonna be in it?," he said, "Yes. We were going to animate the Martian, but now we're gonna do something else…" Here again he didn't tell me that much about it, he was pretty secretive at that point.

By this time, and for years to come, George tended to be kind of close-mouthed on the subject of his future pictures. I'm sure this was a result of what happened to him on *Destination Moon*: A low-budget company called Lippert saw all the publicity that *Destination Moon* was getting and, deciding to cash in on it, they made their own trip-into-space movie, *Rocketship X-M*, which was in theaters ahead of *Destination Moon*. From then on, I think, George was a lot less open about the films he was preparing. In fact, I later learned that he had a safe at home where he locked away scripts of his upcoming pictures.

Before we went our separate ways at that convention, George gave me his phone number at Paramount, and I think that if I had called and asked to visit the set of *War of the Worlds*, he might have allowed it. But, here again, I was so shy. (In fact, the only set I was on with George was *Destination Moon*.) After this point, I didn't see George again for several years; the next time I established contact with him was in 1960, soon after I got out of the Army. He had just produced and directed *The Time Machine* with Rod Taylor as the Time Traveler, and there were rumblings all around town about it. I was so excited about seeing the picture that I got up the nerve to call his office at MGM. The person who answered the phone was Gae Griffith, his secretary, whom I had first met on the *Destination Moon* set. (Gae was so devoted to George — George was her whole life, really.) Gae remembered me from way

George Pal's cast and crew members, including Rod Taylor, pictured here sitting in the Time Machine, were devoted to him.

back and said that she'd tell George that I phoned — and sure enough, he called me back. And he talked to me like we were old friends — "Bob, how are you?," "Bob, it's so good to hear from you!"

When I told him how jazzed I was about *The Time Machine*, he sent Kathy and me invitations to an advance showing in a screening room on the MGM lot. A few of the actors were there, and of course George, whom I approached and thanked for inviting us. So we got to see *The Time Machine* before it was released, and I just melted. *The Time Machine* is one picture that really "did it" for me — I was just blown away by it. It immediately became one of my favorite movies, and the Time Machine itself, co-designed by George and MGM art director William Ferrari, became one of my very favorite movie props. I'll never forget what George told me about the design: When he was a young fellow in the old country, in the days long before TV and even radio, the big event each year was riding around in a horse-drawn sleigh. So George incorporated the look of a sleigh into the Time Machine. Take another look at the Time Machine, now that you know this, and you'll see it immediately. That part of the design was all George.

From that point, 1960, on, George and I talked on the phone like every month. About anything and everything. I grew to love the man. For one thing, he genuinely loved science fiction, particularly science fiction that dealt with exploration. He had an incredible imagination and he loved fantasy in general. He was very happy making the films he made, and I don't think he ever cared to make any other kind — I don't believe he felt the least bit "typed." He loved doing genre pictures, and he was very good at it.

The other thing was, he was innately a sweet, wonderful guy. The best way I can illustrate this is to relate what I was told about him by Wah Chang and Gene Warren Sr., effects guys on many of George's pictures. (Wah and Gene were with Pal from the very beginning, right from the time he first came over to the U.S. — they were with him off and on all through his career.) Wah and Gene said that everybody loved George so much, they wanted to do the best possible job for him. *The Time Machine* was done for $750,000, which is pretty cheap for a movie like that. Part of the reason it was made that inexpensively is that George's crew put 150 percent into whatever they did. Because they *wanted* to work for him. They *wanted* to go the extra mile for him.

On the job, George was the kind of guy who was never bossy. He never told his crew what to do, he *suggested* what to do, which is a whole different way of doing things. If you did a shot that maybe he didn't like, he'd say, "Well, that's really good. But I wonder if maybe we should try it this way and just see what happens…" Never would he say, "That's not what I wanted, you idiots." According to *every*body, he was a very gentle human being on the sets of his movies — and I knew that myself from observing him on *Destination Moon*. You could tell that everybody loved him. Alan Young, who appeared in George's *tom thumb* and *The Time Machine*, said that working with George was one of the biggest thrills he ever had. Rod Taylor felt the same way; that's the reason he agreed to appear in *The Journey Back*, the 1993 *Time Machine* "Making Of" documentary that Kathy and I executive-produced. Rod said, "I would *love* to be able to talk about George." And there was one point in Rod's on-camera interview when, talking about George, he started to tear, and we had to cut. You can actually see it in the show, you see him choke up a bit. Everybody loved George — everybody except the young punk kids who started running the studios in the '70s. I'll get into that later.

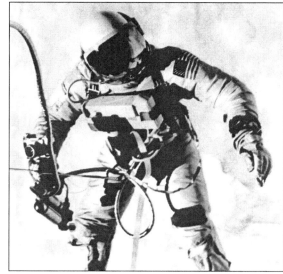

Using these photos, CBS-TV News compared Warner Anderson's spacewalk in *Destination Moon* with the real-life accomplishment of astronaut Ed White.

I was happy to share with George anything I had in my collection. He owned a tape of the episode of the radio series *Dimension X* in which they adapted *Destination Moon*, but he had somehow messed it up. (For a guy who was so "into" science and science fiction, in real life he was not very technically oriented!) I had my own tape of it, so I copied it for him along with the Bozo Records kiddie adaptation of *Destination Moon* in which a little boy and his dad take the trip to the Moon. He was thrilled to get those. But then in 1961, there was a sad incident which later prompted George's wife Zsoka to ask me not to share any more items from my collection with George. In November of that year, the worst brushfire in the history of Southern California swept through Bel-Air. Driven by 50 MPH winds, it destroyed nearly 500 homes, including George's.

George lost everything, not only his home, but also a lifetime of mementos. They weren't just objects to him, they were part of him. He also lost his scripts for a number of forthcoming pictures — *The Disappearance, Lost Eden* and *7 Faces of Dr. Lao.* He kept them in a fireproof safe and, sure enough, the fire didn't destroy the safe. But the fire was so hot that it incinerated everything *in* the safe — there was nothing but ashes when they opened it up. (So a fireproof safe is fine, as long as the fire doesn't get to it!) I felt so bad for him, I began making copies of all the photos I had from *Destination Moon, When Worlds Collide, War of the Worlds*, all his movies, to replace some of the ones he had lost. But then I phoned the house one day when he was out and Zsoka said to me, "Bob, I don't know if it's a real good idea to do this. If something happens to them again…he couldn't handle it." She knew that if he built up a new collection and then lost it a second time, it would just kill him. I

George was a fellow who was always looking to the future. Here's the Pal family sending Christmas greetings from the surface of the Moon.

pondered that later, the fact that George was so sensitive and sentimental that the loss of his mementos had devastated him, and I marveled at the fact that a guy like that was able to survive in a tough town like Hollywood. He wasn't mean enough to be in that business, it seemed to me, and I wondered how he managed to do it.

I have so many wonderful memories of George. In 1965, when Ed White became the first American to walk in space, I was watching the TV coverage with *Destination Moon* in the back of my mind (George had featured Hollywood's first "space walk" in his movie). White not only floated in space, he propelled himself around with a maneuvering unit the same way one of the characters did in *Destination Moon*. Suddenly the network showed a still of White floating in space — and next to it a still of Warner Anderson floating in space in *Destination Moon!* The two stills were so close to being perfectly identical, it was incredible. Then they even showed a clip from *Destination Moon*. I called George to tell him about it, but he'd already seen it and he was as excited as anybody could be about that. He was thrilled to death. It was as if he had been vindicated. The events depicted in *Destination Moon*, the movie some called preposterous when it was first proposed, were all coming to pass.

Of course I was interested in knowing what George's favorite science fiction films were. One was Fritz Lang's *Metropolis* — he thought that was an interesting picture on account of all the then-new techniques that were used in it. (At one point in the 1960s, he announced that he planned to remake it.) Other favorites were Lang's *Woman in the Moon* and William Cameron Menzies' *Things to Come*, which he thought was very innovative for its time. I'm sure he mentioned more, but those were the top three as I recall. Among his own movies, his favorites were *Destination Moon* (of course), *War of the Worlds*, *The Time Machine* and *7 Faces of Dr. Lao* — he just loved *Dr. Lao*, even though it wasn't real successful financially.

George and me on the day he offered me a role in his upcoming film *The Voyage of the Berg*, which unfortunately was never produced.

The two he liked the least were probably *The Power* and (his biggest disappointment, I believe) *Doc Savage: The Man of Bronze*. George had bought the rights to all the Doc Savage novels and his original plan was to film a number of them. And he loved the star, Ron Ely — I remember him saying, "My God, he *was* Doc Savage. He was perfect." But during the making of *Man of Bronze*, Warners took it away from him, rewrote it, put in a lot of "funny" stuff. George wanted it to be pretty straightforward — he wanted Doc Savage to be the sort of hero Indiana Jones would be in *Raiders of the Lost Ark*. Then Warners horned in and turned it into a campy, *Batman*-like thing. I know George wasn't thrilled with that. He never publicly complained about the film; in fact, I remember him going around at conventions, wearing a Doc Savage T-shirt. (He *had* to plug the film, what else could he do?) But the truth was that he was unhappy with the way it came out. Of course, it was a disaster at the box office, which put the kibosh on George's plan to do more Doc Savage pictures.

Tom Scherman inspects the Time Machine, missing its chair, the day we brought it home from the thrift shop.

George was never an aggressive guy, and (needless to say) that worked against him in Hollywood. You've got to sometimes be a son of a bitch in that business, in order to "make it." But George would rather switch than fight. For example, he left Paramount after making *When Worlds Collide* and *War of the Worlds* and a few other pictures there, because they messed *Conquest of Space* up on him. Paramount put in a religious angle, made the commander of the ship (Walter Brooke) a fanatic, and George didn't appreciate that at all. And, being a passive person, the way he took care of that situation was, he left Paramount. It wasn't in him to go up against the studio, so he moved on. But then, years later, MGM

The Time Machine on the set of our 1976 Halloween show "Return of the Time Machine."

meddled on *The Power*, and then Warners meddled on *Doc Savage* — George began contending with this all the time. When he was pretty much independent, like when he did *Destination Moon*, he was fine. On *When Worlds Collide* and *War of the Worlds*, Paramount left him alone pretty much. But later on, everybody started wanting to put in their two cents on his pictures.

I had a chance to be in one of George's pictures, but unfortunately nothing came of it. George used to give talks at colleges and he'd bring along a reel of 16mm clips from some of his movies. Well, one day the film broke — and I was the only guy he knew who had splicers at work (I was still a film editor at CBS then). He phoned and asked if I'd fix it for him, and I said sure. When he arrived, I was getting ready to show a friend my 16mm print of *The Further Adventures of Major Mars*, a seven-minute featurette that several of my special effects artist-friends and I had made (I played Major Mars). I didn't want to bore George with it so I told him, "I'll be with you in a minute, just let me start running this little featurette thing I did." He said, "*You* did it? I'd love to see it!" So I showed it and he loved it — he was howling! And when it was over, he said, "I didn't know you were an actor." I laughed, "I'm *not*. That oughta be pretty apparent!" But George was serious — "No, no, no, Bob, you were wonderful, you were brilliant! If I ever do *The Voyage of the Berg*, there's a comedic part that you're just made for." (*The Voyage of the Berg* was a film he wanted to make about a giant iceberg, the size of a city, that was going to be floated over from the Antarctic to places that had no water.) I'll never forget George saying, "If I do *Voyage of the Berg*, you're definitely going to be in that film," and I'm sure he would have made good on that promise. He wasn't a b.s. guy — that was another thing I liked about him.

George was a fellow who was always looking ahead into the future and there was one time when he made a prediction about *my* future. That story begins on the day in 1970 when I heard about the big upcoming MGM public auction, the now-famous one where they offered the ruby slippers from *The Wizard of Oz*, costumes from *Gone with the Wind*, the different

The Time Traveler (Charlie Dugdale) in our "Time Machine" Halloween show.

In a corner of my basement, I take the Time Machine for a spin.

saucers and ray guns from *Forbidden Planet*, a couple of the chariots from *Ben-Hur* — and, my personal Holy Grail, the Time Machine. George had always told me that he was sure that I would someday add that to my collection, and now here — finally — was my opportunity. Kathy and I scraped up and borrowed a thousand bucks, hoping maybe I could get it with that, and we went to the auction, which was held in one of the buildings at MGM. Finally the Time Machine came up…and when it got to $4000, I said, "Let's go. I don't even want to know." We left before the final bid. It ended up going for like ten grand to a fellow who operated a traveling show, carting movie props around the country in big semi trucks.

George and me on the Halloween show set as the Morlocks prepare to attack.

After the auction, I called George, very distraught, and told him I'd lost out. "Oh, you're still gonna get it," he chirped. "Someday you're going to end up with that machine, I just *know* you are." He was always full of hope — that was George, a positive guy. Well, I said, the chances of that were pretty slim. Then, lo and behold, George's prediction came true. Five years later, a friend of a friend was in an Orange, California, thrift shop looking for props for a movie — and in the back of that place, he saw the dish of the Time Machine. He called my buddy Tommy Scherman and said, "I think I found the machine that your friend Bob's lookin' for."

Two hours later, Tommy and I were down there, sauntering "casually" toward the back of the shop, and there it was. The chair was gone out of it, and the pods were all pretty much melted, but it was the Time Machine all right. The traveling show guy had gone out of business and all his props got re-auctioned, and this thrift shop owner bought the Time Machine because he wanted the barber chair that was built into it.* The shop owner had

---

* George liked the idea of a barber chair because it reminded him a little bit of a pilot's seat. So MGM got a-hold of a barber chair and re-did it, taking it off the pedestal and making feet for it and then "gingerbreading" it. For a look at that same style barber chair minus all the modifications, check out the barber scene in Charlie Chaplin's *The Great Dictator*.

sold the chair out of it to some barber chair collector, but that didn't concern me because George had given me the Time Machine blueprints, which included blueprints for the chair. I knew it wouldn't be hard for us to re-manufacture it.

The shop owner was an older fellow, a short, skinny, craggy old guy; if you were making a movie with a scene set in a big, grungy old thrift shop, he's the guy you'd want to cast as the proprietor! He didn't even know what film it was from, but as soon as I showed an interest, he said, "Well, it's probably a pretty important prop. I would have to get about five, six thousand dollars for it." My heart dropped. Thank God Tommy was there, and that he

The Time Traveler returns: Rod Taylor visits Bob's Basement and sits in the restored Time Machine.

had the presence of mind to do what he did. As soon as the store guy said six grand, Tommy looked at me and he scoffed, "Wait a minute. The chair's gone, the pods are melted — Bob, it's gonna cost us a couple thousand dollars to fix it. It's not worth it. C'mon, let's get outta here." He started to pull me out of the store and, believe me, my heart was going bumpity-bumpity-bumpity! We were about halfway out when the owner finally said, "Wait a minute, wait a minute…let's talk this over." I ended up buying the Time Machine for a thousand bucks — exactly what I'd intended to spend at the auction.

Naturally I called George as soon as I got home. "George, you're not gonna believe this, but I now have the Time Machine," I babbled out to him. "It's in bad shape, but I have it." He had such a great sense of humor: He paused for just a second, and then he said, very grandly, "Of course! You never doubt me! *Never* doubt me! I always *told* you, you were gonna get it." Then he laughed like crazy, that great laugh of his.

I finally had the Time Machine in my collection. Now, to give us the impetus to replace all the missing parts and make all the needed repairs, we decided to make it the centerpiece of the annual Halloween show at my house in Burbank that year. (It probably still wouldn't be finished if not for that Halloween show!) Using the blueprints George gave me, and with the help of Tommy Scherman, Dennis Muren, Mike Minor, Dorothy Fontana, Marc Richards and Lynn Barker, we completely rebuilt it in time to produce the Halloween show

"Return of the Time Machine." David Gerrold, most famous as the writer of the *Star Trek* episode "The Trouble with Tribbles," scripted the show in exchange for getting to be one of the actors alternating in the role of the Time Traveler.

That was in 1976, the year after George's *Doc Savage* played (briefly). Sad to say, there were no more films in George's future. But not for lack of trying. George went from studio to studio, trying to sell them on various projects — *The Voyage of the Berg*, *The Disappearance*, a number of stories. And he always wanted to do a sequel to *The Time Machine*, right back to the time when he made the Rod Taylor original at MGM. *Time Machine II* — that was

That's me at the controls of the Time Machine seen in the 2002 remake. The chair in the new machine is identical to the one in George's original.

his big dream. I own a duplicate of the tiny Time Machine you see in the 1960 movie and I used to loan it to George and he would take it to the studios where he was pitching *Time Machine II*, to have a prop to show them. (George used to own the actual little Time Machine in the film, but that burned up in his fire.)

Unfortunately, this was now the 1970s and most of the studios had changed hands since the days when George worked there. Younger guys were now running the show, and George was just an old man as far as they were concerned. Everywhere he went, it was always, "You're too old." (Okay, he *was* old, but the guy's mind was still so sharp. He could have still done anything, no problem.) And they kept bringing up his last couple of pictures: "Wellll, *The Power* didn't do very well, and *Doc Savage* was a total failure…" They basically just told him he was too old.

George was always a guy who believed in positive thinking — you can tell that just by watching some of his movies. He truly believed, "There's always something great just about to happen." But once he found himself being turned down by studio after studio, I finally started hearing in his phone calls, for the first time ever, that he was getting depressed. Really depressed.

The last time I talked to him, in 1980, he was as blue as I had ever heard him. He had tried to sell *Time Machine II*, and his other projects, one more time, and once again it was no-go. I don't recall if he told me what studio he had been at, it was one of the majors, but he said, "I've never been treated so badly in my life. These young studio execs just think I'm too old and all washed-up…they say nobody likes those kind of genre films any more…" I never heard him so despondent. He was always "up," he was never "down," there was always hope for anything and everything with George. But now, he knew there was no hope left. It was very difficult for me to hear him talking like this. Finally he said, "You know, I finally figured it out…I *am* too old. And I guess I don't have it."

I said, "George, that's not true, man. You're as bright as you've ever been. But you're dealing with guys who don't know the genre at all — they don't know the *business* at all. They're ex-agents, and they're ex-accountants, and they're ex-God-only-knows-what. But they're running the business now. The people running the business are not moviemakers any more." I tried my darnedest to raise his spirits, but he said, "No. No. I'm through. I'm just not gonna try any more. I'm tired of being told that I'm an old man, and a has-been…" I'd tried to lift him up, but there was no way I could do it. After I got off the phone, I felt awful. I told Kathy, "I've never heard George sound this way before. The guy's destroyed…"

And two weeks later, I got a phone call at CBS, in the morning, from Gae Griffith. "Bob," she said, "I have to give you some really bad news…I don't even know how to tell you…

"George died last night."

The business, I think, really did George in. Once he finally started to believe what everybody was saying about him, he was very depressed, for weeks. And then he died.

It was a pretty big funeral, George's — a lot of people turned out. A lot of his crew — nearly all of the oldtime technician guys who had worked for him and were still around were there. Ron Ely was there and I think Alan Young. Forry Ackerman gave the eulogy. It was very sad, it was a collective "We really miss this guy. He was one of the good guys in this world and…he's gone now."

Afterwards, a very few of us went back to the Pal house. It was me and Kathy and Zsoka Pal, and George's son David, and a few other close friends. Also some production people I didn't really know. And Gae Griffith, of course — she was with George to the very end. (She was darn near as broken up as Mrs. Pal was. She and George had like a "work marriage," you might say, because they'd been together for so long and she'd been his girl Friday on so many pictures. She was a wonderful lady.) It was a very sad time. I felt the same way Gae did when she said, "I've lost the best friend I've ever had in my life." I don't think there was a dry eye in the place.

The consensus that day, as we sat around George's big living room, was that he had died of a broken heart. The people running "the new Hollywood" had actually killed his spirit. George had had an incredible spirit…and when that spirit died, he died. I think that's exactly what happened. I'm starting to tear up now, just writing about it. It gets to me, to this day. Here was this guy who was just so full of life and so full of talent *still*, he could have done things. And this town beat him down. That sure helped kill him.

I try not to think about that last part of George's life — I have too many fond memories from happier times. One of my favorite memories of George crossed my mind when I visited the set of the 2002 *Time Machine* with Guy Pearce as the Time Traveler. My makeup artist friend Greg Nicotero worked on the new version, making up Jeremy Irons as the head Morlock, and he offered to see if he could arrange for me to visit the set. And when he called me back about it, he said, "This is really odd. They've been trying to get a-hold of *you*. They'd *love* for you to come over, they want you to see the new Time Machine and find out what you think of it!" So of course Kathy and I went over to the Warners lot, where the producer David Valdes and the writer John Logan treated us like royalty. John took us around and showed us all the sets, and then they showed us the new Time Machine, fired it up and asked what I thought of it. It had crystals that rotated and threw rainbow patterns, a back dish that opened up like a flower petal and spun, a front disc that spun the other way — it was beautiful to see it in operation, I loved it. And their Time Machine paid enough of an homage to George's, I felt. The chair in the new Machine was identical to the chair in George's, and the control lever was of the same design. The rest was different, but there was enough of the "classic" Time Machine to it that you'd think, "Oh, yeah, that's the Time Machine all right." David said, "This is very important to us, Bob…how do you like

I'm proud to say that when George finally sat in the Time Machine for the first time, it was in my backyard.

it? Do you think the fans are gonna hate it, or what?" And I told David and John, "Guys, I'm tellin' you: They're gonna love it."

I was trying to build up the courage to ask if I could maybe get a picture taken by the Machine when all of a sudden David said, "Bob, I want to get some shots of you sitting in the Machine — do you mind?" I almost fainted! I didn't have the nerve to even ask, and here he spoke up and suggested it himself and he brought the still guy over. I was totally thrilled — probably as thrilled as George Pal was when he sat in his Time Machine for the very first time. In my backyard.

This is not only my very favorite memory of George, it's one of my all-time great memories of all of our Halloween shows. George and Zsoka came to watch "Return of the Time Machine" that Halloween night in 1976, and they stayed the whole evening long. The show ran about ten minutes (that's including turn-around time to get the audience in and out) and we did it 35 times that night, starting around five in the afternoon and finishing up at midnight. George just loved seeing people react to it. And after it was over, the man who created that marvelous movie sat in the Time Machine. It was something which he had never done during the making of the movie — he just never got around to it, or maybe never even thought about it. It was a thrilling moment for all of us. When he sat in that machine, he was like a kid in a candy factory — I had never seen him so excited. That excitement actually shows up in the pictures that my friend Joe Viskocil took that night. And one of Joe's shots instantly became George's favorite, He had it duplicated, and from then on, for the rest of his life, that was the one he sent out to anyone who wanted a picture, In fact, in 1978 when *Starlog* ran an article on my Halloween shows, and used that photo as part of the montage on that issue's cover, George called me, very excited,

"Bob, I want to thank you so much," he said.

"Thank me? For what?"

"You made me a *cover boy*. I *always* wanted to be a cover boy!" That was his sense of humor.

I don't think I've ever met a finer man than George Pal. He and Glenn Strange, to my mind, were two of the nicest, most upstanding human beings on the face of this Earth. Any goodness I may have, I picked up from Glenn Strange and George — I'm a much better person for having known them. If I ever wanted to be like anybody, it would be like both of those gentlemen.

Gemora the Invincible

Charles Gemora as he appeared in Abbott and Costello's *Africa Screams.*

As a kid growing up in Oklahoma and California, I always loved jungle movies because I always loved the gorillas. And once I began meeting actors and makeup artists and other people who worked in the movie industry, I made it my business to find out who Hollywood's "gorilla men" were. I knew from Glenn Strange that "Crash" Corrigan played gorillas in a lot of pictures, and I knew about Emil Van Horn (*Perils of Nyoka, The Ape Man,* etc.) from Roy Barcroft. I found out all the names through perseverance, mostly by asking the makeup guys. And whenever I would ask about one of my favorite gorillas — "Who played the gorilla in *Murders in the Rue Morgue?*," "Who played the gorilla in *The Monster and the Girl?*," "Who played the gorilla in *Phantom of the Rue Morgue?*" — the answer would always come back the same: Charlie Gemora.

I started gelling friendly with the various makeup men in the early 1950s, when I was about 18. One of them was a fellow named Emile LaVigne, who had worked on some of the Universal Frankenstein films and later made-up the mutants for *World Without End.* He'd been around a long time and I'd known him since I was a kid. One day he told me, "If you want to really learn about this stuff, they always need people to sit in for makeup tests. They don't care how old you are, they just need a face." He made a call for me, and soon I was sitting in for tests at the makeup union.

Makeup "interns" — young guys trying to get into the makeup union — would take a makeup test consisting of an oral test, a written test and then of course the makeup itself. They would do hair work on me, the bald caps, the beards, the cuts, the bruises, all that kind of stuff. A lot of people didn't like to do it — it is pretty uncomfortable — but I didn't care, I loved it. In fact, the more junk they piled on me, the *more* I loved it! After the interns finished up on me, the old makeup guys would come in and see how the hair looked and examine the bald cap looking for "ends" and so on, then grade the interns. This was before there were makeup classes at places like the Joe Blasco Schools; back then, the only way you could pick up makeup tips was by sitting in for these guys. It only paid ten bucks a day, but I knew I'd start getting an inkling how to do this type of work, and that was the idea.

The way I was introduced to Charlie Gemora was, again, through an old makeup guy I knew, Abe Haberman. In talking to him one day, I mentioned Charlie doing apes, and Abe said, "He's over at Paramount now." I'd had no idea. I knew Charlie did the Martian for *The War of the Worlds* at Paramount, but I thought Paramount just called him in for that — I didn't know he *worked* there, but he did: At that time, 1957, Wally Westmore was head of makeup at Paramount, and Charlie Gemora was head of the lab.

Once Abe realized how interested I was, he said he'd make a call for me — and he did. Charlie said, "Sure, come on over!," and we arranged to meet at Paramount a couple of days later. I had a pass that got me through the famous Paramount gate and I proceeded to the makeup lab. I knew him as soon as I saw him, mainly from his size — he was only about five-five, a very short man. He was Filipino, and at that time 54 or 55

Charlie's passport photo (1920s).

years old. It was really exciting for me; and, funnily enough, *he* was really excited that *I* was excited, because he probably didn't have a whole lot of fans asking him about his work. He said a few people had talked to him about making the *War of the Worlds* Martian suit and playing the Martian in the movie, but nobody had ever talked to him about doing the gorillas — nobody had ever even *mentioned* that. I was the first "fan" ever to bring up the gorilla side of his career. So we got along famously.

We talked right there in the lab: He had a little desk in a corner of the room and that's where we sat down, across the desk from each other. I pulled up a chair and we sat and talked for hours. Man, sitting across from Charlie Gemora — how cool is that? He asked, "Well...

Early in his career, Charlie (far right) headed up the crew that built Universal's Phantom Stage.

what do you want to know?," and I told him I thought he made the greatest gorillas in the world. And once I told him that I was hoping to someday build a gorilla suit, it opened up that whole avenue. He began telling me *everything* he knew about gorilla suits, what to do and what *not* to do and so on and so forth.

Charlie got started building gorilla suits back in the 1920s, when he realized that there was a need for them. On some picture that he was working on as a makeup man, somebody said, "We need a gorilla suit" — and so Charlie built one! I've seen photographs from silent films with gorillas that aren't Charlie, so obviously costumers built gorillas from the '20s

Frank Merrill was Tarzan in a 1920s jungle adventure with Charlie in an early gorilla role.

Bela Lugosi, king of Hollywood's horror men, and Charlie, lord of the jungle, menace Sidney Fox in a *Murders in the Rue Morgue* posed shot.

on, and probably put extras in them most of the time. But Charlie was the first to actually build his own gorilla suit and then portray the gorilla as well. He was a makeup artist who simply thought to himself, "Well, there's a need for a gorilla suit, so I'm gonna build one." It was a great idea, one that gave him a whole second career.

My main questions were about building gorilla suits, and Charlie was very open about it. He had no secrets at all, he told me everything. He said, "You're going to need a cast of your face if you want it to fit well. That's one of the main things you gotta worry about. If you have daylight through those eyeholes, you're in trouble." That was one thing that put Charlie's gorilla suits above all the others: His eyes fit right up against the eyeholes. You could shoot an extreme closeup on his face and his eyes blended right in with the gorilla face, and it didn't look like a mask. All the other gorilla guys, if the camera got too close, you could tell there were eyeholes. But even in the early days, you could get real close on Charlie's face and it would look great. The only guy that came close to that was George Barrows (*Gorilla at Large, Black Zoo,* many more), because he also did a casting of his face and it worked pretty good. So when I did my first gorilla head, one that Don Post Sr. made for me, we took it off my head cast and it was perfect. The inside of my gorilla face was a perfect "negative" of my face, so it fit very close around my eyes. You could get closeups, everything, without a problem. That was because I listened to Charlie.

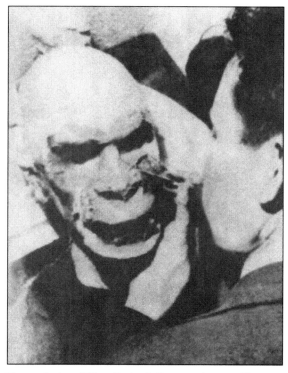

Rare photo of Charlie building up the gorilla face on a bust of his own head.

To make his gorillas bulkier and more imposing, Charlie padded himself with kapok, the silky stuffing they used to use in sleeping bags. It's fine, it's good padding, but you sweat to death because *insulation* is what it is! He told me, "*Don't use kapok,* what*ever* you do. It'll kill you!" That was a very good suggestion, and I certainly didn't use kapok. Unfortunately for Charlie, kapok was probably about all he knew in the early days, and he just didn't think about changing. Something else he advised me against doing was wearing the "iron mask" that he and Emil Van Horn and "Crash" Corrigan wore, a metal armature with the rubber gorilla face glued to it. What I did instead was make a gorilla face that was all rubber — a dense foam rubber, a thicker type of foam. Instead of having on my face the metal armature that the gorilla face fit on, my foam rubber gorilla face fit right to my face.

Charlie was also the first guy to ever come up with what he called "a water bag." He put it in the stomach of his later gorillas so there would be totally realistic movement — it moved the way a chubby person's stomach would if he was bouncing around. It was incredible, the extra realism he got by having the belly move. I think the first water bag was in his *Monster and the Girl* suit — at least, that's when I first noticed it — and it was also in the *Phantom of the Rue Morgue* suit. Charlie also did extension arms, because gorillas' arms are a lot longer than human arms. You don't need them on a gorilla suit unless you have to walk on all fours, but *then* you really do, because the human body doesn't bend the way a gorilla's does. Emil Van Horn used arm extensions, and George Barrows later on, but (again) Charlie was probably the first because, here again, he wanted it as realistic as he could get it. The gorilla actor's hands reach down the gorilla sleeve to about the elbow, and there would be a grip that he would hold onto. The arm extensions would go on down the rest of the way from there. Usually the gorilla hands were in a clenched position, because gorillas clench their fists when they're walking. Charlie only used them when he was moving around; otherwise he didn't have to use them at all. Believe it or not, he could go back and forth between regular arms and extension arms in the same movie, all depending on the scene. For some reason, you can get away with that, audiences just don't notice it. For example, in *Phantom of the Rue Morgue*, he isn't wearing the arm extensions for the scene where he's in his cage, reaching through the bars and touching Karl Malden and Patricia Medina. But in later scenes where you see him walking on all fours, he *is* wearing them.

Charlie made all of his own suits from scratch, every one of them. Heads, hands, feet and the suit, he built; the only thing he didn't build was that "iron mask" armature. In addition

Appearances to the contrary, Laurel and Hardy loved Charlie, and Charlie loved them. (From the 1932 short *The Chimp.*)

to telling me everything I wanted to know about building a gorilla suit, he gave me lots of advice on how to move. For gorilla guys, the right "body English" is essential, and Charlie had it down pat because he'd done his homework: He used to go to the San Diego Zoo (the only place in California that had gorillas in those days) to observe them; he studied up on gorillas as much as he could and he even got some scientific pictures. That was back in the '20s and '30s, when gorillas were still very "mysterious." (Back then, people used to think they were monsters and hunt them just because of their size and the fact that they were pretty ugly, grisly-looking things. You can tell that by the early movies, where the gorilla was always the monster — always.) The fact that Charlie had done his homework showed in his suits and also in his performances.

According to Charlie, what "makes" the performance is 90 percent body English and eye movement. He told me to do a lot of head movements and things like that; open and close your eyes; and, if you want to make the gorilla look really mean, when you open the mouth, throw your head back so that people are now looking up inside the mouth. It gives the illusion that the mouth is open a lot wider than it actually is. Just tilt your head back, open your mouth as wide as you can get it, and it looks like you're really growling. I had seen him do these things 100 times in his movies, and yet these were things that I'd never thought about. Ever. And it was all true. People think that the gorilla brow moves up and down and everything. But it doesn't move at all, it's strictly an illusion! When I played gorillas, I've heard people say about me, "Man, that gorilla really looks mean. Look at that brow!" — when the brow wasn't doing *any*thing. It's strictly the eyes and your body English. My gorilla faces were exactly like Charlie's as far as movement went: The mouths of my gorilla suits opened and closed, and that's all they did.

Charlie got up out of his chair and moved around and did all his gorilla stuff. He showed me how he walked and how he beat his chest and how he threw his head back — he demonstrated all of that for me. I think he was having a lot of fun. The other guys in the makeup lab, I don't remember if they watched — I was so engrossed, I don't even know if they were even still there.

I was flabbergasted. Here was the God of Gorillas, showing me how he did his gorillas. To me, it was like the biggest thing in the world. I think he had a lot of fun. I know I sure did!

Charlie built at least six gorilla suits; he could have made more than that, but no less. He did three in the silent-early sound days (the one he wore in a Tarzan picture, the one he wore in the 1930 *The Unholy Three* and *Murders in the Rue Morgue*, and the one that was in the Laurel and Hardy short *The Chimp*), Then he did one for *The Monster and the Girl*, which

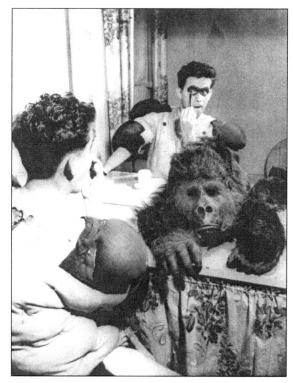

"Raccoon" makeup and shoulder pads were part of Charlie's preparations for playing his amazing apes.

was the best gorilla suit he ever built; one that ended up in *Africa Screams* and some other films; and then the *Phantom of the Rue Morgue* suit, which was the last one he made. He might have built more suits in between that I'm not familiar with, but I know he did at least those six.

Gemora battles a dragon (Wah Chang) as Mae West and Marx Brothers puppets look on in the unfinished short *Magic Island*.

Of course, he also talked about some of the experiences he'd had making those movies, and some of the stars he'd worked with. He was in Lon Chaney's *Where East Is East* and the talkie version of *The Unholy Three* and said that Chaney was a very generous, kind man. Laurel and Hardy he loved to death. He absolutely adored those guys and told me that they were two of the nicest, friendliest men he'd ever met. I knew Stan Laurel real well, and that was exactly the same thing Stan used to tell me about Gemora, that Charlie was the sweetest, greatest guy that *he* ever worked with. Charlie worked with them twice, in *The Chimp* and then in *Swiss Miss*, where he played the gorilla on the suspension bridge. He loved working

The Monster and the Girl gave Charlie his biggest role, as a gorilla with the brain of an unjustly executed man.

with Laurel and Hardy and he talked about them more than he did anybody else.

I don't know how physically strong Charlie was back when he was in his prime. When you're playing gorillas, it helps a lot if you are, but you don't have to be. You have to be in pretty good health, though, and obviously Charlie was because he did it a number of times in the '20s, '30s and '40s. It's hard work, I can certainly vouch for that. He didn't mention any injuries, even though I don't believe he was stunt-doubled very often in his gorilla roles. In *Murders in the Rue Morgue*, Charlie did tell me that strongman Joe Bonomo doubled him in the scenes where he's climbing up to the Paris rooftops. But the thing about *Murders in the Rue Morgue* that stuck in Charlie's craw a little was the fact that closeups of an actual chimp were inserted into the movie instead of the closeups they'd shot of Charlie in his gorilla suit. He didn't know they had done this until he saw the movie; when he did, he said he was in shock because all of a sudden the movie would jump from a shot of him in his gorilla suit to a shot of that very different-looking chimp. He wasn't too pleased with that, and could never figure out why they did it. His gorilla face was perfectly mobile. It could do the expressions that were needed. And *did*.

One of Charlie's more unusual credits was *Magic Island*, which was shot in color around 1935. It was a short in which puppets of various movie stars (like the Marx Brothers and Mae West) are menaced by a giant gorilla (Charlie) and a dragon (played by Wah Chang, who built his own dragon suit as well as the puppets). It was directed by LeRoy Prinz, a choreographer who had to shoot *Magic Island* at night because he was shooting dance sequences for other movies during the day. I never talked to Charlie about *Magic Island* — I didn't even know that it existed until Wah Chang told me about it much later. Wah recalled that in one scene he and Charlie had a fight, and that at one point Charlie fell on top of him. Poor ol' Wah was a very thin little guy, and he said the weight of Charlie and his gorilla suit almost squished him! Wah didn't think that *Magic Island* was ever completed, and I can believe that; I've never seen it, and never talked to anyone who has.

Charlie's favorite of all his films was also my favorite: *The Monster and the Girl*. He said he thought he "nailed" playing a gorilla there better than anywhere else, and so he just loved the film. He also liked the premise (a man's brain is transplanted into a gorilla) and the fact that, in his own words, "I probably got more gorilla time in that film than any other movie I ever did." One cute story I remember him telling concerned the little dog in the movie that follows the gorilla everywhere he goes. Charlie said they were worried that that dog might be scared of him, or maybe try to attack him; for some reason, animals are funny around people in animal suits, and you never know what's going to happen. The dog's trainer was very concerned, and suggested that they first introduce

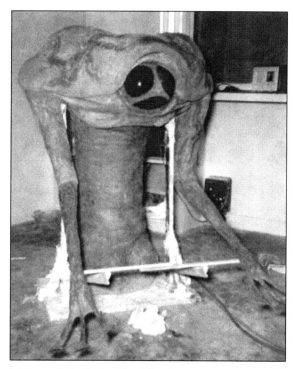

Makeup lab shot of the Martian costume created and worn by Charlie in *The War of the Worlds.*

the dog to Charlie without the gorilla suit, so the dog could get Charlie's scent and know who he was. After they did that, Charlie put the suit on, and very tentatively they sent the dog over to sniff him out and see how the dog would react. Well, that dog went right up to Charlie, the little tail wagging like crazy! That dog loved him. Evidently it did get his scent. and after that, they couldn't keep the dog away from him. In the movie, when the dog is

Charlie as the fearsome Sultan, Phantom of the Rue Morgue.

following him, it's *really following him* — that was a bit of directing that the director didn't have to worry about. Charlie said that dog was always there, every time he looked around. If he sat down and took a break, the dog came over by him. It was an amazing thing. He called that dog "the cutest little dog in the world," and the dog loved him too. You can see it in the film, it really looks like that dog loves that gorilla — because it *did*. Charlie found that film a very pleasant experience and thought it was great because he got to do a realistic gorilla for a change. And that was his best suit ever. Rick Baker, the makeup and special effects artist (*Schlock, Greystoke, Gorillas in the Mist*, the 1998 *Mighty Joe Young*), has always

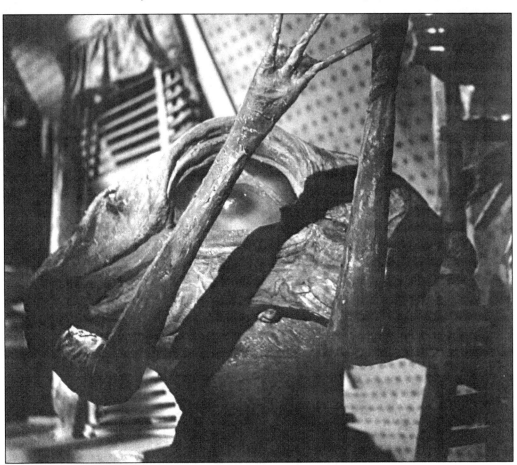

Charlie's frightening Martian as it appears in *The War of the Worlds*.

had a fascination for gorillas, and Rick too thinks that the suit in *The Monster and the Girl* was Charlie's best ever.

Phantom of the Rue Morgue was the last gorilla portrayal Charlie did. He had suffered a major heart attack some time before he began work on that movie, so Nick Cravat, the actor-acrobat who worked with Burt Lancaster in swashbucklers like *The Flame and the Arrow* and *The Crimson Pirate*, doubled him in the more strenuous scenes. Charlie did all the closeup work, like the scene I mentioned where he and Patricia Medina are touching each other through the cage bars. At that point in his life, Charlie could do only minimal movement in that role — he could do some stuff, but he couldn't do any of the stuntwork, like scaling the side of Karl Malden's house or climbing the tree or tearing up the mannequin in the dressmaker's shop window. Nick Cravat doubled him in all those physical scenes. (Cravat was uncredited, of course, as was Charlie. I believe the only time Charlie got screen credit for playing a gorilla was *Swiss Miss* — and there they misspelled his name!) Charlie did a very minimal of work in *Phantom of the Rue Morgue*, but all the closeups were him because nobody could do the body English the way he did.

The only monster Charlie ever played was the Martian in *The War of the Worlds*, and of course I was real interested in that too. And, again, he filled me in on the whole story, including how he made the suit. (There was no secrecy about this man — none at all.) Building a Martian suit for *War of the Worlds* was a last-minute decision. Since George Pal had done the Puppetoons, the original idea for the Martian was to stop-motion-animate it the way the Puppetoons characters were animated. But then they decided that animation would be too costly — Paramount already had a lot of money in the film anyway — and that they would go ahead and make a Martian suit instead. Art director Al Nozaki quickly designed the Martian guy and Charlie built it just as fast. He made a wood armature and a chicken wire framework and laid what he called rubber sheeting over it. The Martian's three-color eye was made out of plastic and glass. (I'm sure somebody in the Paramount prop shop, not Charlie, made that.) For the Martian's pulsating veins, he used very, very thin rubber tubing — off-camera, Charlie's daughter Diana, 12 years old at the time, worked the tubes, sucking the air out to make them collapse and then letting air back in again. That's what made them fluctuate and look like pulsating veins.

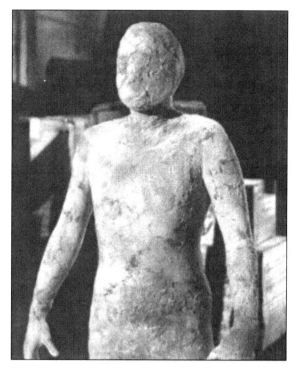

Charlie created the costume worn by stuntman Bob Bryant in *Curse of the Faceless Man*.

Charlie built the suit from Al's design and also wore it in the film (again uncredited, of course). I believe the reason he played the Martian was because of the time constraints. He was used to wearing gorilla suits, so he knew it wouldn't bother him, and it was easier to build it for himself than to build it for somebody else. He didn't say that to me, but that's my speculation. Also, Charlie would know how to manipulate everything. If Paramount had put an extra in that suit, it would have probably taken him hours or days to figure out how to work it. So it was just easier for Charlie to do it.

It's producer William Alland (right) who ought to be giving Charlie a big hand for his work on *The Colossus of New York*.

People have sometimes wondered what the bottom of the Martian looked like — you only see the top half of it in the movie. Well, a bottom half was never designed, there *was* no bottom to the Martian. The suit went down below Charlie's waist to probably just a little bit above his knees. Here again, as with his gorilla arm extensions, his arms went into the sleeves of the Martian suit but his hands went only to the elbows. At the elbows, there were three little rings that he put on three fingers. By pulling on those rings, which were attached to cables, he could make the Martians' fingers move. If he moved his fingers inside, opened and closed them, the Martian hands would open and close. When they were ready to shoot the scene, Charlie knelt down on a small dolly, and a couple of grips using pull wires began wheeling him around on it. At the end of the scene, when you see him streaking out of the room, they literally just yanked him across the room on that dolly! Balancing himself on his knees the way he was, he almost fell off and busted his head. He said that was perhaps the only time in his gorilla-monster career that he almost did get hurt! But Charlie thought playing the Martian was real fun. He said it was a quick and easy scene, that there wasn't really all that much to it, and that they got it done in just one day. I also remember him telling me that the Martian was made so fast that it literally fell apart right after the shooting.

A very rare shot of Charlie taking his gorilla head and hands into the portrait studio on the Paramount lot in the early 1940s.

I sat with Charlie in the Paramount makeup lab that day for at least four or five hours. We even went to lunch at the studio commissary — his treat. Like Stan Laurel said, he was absolutely the sweetest guy on Earth. He was a humble man — extremely humble — and very, very nice. In fact, I think he was maybe even a little bit embarrassed, because I don't think he was used to having fans wanting to talk to him. That was the feeling I got. It's so neat when you finally meet someone whose work you admire so much, and they turn out to be that kind of person. Often you meet people you think are going to be great, and they turn out to be so full of themselves. But he was just the opposite. In our meeting, he even promised to send me some photos of himself in his various movies, and sure enough he mailed them to me about a week later. I still have them today. I saw Charlie just that one time, but I talked to him at Paramount on maybe five or six occasions over a period of the next few months. I would think of another question about gorilla suits — what about the padding?, what about the size of the hands?, that kind of thing — and he was always extremely nice. If somebody else would answer, no matter what Charlie was doing, he'd come right to the phone.

Charlie worked as a makeup man and mask maker on other science fiction and fantasy films after I met him (*The Colossus of New York, Curse of the Faceless Man, I Married a Monster from Outer Space, Jack the Giant Killer* and others), but his days of working in front of the camera were over. He was the makeup man on a movie called *Flight of the Lost Balloon* with Marshall Thompson and Mala Powers, and one of Charlie's old gorilla suits was also used in the movie. But I doubt very much if it was Charlie wearing it: They weren't his mannerisms at all. He never did another gorilla after *Phantom of the Rue Morgue* that I know of. He'd had his heart attack in the '50s and *Flight of the Lost Balloon*, shot in May-June 1961, was one of his last films. I don't think health-wise he could have played the gorilla.

Charlie passed away in August of 1961. When I heard that he had died, I was devastated. Even though I couldn't say he was a close friend, I felt like I had lost a close friend because I had followed his career for so many years, and then he'd been so kind to me. It was like "The king of gorillas is dead. The King is dead. There'll never he another one like him." And that's true — I don't think there ever will be another quite like Charlie Gemora.

In his obits, it was reported that his last work was as a makeup man was on Paramount's *One-Eyed Jacks* with Marlon Brando — and that he had "achieved his first measure of fame as the oversize gorilla of the film *King Kong*." Charlie never in his life said he played King Kong — never — but for some reason, people believed that he had played Kong in some scenes. According to the rumor, it was Charlie climbing up the side of the Empire State Building. Well, I've got a picture of Buzz Gibson animating the Kong puppet for that scene! There was *never* a guy used in a suit in that film, ever. Charlie was never even sure how the rumor got started, but it had gone around for a long time. At some point, maybe somebody who knew that Charlie played gorillas was talking about *King Kong* and said, "It must have been Charlie Gemora…," and the story spread from there. Charlie never claimed that he played it, and when people would mention to him that he did, he would tell them emphatically, "No, I did *not* play King Kong. I never played King Kong." That was a sore point with him. He would always say, "*No*, I had *nothing* to do with that film…"

What Charlie did with his gorilla suits, I don't know. I think most of them rotted away. The last one, the *Phantom of the Rue Morgue* suit, ended up years ago with some makeup artist at NBC. I don't know how or where he got it, but he brought it over to Don Post Studios one day. It was just totally rotting away — the face was about gone. It was in real bad shape, and it's completely gone by now, I'm sure. What ever happened to the rest of his suits, I never even thought to ask him, and he didn't say.

Charlie Gemora was *the* gorilla guy, the most realistic of any of 'em — Emil Van Horn, "Crash" Corrigan, whoever. Probably the one who came closest to acting like him was George Barrows. George did a pretty darn good gorilla, and he was probably the only one of the latter-day guys that tried to do a real gorilla. (I never really got to try to do a real gorilla; whenever I played a gorilla, most of what I did was comedy. But that was okay with me.)

Unfortunately, I didn't make my first gorilla suit within Charlie's lifetime. We didn't build my first suit until 1962, when Charlie had been dead for several months or a year. Don Post Sr. sculpted my original head, hands and feet, and Kathy built the costume.* We were over at Post Studios when we first got the suit all together. Once I got it on, I looked over into one of those big, full-length mirrors and I saw myself for the first time, and I got a thrill that I've never gotten over. I had chill bumps on top of chill bumps. Here was a lifelong dream fulfilled: I was looking in the mirror, and looking back at me was this incredible gorilla.

And as I tried that suit on for the first time, who was I thinking of but Charlie Gemora. He was in the forefront of my mind. I was asking myself, "Now, what would Charlie do? How would he move? How would he tilt his head?" And I did every move he did — or *tried* to, anyway. I wasn't thinking about real gorillas and how real gorillas moved, I was thinking about Charlie Gemora. I emulated him the whole way.

* It was kind of weird, the way she built the suit. There were no such thing as "gorilla patterns," not in those days, so she based it on a clown suit, because clown suits are kind of "full."

Near the beginning of his outré acting career, Charlie worked with a star who was at the end of his: Lon Chaney in 1930's *The Unholy Three.*

Below: Seventeen-year-old Charlie Gemora went to work for Universal as a sculptor.

Charlie and wife
Isabel on the set of
Cecil B. DeMille's
1935 epic *The
Crusades.*

Gemora's music
soothes the savage
Harpo Marx behind
the scenes on 1939's
At the Circus.

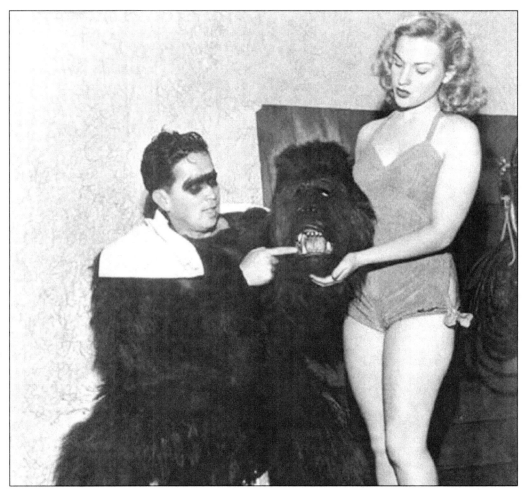

The kind of publicity shot Hollywood doesn't take any more: A swimsuited starlet is on hand as Charlie dons his *Monster and the Girl* gorilla suit.

As visitors to his home watch, Charlie monkeys around.

The Monster
(Charlie) closes in
on his last victim
(Paul Lukas) in *The
Monster and the Girl.*

Charlie poses with
one of his own
simian simulations,
circa 1947.

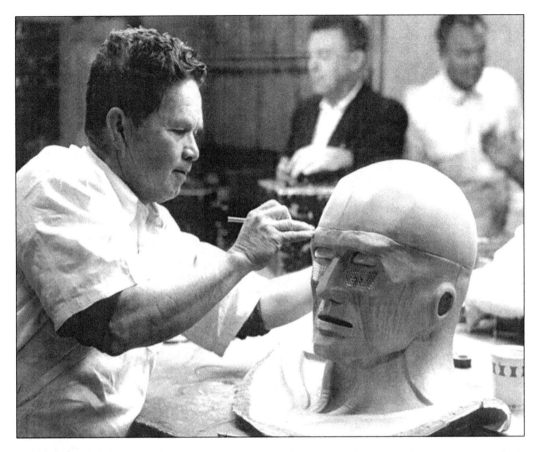

This pair of behind-the-scenes shots, taken during the making of *The Colossus of New York,* showcase Charlie's attention to detail as he sculpts the oversize head and paints on the finishing touches.

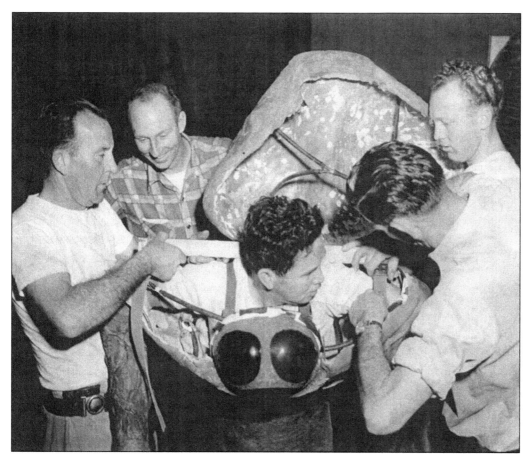

Above: *War of the Worlds* crew members help Charlie into his Martian costume as they prepare to shoot the movie's frightening farmhouse scene.

Left: Creating the she-fish for *Mr. Peabody and the Mermaid.*

Right: Charlie and Wally Westmore aged James Dean for his role in *Giant.*

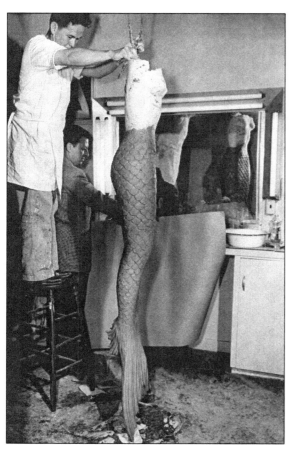

Another unforgettable movie menace that emerged from Charlie's lab: The alien invaders in *I Married a Monster from Outer Space.*

The Faceless Man strikes down a policeman.

In 2001 I did an article about Charlie for *Monsters from the Vault* magazine and the best upshot of that was that his daughter Diana read it and contacted me. We've become great friends and she's visited me at my home (pictured).

Castle
of Horrors

People might not have been using the term "cult movies" yet in the late 1950s, but William Castle was producing them one after another and, within the short space of just a year, had coronated himself the King of Gimmick Horror Pictures. By the end of 1959 I'd already seen Castle's first horror movie *Macabre* and, like everyone else who bought a ticket, was issued a $1000 life insurance policy payable in event of my death by fright during the performance of the film. Even wilder was his *House on Haunted Hill*, presented in the miracle of Emergo — which meant that a cardboard skeleton glided on wires over the audience during a key climactic scene. Well, that was the plan, anyway. In the Los Angeles theater where I saw the movie, the skeleton got about halfway and then got hung up in the wires, and just dangled over the heads of the people in the auditorium for

It was *Shock Theater* host Joe Alston (left) who paved the way for me to meet William Castle. That's me as Joe's sidekick, Ygor.

a while. People were throwing popcorn, popcorn boxes and every other thing at it!

Those were Castle's first two horror movies but I'd become aware or him years before that: I'm a nut for 3-D movies and he'd made a few of them back in the early '50s, the heyday of 3-D. So between the 3-D pictures and now the gimmick horror movies, by 1959 I felt as though I had a lot in common with this man I'd never met. And the circumstances under which I did finally meet him were almost as unusual as the plots of some of his pictures.

The "build-up" to my meeting with Bill Castle is a bit of a long story but since it involves monster sketches, gory makeup prosthetics, *Shock Theater* and (the ultimate horror!) a draft notice, I hope you'll bear with me. In 1958 I received that dreaded letter which began "GREETINGS FROM THE PRESIDENT. YOU'VE BEEN SELECTED..." In other words, I got drafted.

I went into the Army, kicking and screaming of course, and soon found myself getting my basic training at Fort Ord, up near San Francisco. The way the Army works is funny: I found out that they needed a film editor and, jumping at the

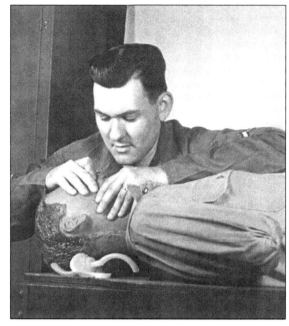

Performing CPR on a dummy with my face was really weird!

opportunity, I said, "That's what I do for a living!" To which they replied, "Oh, no, no. No, we'll train somebody." What the Army wants is someone who'll do it the Army's way. So instead of putting me in film editing or some other field where I might have done 'em some good, they put me in Medical Supply, which was a "great" place for me to be! It's a good thing I didn't dispense medication — God only knows how many G.I.s would no longer be with us if I had!

My Medical Supply training began at Fort Ord and then continued at Fort Leonard Wood, Missouri. We used to call it Fort Lost in the Woods because we were 93 miles from

As part of Fort Sam Houston's "Training Aids" division, I helped build the Brooke Army Medical Center's float for a local parade (saucer in front, planets in middle, futuristic helicopter at rear).

the nearest town — this was nothing but a place in the Ozarks where you got bit by chiggers all the time. And from there they sent me to Fort Sam Houston in San Antonio, Texas, which is where I was going to be stationed.

While taking the last of my Medical Supply courses at Fort Sam, I did what I always do: I doodled all the time, monsters and stuff like that. One day, the sergeant caught me. I thought I was in for it, but instead of letting me have it, he said, "Wow…that's pretty good!" And then he asked, "Could you maybe do some sketches for my little boy? His birthday's coming up." I thought about it for a moment and then suggested, "What if I did creatures

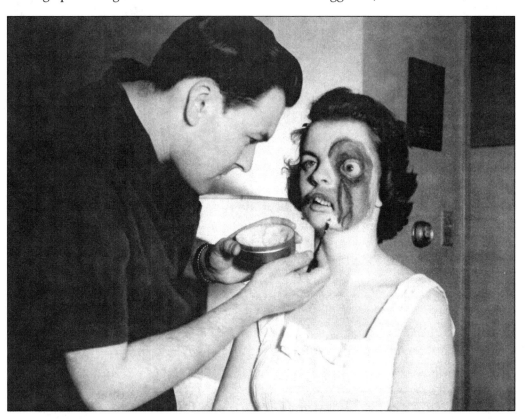

With a little makeup magic, I transformed Kathy into the KENS-TV *Shock Theater* mascot, Miss Shock.

from all the different planets?" The sergeant said that would be cool. So I did the sketches, and he invited me over to his place (off the base) for dinner the night of the kid's birthday party — that's almost unheard-of, a draftee like me conferring with an enlisted man. But this sergeant was a real nice guy, one of the few nice guys I met in the Army. I gave the sketches to his little boy, who was thrilled, and then the sergeant said, "You know, you're wasting your time here. You shouldn't be in Medical Supply. You've got talent. You belong in Training Aids."

What the men in the Training Aids division did was build any and all kinds of stuff for the Army, from the smallest items to the yearly float that Fort Sam had in the San Antonio "Fiesta Flambeau" Parade. The sergeant thought I'd be perfect for projects like that and he talked to the head captain and, sure enough, I got transferred out of Medical Supply and over to Training Aids.

As luck would have it, at that time they were just beginning a new initiative designed to make the instruction for medical trainees more effective. Up until then, simulation exercises consisted of attaching tags to the soldiers who were playing casualties ("THIS MAN HAS A GUT WOUND," "THIS MAN HAS A HEAD WOUND" and so on), and then the young medical trainees in the field would have to "treat" them. Well, doing it that way, these guys just couldn't take it seriously.

Things changed when some Canadians started a program called Simulated Casualty where wounds made out of rubber were applied to the "injured" soldiers. Fort Sam Training Aids ordered some of these pieces — a couple of gut wounds and some leg wounds — and they were really pretty bad. Since I had makeup experience, I was asked, "Do you think you can sculpt some better stuff?" I said, "Well, I know I can do better than *this*!" So we made molds and we made our own "wounds" and got 'em pretty darn realistic. I had to see photographs of the real stuff — for instance, we saw photographs of a guy with a gut wound, with his entrails hanging out, and we had to duplicate that. Then we made up our own blood formulas. My "claim to fame" there was my glycerin and oatmeal vomit!

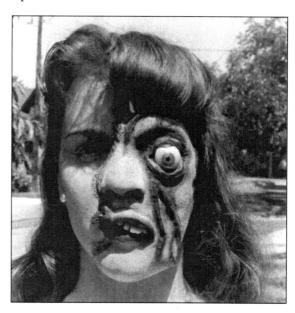

By this time I'd been promoted from Private First Class to Specialist Fourth Class, which meant that I was permitted to live off the base. Once I got that promotion, I had Kathy come out and we got a little apartment about ten minutes from Fort Sam. One night, we were watching the local *Shock Theater* on KENS-TV Channel 5, San Antonio's CBS affiliate. The "horror host" was Joe Alston, who looked a little like Orson Welles and sounded very much like him. But all he would do was dress in a cape and a Homburg hat, sit in a chair on a little haunted house set and say "Good eeevening…" and "We hope you're enjoying the movie…" and so on — the usual "horror host schtick," a lot of nothing. One night I said to Kathy, "You know, we could *help* this show. I bet if we could talk them into paying for the supplies, we could give them a monster every week. When they show *The Mummy*, I could be there wrapped in bandages. When they show *Frankenstein*, I could dress as the Monster. When they—" Kathy said, "Well, let's *call* 'em."

We called, and we got an appointment at KENS-TV. Joe Alston turned out to be just the nicest guy. In those days, the 1950s, the TV station announcer was the jack of all trades, and Joe was no exception. Joe did live commercials, he did *Shock Theater*, he even had an afternoon kid's show called *Captain Gus*. We met Joe and the *Shock Theater* producer-director, another nice guy, and they said, "Let's give it a shot and see what happens." On my first *Shock Theater*, I believe I played a mad doctor, with a very simple makeup. It wasn't anything special at all, but KENS got some letters and calls about it — *Shock Theater* viewers actually thought it was pretty cool that there were now little skits. We started getting a bit more elaborate, and pretty soon the station bosses said, "Okay, it's a go. We'll pay for all your supplies."

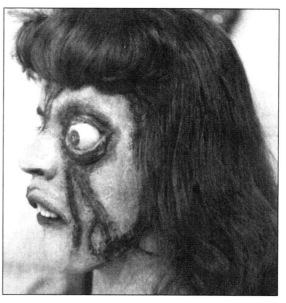

While we were doing *Shock Theater*, the manager of the Texas Theater (the biggest theater in San Antonio at that time) called KENS-TV and talked to the show's producer. He said that he was going to be playing William Castle's new picture *The Tingler* and Castle was coming into town to plug it. "I'm wondering…" the theater manager said, "is there a chance you could send somebody from the *Shock Theater* cast out to meet him at the airport? And could you have the KENS news crew cover it?" The *Shock Theater* producer immediately called me and told me what was going on, and he asked, "Would you and Kathy go out and meet William Castle?" Of course I said, "Well…*yeah*!" As I mentioned before, even in '59 I knew who he was and I was a big fan. I was just thrilled to death.

Just for fun, I thought I should present Castle with something, like a Key to the City. And the idea I came up with was, "Why not a *Skeleton* Key to the City?" In the Training Aids division, I used to have to repair skeletons — the practical jokers among the interns would hide the medical division's skeletons into their buddies' beds, and when the buddy came home at night, he'd lie next to it, or *on* it, and get spooked. I had boxes and boxes of broken skeleton bones — "spare parts" — so that was my notion, to make the key out of skeleton bones. A hip bone became the main part of the key, and finger bones became the ring of the key. I made this thing up, and then we did a special "Seal of the City" to go with it.

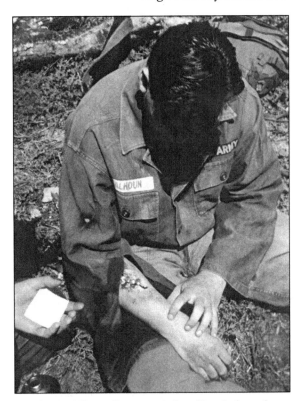

Bob burns! In an Army training film, I played an injured soldier (after doing my own "casualty" makeup).

And on Sunday night, December 20, 1959, our little "delegation" was waiting to greet William Castle as his plane landed at the International Airport. I was there, wearing a werewolf mask and gloves; Kathy was made-up as "Miss Shock," with scars on her face, crooked teeth and a big bulging left eye hanging down over her cheek; and an Army buddy of mine, a Texan named Paul, was done up in greasepaint and wig to play an Ygor type. There were even a couple folks from the Texas Theater dressed as a hooded executioner and a devil; a hearse; and a big banner made up by the theater manager:

WELCOME KING OF HORROR MAKERS
WILLIAM CASTLE BRINGS SAN ANTONIO
THE TINGLER

As Castle stepped out of that plane and started down the stairs, there we all were. Kathy went up to him and said, in a spooky voice, "Mr. Castle, we would like to present you with the Skeleton Key to the City…" — and he just loved it. He waved the key around and carried on and looked like he was having the time of his life. A KENS-TV cameraman captured it on 16mm while some of the people who came on the plane with Castle — Columbia Pictures publicity relations people, I assume — took lots of still photographs. The local newspapers probably had photographers on hand there too, because flashbulbs were going off all over the place. Castle being a showman, a guy who put as much effort and imagination into selling his pictures as he did into making them, this was the kind of stuff he loved. A reception like this was just perfect for a guy like him, and he ate up the attention.

We were supposed to meet Castle, give him the Skeleton Key and split — that was it. But as Kathy. Paul and I started getting ready to leave, he said, "Whoa. Where you going?' I said, "Well, our job's done. This is it." He said, "No, no, no! I'm going to the hotel, and you guys are comin' with me. I want some more pictures of this!" So we rode back into town in his limousine with him. Here's a werewolf and Miss Shock and Ygor, all riding in a limo with Bill Castle! And when we got to the Menger Hotel back in San Antonio, we went into the banquet room and he had a whole 'nother batch of pictures taken or us there.

After Castle's people took all the pictures that he wanted, Kathy, Paul and I just hung around. They had a big spread set out for him there in the banquet room, the manager of the theater was there, the dignitaries of the town of course — a lot of people. (I had unzipped and taken off my werewolf mask, but Kathy and Paul "stayed in character" — Kathy's makeup was glued on, and Paul's was just greasepaint.) And Castle kept coming over to us, because he thought that what we did was just the neatest thing. Over and over he said, "I can't believe you guys did this." We spent the rest of the evening at the hotel with him, and he was just as nice as he could be. He wasn't snooty, he wasn't your "typical producer" at all.

Towards the end of the evening, I said, "Is there any way I could get any of those pictures you took?" and he said, "Give me your address, I will send you some." And then he said, "Oh, by the way, in the morning, at the Texas Theater, we're going to be wiring up the seats." (That was the gimmick for *The Tingler*. In each theater playing it, x-number of seats were wired to vibrate at key moments in the movie. He called this gimmick Percepto.) When Castle asked if we'd like to stop by and see how it was done, I said absolutely. Luckily I was off the next morning, so Kathy and I were able to go over to the theater and watch them setting things up.

Castle was there, of course, standing in the lobby engaged in a conversation with the manager and some of the theater personnel, telling them what needed to be done. (I could have reintroduced myself, but he was busy. I can't be certain he even knew who I was because he was seeing me out of makeup for the first time. The night before, even after I took the werewolf

I helped wire the seats that tingled with Percepto.

mask off, I still had black around my eyes.) So we went and watched the technicians work. I don't know how it was at other theaters, but at the Texas Theater they only wired up 13 seats or so, scattered all over the auditorium. And what made the seats shake, I learned, was a vibrating gizmo a little larger than, say, a Coke can, attached to the bottom of each

Presented with the Skeleton Key to the city by a werewolf (me) and Miss Shock (Kathy), William Castle has the time of his life.

selected seat. Just by looking at them I could tell that these were not things that Columbia made-up, they were things that they'd somehow gotten their hands on, and so I asked one of the technicians, "What *are* these?"

It turns out they were vibrators that were used during World War II to de-ice the wings of airplanes. They had off-set cams in them, they were installed inside the wings of planes and, when activated, they would vibrate and shake off the ice. (I don't know who came up with the idea of using these things for *The Tingler*. My guess is that Castle came up with the idea of vibrating seats and somebody else figured out they could use de-icers to do that.) Anyway,

A *Tingler* pressbook ad touts the power of Percepto.

that's what they were, and I got to help install a couple of them. The technician asked, "Do you want to help put 'em in?" and I said, "Yeah!," and we just literally screwed them onto the bottoms of the seats. They laid the electric wires across the theater floor, taped them all down and ran them back to the projection booth, where there was a wooden "control board" with 13 little switches. I sat in one of the seats just to see what it was like, before the show, and that seat shook. It wasn't just a little vibration, you really moved when the power was turned on to that little de-icer.

That was Monday morning. And three days later, on Thursday evening, Christmas Eve, Kathy and I came back to see *The Tingler* on its opening night there. As you passed through the lobby, they had people dressed like doctors and a nurse "standing by," and then in the auditorium Castle gave a little talk just before the start of the picture: "I hope you enjoy *The Tingler*" and so on. It was a typical publicity junket-type appearance, but the crowd was very receptive because they liked the fact that a "big Hollywood guy" was there in San Antonio. Then the picture started — and when the Percepto moments came up, it was just amazing what happened. There were 13 seats hooked up, and they would hit the switches randomly. Like maybe the operator in the booth would hit 1, 5, 9…then 3, 10, 15…and so on. And what happened was the old "bit" where one guy screams, and then the guy who's next to him screams — it was contagious. It was like an infectious thing, and then finally it became a *collective* thing — soon everybody, including me, was screaming! I'm sure there were people who *thought* they felt it, but didn't really feel it — the power of suggestion is very strong! It worked extremely well. And, naturally, there was a "plant" in the audience, a gal in an aisle seat who screamed and "fainted" and fell out into the aisle. The "nurse" and the "doctors" came rushing down with flashlights and got her to her feet and, one on each side of her, helped her walk up the aisle and out of the auditorium.

That whole evening was really a neat experience — a wonderful "early Christmas present" for this Army-weary soldier! Thirty-odd years later, after Joe Dante did *Matinee*, I kiddingly told him, "You did that movie for me!" because for me it was like *déjà vu* to see John Goodman, starring as the William Castle-like filmmaker, setting up shockers in theater seats to go along with *his* movie. It was just exactly the way it really happened. That's why *Matinee* is one of my favorite films, on account of that scene being so dead-on and bringing back so many memories.

During the several days that Castle was in San Antonio, another cute thing he did was go down to the KENS-TV studio and, donning an old Don Post Frankenstein mask, appear in a "Mystery Photo." They photographed and videotaped him wearing that mask, standing next to Joe Alston and holding a big cane up in the air in a threatening pose. KENS then announced its contest, "Identify This Man" (see ad on right). They ran the tape on TV all during the week as a commercial, and they also advertised it in the newspaper.

After a week of playing that commercial and running that newspaper ad, on the next *Shock Theater* they played the videotape in its entirety: At the end of it, "Frankenstein" took

Another incredible pressbook ad promoting *The Tingler.*

the mask off and, of course, it was Bill Castle, and somebody somewhere won a $25 savings bond. It may seem goofy now but it was just one of the many crazy gimmicks which made that such a fun time.

That night at the Texas Theater was the last time I saw William Castle although, about three weeks later, true to his word, I got in the mail a big envelope from Columbia Pictures with a note from Castle saying, "Here are the pictures. Hope you enjoy 'em." It was the photos of us that I'd requested. I'd asked for them thinking he was probably your average Hollywood producer and that I'd never hear from the man, but here were seven or eight shots of us and a nice note which went on to say that he didn't realize until afterwards that the Skeleton Key was made up of real skeleton bones — somebody had subsequently told him. He thought it was *really* funny then. And he must have kept copies of the photos for his own personal collection, because years later he used one of them in the hardcover edition of his autobiography *Step Right Up! I'm Gonna Scare the Pants Off America.* Another souvenir of that fabulous night: The KENS-TV news director gave me the black-and-white 16mm footage that the news crew shot at the International Airport. It's only about 30 seconds of footage, not very long, but it's great to have. Castle stands under the big WELCOME banner waving the key around, and then he's menaced by the five of us — the werewolf, Miss Shock, Ygor, the executioner and the devil — as he makes his way to the back of the hearse. You can see this footage in the 1999 documentary *Scream for Your Lives!* that Jeffrey Schwarz made for inclusion on Columbia's DVD of *The Tingler*. Until that DVD came out, nobody had ever seen that footage outside of the San Antonions who saw it on the KENS news show 40 years earlier.

At the Menger Hotel soiree for Castle, Miss Shock and I, and others, give him a less than dignified reception.

Needless to say, I continued to follow Castle's career and I saw every one of his later pictures. *13 Ghosts* was fun just on account of the fact that I love gimmick pictures and I thought the gimmick in that one, the Ghost Viewer, was very cool. *Strait-Jacket* with Joan Crawford was well-done but *Homicidal*, the one with the male impersonator, I thought was a *very* good movie, because the twist ending took me completely by surprise. I'm pretty good at guessing surprise endings, but that one I didn't expect at all. And of course *Rosemary's Baby*…Castle just produced that, he didn't direct it, but that was a great film. Those are some of my favorites from among the later Castles.

I can't stress enough how nice a guy William Castle was. He was very kind to everybody and he seemed very thrilled and honored that people took the time to meet him at the airport the way we did. When fans think of him, they think immediately of what a great showman he was, but the first thing that *I* remember is what a delightful *man* he was. Hollywood may remake his movies, but they'll never produce another fabulous character like William Castle.

Creep in the Heart of Texas

I dressed as the She-Creature (in the film vault of KNXT-TV, Los Angeles) the night of my 1956 television debut.

The first time I was on television was in 1956, when I made two promotional appearances on local L.A. TV wearing the scaly sea monster costume that my friends Paul and Jackie Blaisdell built for the then-new movie *The She-Creature*. But I became a TV regular for the first time on Joe Alston's *Shock Theater* out of San Antonio, Texas, during my Army hitch at nearby Fort Sam Houston.

I had the proverbial acting bug from the time when I was a kid, cutting up one of my mom's wigs and gluing the hair to my face in a ten-year-old's attempt to duplicate the makeup worn by Lon Chaney's Wolf Man. On *Shock Theater* I would again become a werewolf…and a mummy, and the Frankenstein Monster, and several other characters, over a period of almost a year and a half. Not only was it tremendous fun, but it helped me keep my sanity during those stressful months that, for some unimaginable reason, Uncle Sam Wanted *Me*.

Once Kathy and I got involved on KENS-TV's *Shock Theater*, the wraparounds became much more elaborate. Early on, Joe Alston (playing the ominous caped character The Host) merely sat on a small haunted house set, greeting viewers and then making occasional comments on that night's movie. But after Kathy and I talked our way onto the show's production team, there were comic skits, "guest star" monsters and even bigger ratings for this already popular Friday night showcase for the classic Universal and "Poverty Row" horrors.

Al, the show's director, was a nice guy who developed a lot of the gags and wrote up the scripts. But it was a collaborative effort: Joe Alston and I, and even the KENS program director, would also get involved in the writing. Joe was especially helpful; after Al, he was probably the #1 guy as far as coming up with ideas: "Why don't I say *this* instead of *that*?" and so on. Joe carried the show and he was a real professional. He would be the butt of all the jokes, but he didn't care. Over the year-plus that I was on *Shock Theater*, Joe and I did a lot of schtick, a lot of what we used to call "rimshots" — and I began having the time of my 23-year-old life.

The first night I appeared, I believe the movie was Universal's *The Mad Doctor of Market Street* with Lionel Atwill. Since there was no monster in it, I wore a smock and grayish ghoul makeup to play a weird-looking doctor on a "mad lab" set, getting ready to do some experimenting. It wasn't very much, but it was enough that KENS got a good response from viewers who liked the fact that there were now gags and schtick, that there were now comedy bits during the breaks in the movie. And I wasn't nervous at all about it, even though this was one of my first times on TV. As long as I know what I'm doing — or at least *think* I know what I'm doing! — I generally have confidence that I can handle it.

Each week, needless to say, we tried to tie in our skits with the theme of that night's movie. The brainstorming sessions went something like this:

"We're showing *The Mad Monster* next week. What can we do?"

"Well, it's a werewolf movie. We're going to have to have a werewolf in the skits."

"Okay, so what's the werewolf gonna do?"

And so on, as ideas and suggestions were tossed out, and a script slowly began to come together. Actually, *The Mad Monster* was one of the more ambitious *Shock Theater* experiences. I already had my werewolf mask, so it was a no-brainer that we'd use that, but I also had some 16mm footage of myself turning into a werewolf: In 1956, Paul Blaisdell and I had shot it at his house with my brand-new 16mm Bolex. (Neither Paul nor I knew exactly how to work the lap dissolve feature so it didn't come out as well as we'd hoped, but it was still kind of cool.) The *Shock Theater* guys knew we needed to find a way to utilize that footage on the show and we did.

Right from the very beginning of that particular show, they used a thunder soundtrack to establish that it was a rainy night outside the haunted house. Playing a regular guy, I showed up at The Host's door, explaining that my car has broken down and asking, "Can

Here I am posing for a phearsome photo the night of the *Mad Monster* telecast.

I stay here until the rain stops?" For most of the show, The Host would comment on the movie and do funny stuff, and I'd just be sitting there in a chair, waiting for the storm to let up. Near the end, The Host got up, looked out the window and said, "I see the rain's stopped. And, gee, there's a full moon tonight!" The director then cut to the 16mm footage where I transformed into the werewolf. By the time that footage ended and they cut back again to the haunted house set, I had put on my werewolf mask, and now I jumped up and throttled The Host. Then, for the closing "tag" of the show, instead of The Host sitting in his chair with his Homburg hat and his cape, it was me as the werewolf sitting there with the hat and cape,

and in a growly sort of "werewolf voice" I said, "Good niiight, everybody…!" (We did a lot of shows where we would kill The Host off at the end, but of course he would always come back the following week.) That was one show where the timing had to be just right (the running of the 16mm film, the action of the actors) in order for the gag to work, and it did.

Another night, when the featured movie was (again) just a generic mad doctor movie, possibly *The Man They Could Not Hang* with Boris Karloff, we decided we wanted to have a heart in a water-filled tank — *that* old bit, like *Donovan's Brain*, but with a heart in the tank instead of a brain. We got an aquarium and filled it with water, and the prop man went out to a butcher shop to buy a pig's heart. And he came back with an *enlarged* pig's heart — the thing was gigantic! We placed the pig's heart into the aquarium water, and I put an air hose into one of the valves of the heart so that a stream of bubbles would rise up from it. A prop like that always looks better when it's doing something.

Amazingly, what happened on the show was that the submerged heart expanded as it filled with air — and then, after it filled to a certain point, the heart valve was forced open and the air escaped all at once and the heart collapsed a bit. Then the process began again. In other words, the heart looked exactly as though it had started beating! It was so weird! But it worked out beautifully for us. It was just supposed to be a heart in a tank, and The Host had lines like, "I'm never going to get this heart to beat again…" Well, it was never

supposed to start beating — but it did! So Joe Alston started ad libbing new dialogue to me: "My God! Igor, look! It's beating! It's actually
beating!" The camera went in for a closeup, and sure enough the heart
was beating! (At the end of that show, I did the typical Dwight Frye-
"Fritz" thing: I went to move the tank but I dropped the whole thing,
and it shattered and splattered all over the floor.) KENS got a lot of
letters on that one, many of them asking, "What in the world did you
do to get that heart to beat?" — and we had no answer. It was strictly
an accident. If it had been our plan to make that heart beat, it wouldn't
have happened in a million years!

Meanwhile, back in the real world, not everything was rosy: At Fort
Sam, the man in charge of the Training Aids division was a sadistic
drunk Army lifer. Sgt. Raymond had been in the Army for almost 30
years but he was still just a sergeant; the story I heard was that, over in
Europe during World War II, he went AWOL for two days, and when
they found him in a bordello, they broke him down to private. It took
Raymond several years to get back up to sergeant again — and now
he was my sergeant. He was an alcoholic, a bad alcoholic, he came in
drunk all the time — and he hated draftees.

I was a draftee, the only one under his command.

During the first week that I was in the Training Aids building, Sgt.
Raymond was very unfriendly to me. Then one day he finally came over
to me and laid it on the line:

"I'm gonna tell you something," he snarled. "You're gonna be my scapegoat. I need a scapegoat, and you're a draftee, and you're *it.*"

I was completely taken aback. "What are you talking about? What do you *mean?*"

"*You'll* find out," he sneered.

KENS-TV's ad for *The Mad Monster* depicted me in my werewolf mask rather than the movie's star Glenn Strange!

Claws for alarm! In werewolf mask, I attack horror host Joe Alston during a *Shock* skit.

Well, I did find out: He soon had me doing every crap job in the place. For instance, he would go out at night, take an Army vehicle off post, throw up in it — and I'd have to clean it up. He did that kind of stuff to me all the time. He kept this up for almost a year, and did more things like that to me than I care to describe. True to his word, he made me his scapegoat and his personal slave, on and off duty. I needed the diversion of *Shock Theater*, because I knew that without it, I would snap and end up court-martialed.

There was one small bright spot in the midst of the nightmare that was Sgt. Raymond. After I had been doing *Shock Theater* for four or five months, he found out about it by

A candid shot of The Host (Joe Alston) and me as the generic ghoul Igor.

The *Shock Theater* set. My involvement with the program provided a diversion from the sadistic Sgt. Raymond.

overhearing some of the other guys on post. Once he knew that, every Friday night he'd stick me with some kind of duty — he'd assign me to K.P., or to secure the quarters, because he thought I did the show on Friday nights. But the show wasn't live; we did it on Monday nights, it was taped on two-inch videotape, and then it aired Friday nights at 10:30, after the local news. (We had a couple TVs there on post so my buddies and I got to watch all the shows together, and of course Kathy would watch it at home.) But Sgt. Raymond didn't know about taping; he was just a simple guy who figured that if he was seeing me on TV, that meant that I was at the TV station in San Antonio. Every time he'd watch the show

The Host (Joe Alston, center) runs through a *Shock Theater* skit with director Al and me.

and see me on there, he'd race out of his house, back to the post — and, of course, there I was, doing whatever extra duty he'd assigned me.

"How'd you get back here so fast?" he'd growl.

I did some of my best acting at those moments. "What are you talkin' about, sarge?" I'd ask innocently. "I've been here all night." "Oh, no, you haven't! I saw you on TV just a while ago, Less than a half an hour ago, I saw you!"

"Sarge, I don't know what you're talkin' about, man…"

This drove him crazy. And he never caught on. I'll never forget one particular Friday night: My buddies (all of whom hated Raymond almost as much as I did) knew he was going to show up once *Shock Theater* began, and one of them, Mike, said to me, "Look, here's what you do. You go and take a break. Go get coffee. I don't want you to be here when he walks in." I wasn't sure what he had in mind, but I said okay and off I went. Pretty soon Raymond came in, looked around and demanded, "Where's Burns?"

"Jeez, I haven't seen him in a while," Mike answered. "I don't know where he is."

Raymond instantly became euphoric. "Ah-*ha*! I've caught him at last!" — and he actually started stomping and dancing around, very much like Fred Gwynne would later do as Herman Munster! "I've got him, I've got him, I've got him!"

"What's going *on*, Sarge?" Mike asked.

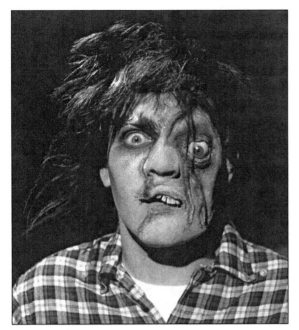

This is me (before a botched brain operation!) as I appeared in one of the *Shock Theater* skits for *The Black Sleep*.

"He's doing that damn TV thing!" Raymond babbled. "I've got him this time! He couldn't get back from town fast enough this time, and now I've got him!"

Well, by this point, one of the other guys came and got me and brought me back over, and I walked in on this scene with a cup of coffee in my hand. Raymond's face fell. "Awwww, *Jeee*-sus…" he moaned — the man was destroyed!

"Where the hell you *been*?" he snarled.

"Didn't Mike tell you?" I said nonchalantly, "I was over getting some coffee."

Mike chimed in, "Oh, gosh, *that's* right — I forgot. That's where Bob was." Mike's plan worked beautifully: Sgt. Raymond's hopes had been were raised sky-high and then instantly dashed. Raymond never found out that *Shock Theater* wasn't live, and he spent many a Friday night trying to catch me sneaking off base. So I got back at him a little that way.

Shock Theater got to be more and more of a blast as the months went by. The week they played *King Kong*, we knew that doing a big Kong would be impossible, so I got a dimensional cardboard haunted house (a Hallmark table centerpiece) and I cut holes where the windows were. Then we put inside of it a special candle that would create the illusion of movement in the cut-out windows. This was our "miniature" of The Host's haunted house. After *Kong* ended, The Host said, "Whew, I'm sure glad the airplanes *got* him. I wouldn't want him around here!" No sooner did he get the words out than you heard the Kong growl. The Host stammered, "W-w-what?!"

Cut to a shot of Kong from the film. Cut back to the haunted house, where the walls were beginning to shake. And then cut to the Hallmark haunted house, which after a moment was suddenly crunched by Kong's hand. (I made that gorilla hand over a surgical rubber glove.

My Kong-sized hand (at the top of the photo) prepares to wreck The Host's house following a showing of *King Kong*.

I put fur and fingernails on it, and it was on my hand when it came down and crushed the house.) Then cut to back inside, where off-camera guys up on ladders were dropping dust and debris in front of the camera.

We used animal parts again the night they showed *The Black Sleep*. In the skits, I was supposed to be the sailor character (George Sawaya) who becomes a monster in that movie. I wore the appliances that I made for Kathy when (as Miss Shock) she greeted William Castle — the droopy eye, crooked teeth, fake nose and all. The Host wore a surgical gown and I sat there in a chair, acting like I was in a daze. The Host said, "I'm gonna operate on this guy and see if I can do something for him." I had a wig on, and under the wig I wore a squared-off headpiece that made it look like the top of my skull had been cut off. And we actually had some real pig brains set inside the headpiece. The Host started poking around in my open skull, wielding his scalpel, and every so often he'd say, "I don't think he needs this part" — and pull out a bit of pig brain and throw it aside! He kept doing that all through the show and by the end I didn't have any brains left at all. The Host stepped back and looked at me and asked, "How do you feel now?" — and of course I didn't even move. And, after a moment, The Host shrugged, "Well…at least he's not gonna have any *problems* any more…!" It had worked well, and again we got a lot of letters about that. I also remember how bad those pig brains smelled!

This shot of me in my werewolf mask and costume reflects my attitude at the time toward Sgt. Raymond.

Right at the height of the *Shock Theater* experience, my life took a very dramatic turn. On Saturdays I was normally off from Fort Sam, and so Kathy and I planned to leave on a Saturday on a trip to my grandfolks' place in Oklahoma. I had put in for a couple days off (that coming Monday and Tuesday), and even arranged with the *Shock* folks to be off on that Monday (Joe was going to handle it alone that night). This would give me and Kathy a four-day vacation. It was something we very much wanted to do and were very much looking forward to.

Friday night I was in the Training Aids building when Sgt. Raymond swaggered up to me. "Oh, by the way, Burns," he said, "you come in here tomorrow. You've got to paint the place." Right away I knew he'd heard me tell people that Kathy and I had this trip planned.

I should have known better than to try to appeal to the man's better side — he *had* none! But I said, "Wait a minute, sarge…I've got plans for tomorrow — "

"I know that," he sneered. "That's why you're coming in here."

I began to see red. "That's not fair. Now, that's just not right," I told him, as the anger continued to build. "I've cleaned the barf out of your trucks, I've done stuff like that, but this isn't right, man. Kathy's looking forward to it. This isn't right."

"Of *course* it isn't right," Raymond said with a smirk. "But that's the way it is. I'm a sergeant…you're *not*."

That did it. I blew. This had been going on for almost a year, and finally I snapped…and I went after him. He saw the fire in my eye and broke into a run. I chased him outside, where his car was parked — he had a car called an Angela, a little British car, even smaller than a Volkswagen. He jumped in that car, but I got to it before he could pull away. I had so much adrenaline pumping, I almost rolled the car over. I lifted it up and up, and just as it started tipping, some of the other Training Aids guys came out and grabbed me and pulled me away from the car. "Don't do this, man," one of them said, as Raymond took off in his car as fast as he could pump that pedal. "Don't *do* this! You'll end up in Leavenworth!"

Leavenworth. The word was still ringing in my ears the next morning when, sure enough, I was called into the Company Commander's office. The charge: harassing a sergeant. The consequences if convicted: prison. Expecting to be arrested at any moment, I stood at full attention before the Company Commander. The fire was now in *his* eye as he demanded to know how I dared to pick on poor Sgt. Raymond.

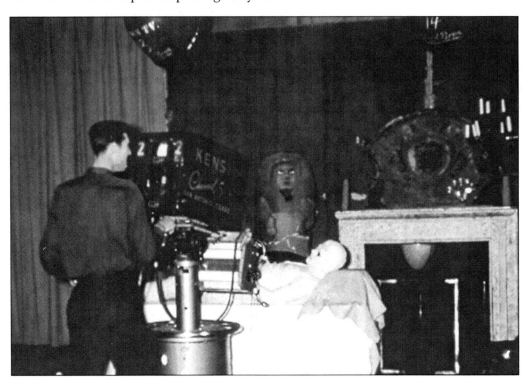

Taping my Mummy resurrection scene.

"Do you want to hear *my* side of the story?" I asked.

"No," he said flatly, "I don't."

Fortunately for me, you do have one recourse in the Army, the *only* recourse an enlisted man has: If you feel you have a real grievance, you can ask to see the Inspector General. The Army can't stop anyone, not even the lowliest dogface, from doing that. I told the Company Commander, "Sir, I demand to see the I.G.," and again, just as flatly, he said no. I came back at him with, "Waaait a minute. I've read the manual. I can *do* that." Finally he shrugged, "All right. Go 'head."

I gathered my wits about me and that afternoon I walked over to the office of the Inspector General, where I made a statement describing what had been going down that whole past year; there was a WAC stenographer there, taking down every word. The I.G. seemed half-way-sympathetic when he said, almost with a sigh, "Well, yeah…we hear about this kind of crap going on…," but then he was all-business again when he told me what my options were:

"If you want to sign this statement, we have to check into it right away. If you *don't* sign it, we'll get around to checking into it whenever we can. But I've got to warn you: If you *sign* this statement, and you *lose*…you'll probably end up in Leavenworth."

Leavenworth. That word again.

I took a breath. "Give me the pen," I told the I.G. "I have nothin' to lose."

Every day for the next four months, I sweated. I didn't know what was happening or where I stood. I thought that every new day would be the day I'd be arrested by the MPs.

Every morning as I left for work, I told Kathy I might not come home that night. It was real hell. Without *Shock Theater*, I would have lost my mind from the stress.

There was, of course, the occasional debacle. The week they showed *Bride of Frankenstein* was the week Kathy and I learned that the KENS art director was real jealous of us. This guy used to do all the work on *Shock Theater* until we came on the scene; well, it turned out that he was pretty perturbed about this. He still designed the new sets and things like that, but he'd been eased out of his other responsibilities and was not happy about it. The week of *Bride of Frankenstein*, he got a bug up him for some reason and he went to the station

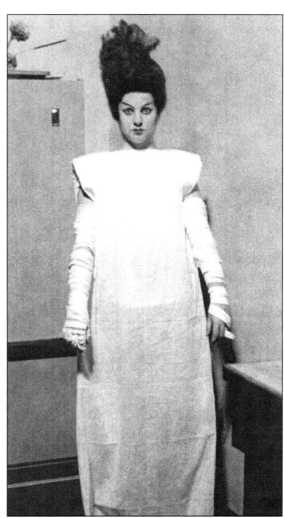

manager and said, "I want to do the wig for the Bride." Kathy had real long hair at the time and our original plan was that she was just going to tease it and spray it real good so that it would stand up. But this art director demanded that he be allowed to make the wig; he made a big deal out of it, claiming that he knew a way of doing the wig that would be just perfect. We gave him the go-ahead.

My lovely "Bride," Kathy, done up in an atrocious steel wool wig.

Kathy made a great Bride outfit and I did the makeup on her — it worked out so good, she actually looked a little like Elsa Lanchester. (Kathy's as much a ham as I am. She loved doing Miss Shock, she did the Bride of Frankenstein, and one night we did a witch makeup on her when they were running some witchcraft picture. She loves being in makeup as much as I do.) And the art director, just as we were getting ready to tape the show, brought the wig in. He'd made the thing out of steel wool — the worst thing you could possibly imagine. And for the white, lightning-like streaks in the Bride's hair, he just cut paper out. It looked awful. Here was Kathy — the makeup looked great, the costume looked great, and this hair was the crappiest thing you ever saw. *And*, because it was steel wool, it was gray. I told the guy, "That's not even the right *color*. It's got to be black!" So he sprayed it with black spray paint but of course, being steel wool, the paint wouldn't really adhere. There was nothing more we could do; it was time to tape the show, and so we had to use it.

The highlight of that show was the creation of the Bride. We had a slanted operating table and Kathy reclined on it the way Elsa Lanchester did on hers in the movie. With the lights flickering and a Jacob's ladder buzzing, The Host and I "endowed her body with life," as Henry Frankenstein might have said. And as she came to life, she didn't look up at The Host and scream, which is what you'd expect — she looked at *me* and screamed. That was the gag.

Egyptian-style props (and a bandaged Bob) added to the fun when *Shock Theater* showed *The Mummy's Curse.*

The skit went well but the Bride wig was pitiful. And to make it even worse, for the next day or two, Kathy was digging pieces of metal out of her back. The whole time she wore the wig, little bits of steel wool were flaking off and getting down her neck, and it really irritated her back. That art director was a real jerk. But at least we didn't have to worry about him again after that, because once everybody, including the director, told him the wig was a pile of crap, he never again asked to do anything except the sets.

My debacle was my first Mummy suit, made for the week that *Shock Theater* ran *The Mummy's Curse*. I fabricated the mask, and Kathy and I made the costume over a pair of long johns, just the way Paul Blaisdell did for the monsters in *Day the World Ended* and *The She-Creature*. Kathy actually sewed the bandages onto the long johns…while I was *in* them. And she stuck me about every other time. She'd pull the long johns away from my body a little for each pass of the needle, but sometimes she'd get me. I'm sure I looked like a junkie by the time she got done!

Once she sewed the thing, we decided to paint it with a "liquid clay" called Slip. We thought that would give it a nice gray, "dead" look — and, after all, that's pretty much what Jack Pierce did when he made his mummy suits for the original *Mummy* and the Kharis pictures. I stood in the bathtub at our apartment as she painted me with liquid clay, and I had to wear it at home for two hours waiting for the clay to dry, which was no fun. By the time we were done, the outfit looked great — but what we didn't realize is that every time I moved, the dried clay would flake and crumble. I left a long trail of "mummy dust" from our apartment to the car port; we put newspaper all over the seat of the car, but I still got it everywhere; and then I left another "mummy trail" from the KENS parking lot right into the station. And by the time we were done with *Shock Theater* that night, the KENS stage was just full of dust! The Mummy suit looked great but the dust got everywhere. It was just not practical! Years later, when I made another Mummy outfit just for fun, I just painted the suit a tannish brown, and it was a lot easier because it didn't shed any more!

The night everything went well was the night they showed *Invasion of the Body Snatchers*. I took some wire, made a framework and then, using a lot of white glue, wrapped it with

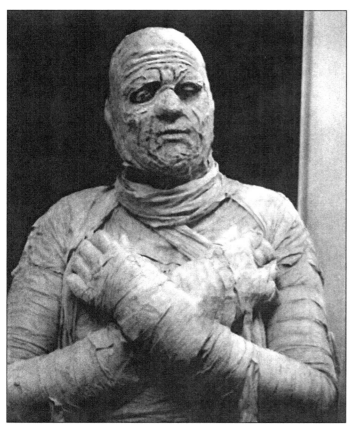

Kathy and I created my *Shock Theater* Mummy costume based upon my sketch.

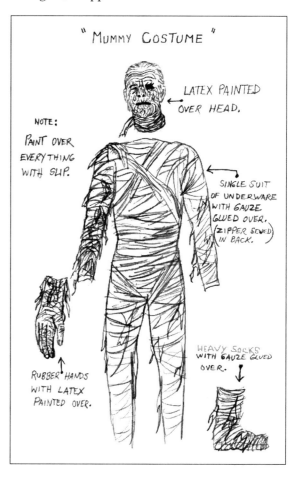

heavy wrapping paper; this became our giant "seed pod." Then I took a casting of Joe Alston's face, made a life cast of it and put it inside the seed pod. At the beginning of that night's *Shock Theater*, The Host got this pod (closed, of course) delivered to his haunted house. It was propped up against a small table on the right side of the set and throughout the show, slowly but surely, it proceeded to open. Late in the show, this partially open pod began bubbling over with soap suds and glycerin, almost like the pods did in the original film. And yet even at that point, you could barely see the life cast — you knew there was a face in there, but it still didn't register too much.

Then of course, at the very end of the show, The Host said, "Well, *we* know pod people don't exist. This is a great movie, it's fun, but — hey, come on, there's no such thing as a pod person....Boy, I'm getting pretty sleepy. I might take a nap. I'll see you guys next week." And at that point, they panned over from a closeup of his sleeping face, then dissolved to another camera, and now the pod was fully open and you could see the life cast in closeup and the soap suds running down. It really looked neat. We got very ambitious on some of the shows, this one for instance, and the reason we did was because the response was still so good. We were getting letters and phone calls. People were really digging the show, and it was becoming a real hit.*

There was even a happy ending — a couple of happy endings — to the Sgt. Raymond nightmare. One day about four months after I signed my statement for the Inspector General, there was an I.G. inspection at Fort Sam. For an I.G. inspection, everything has to be spit-and-polish — you have to be dressed to the nines, you better have your shoes polished and your uniform pressed and your brass shined, everything. Raymond arrived for I.G. inspection after having been out on a bender all night. He'd barfed all over his uniform…he looked like hell…

The Host emerges from an *Invasion of the Body Snatchers-*type pod.

he reeked…and, while trying to line up, he was stumbling all over the place. The I.G. and his staff came by him and they got a load of him; and then they came by me, and I was shaking because I was so nervous. I knew in my heart that one day soon, I was going to jail. The I.G. took one look at me and he asked, "What's the matter, son? You look pretty nervous." I stammered out *some* sort of reply, and then the Company Commander caught my eye and said, simply, "Don't worry." That was all he said. And then they went on by and inspected the other troops.

Two days later, I was called into the Company Commander's office. "I'm not going to apologize for anything, 'cause that's just not my way," he said. "*But*…mistakes were made. They'll be rectified. And I can tell you…you have nothing to worry about." That was the end of it — it never came up again. Sgt. Raymond was still there at Fort Sam, but we never spoke after that. He left me alone, probably because they gave him a reprimand too — I'm sure he was told, "Don't you dare harass this guy again."

Then, a year or two later, long after I'd gotten out of the service, Ralph, an Army buddy of mine, came by to see me at my house in Burbank on his way up north. Ralph and I were in my living room talking when he said, "Oh, by the way, did you hear what happened to Raymond?" I hadn't.

---

* I must add at this point that, for everything I did on *Shock Theater*, I give all credit to Paul Blaisdell. Without the training he gave me, I'd have never even attempted it. The way I made my monsters and props was exactly the way I saw Paul build *his* stuff. If it hadn't been for Paul, I'd have never done any of it — I wouldn't have known *how* to do any of it. He was a marvelous teacher.

It turned out that the Army had started checking into Raymond's past as a result of my signing that statement, and they discovered that at least three times in the past, he had done the same sort of thing to other guys at various posts. Once the investigators found that out, they threw the book at him. Again he was knocked him down to private…and then sent to Korea! (This was after the Korean War, but still, it was the armpit of the world.) I guess that's where good old Sgt. Raymond spent his last Army days. The funny part is, at that point I was still having nightmares about Sgt. Raymond — I was more than a year out of the Army, and I was still dreaming about those horrific days. But as soon as my buddy told me that

Three of the *Shock Theater* masks: Kathy's Miss Shock half-a-face affixed to a sculpt of *my* face, plus the mummy and werewolf masks.

Raymond had been busted and shipped off to Korea…the nightmares stopped. I believe it was Providence that made my buddy stop by my place and tell me about Raymond, because otherwise I'd have never known that he'd finally gotten his comeuppance.

Kathy and I were never paid anything for our work on *Shock Theater*, they only paid for our supplies. And, sad to say, none of our *Shock Theater*s exist any more — each week they degaussed the tape and then used it for the next show. The only thing I have is photographs — those, and a million memories. I loved that whole *Shock Theater* era; I loved making the monsters and the props; and I loved Joe Alston, who put his whole heart into doing this stuff. And, perhaps most importantly, it may have been the thing that saved me from getting court-martialed, because it took my mind off the Army and gave me something to do. (Kathy's certain of that — she says, "Without it, you'd have been in Leavenworth for sure.") I look back at Joe Alston's *Shock Theater* today and I'm as thrilled as I can be, to have been a part of it.

Three more shots of me as the *Shock Theater* mummy: Discussing the upcoming episode with Al the director and Joe Alston; posing on the set; and reaching through The Host's window.

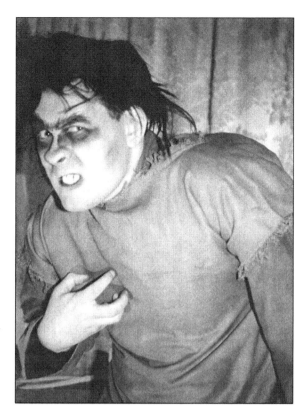

Above: Two views of me in my Igor makeup and costume.

I wore Kathy's Miss Shock half-a-face in *Shock Theater*'s wraparounds for *The Black Sleep.*

The Lost Words of Jack P. Pierce

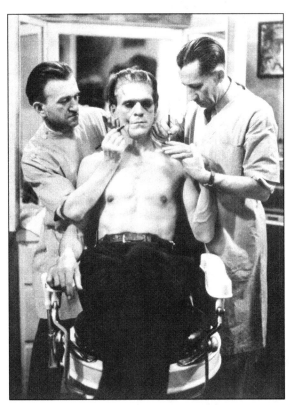

Jack P. Pierce and an assistant work their makeup magic on a "mon-star" in the making: *Frankenstein*'s Boris Karloff.

My fascination with the Men Who Made the Monsters began at an early age: I was probably not much older than eight or nine years old when I began checking the screen credits of horror movies to find and commit to memory the names of the makeup artists. The same name popped up time and again, whenever I was able to catch one of the Universal monster classics: Jack P. Pierce.

I'm not old enough to have seen most of the Universal Horrors when they were first released, but when they were reissued by Realart in the late 1940s and early '50s, I saw almost every one of them at the Loma, the Magnolia and the Burbank Theater. Long before these movies came to TV via *Shock Theater*, I was lucky enough to get the great thrill of being in the theater with them.

I can remember the very first of the Universal Horrors that I saw: It was *Frankenstein Meets the Wolf Man*…and it scared the shirt right off my back. Bela Lugosi's Monster didn't bother me too much, but Lon Chaney's Wolf Man really frightened me. It frightened me, *and* it inspired me to try to duplicate the Wolf Man. The trouble was, I didn't know what materials to use…so I used my mom's wig. I came home wanting to do a Wolf Man makeup and needing hair, and once I saw Mom's wig I thought, "Oh, man, this'll work." So I cut it all to pieces. But I didn't know how to stick it on my face, so I used white glue. That was my Wolf Man face: brown shoe polish for the makeup and hair from my mom's wig, affixed to my face with white glue. It was really awful, I'm sure, but to my ten-year-old eyes it looked pretty cool. Once my mom saw that I destroyed her wig, though, she got very mad at me. And, of course, since I used white glue, I wore it for a couple of days, because it wasn't water-soluble and didn't want to come off. I missed school the next day on account of the fact that I couldn't get that glue off. And all because I was so impressed with Jack Pierce's makeup for the Wolf Man.

By the 1950s I was making $10 a day acting as a "human guinea pig" for wannabe makeup men at the makeup union, and getting friendly with many makeup veterans. They all said they thought that Jack Pierce was the best, the king, the top dog. Mention Jack Pierce's name among makeup people and everybody knew who he was. Abe Haberman was a makeup artist who had actually worked with Jack on a couple of films, so I particularly remember his comment: "Oh, Jack Pierce is the best. There's nobody better than Jack Pierce." Everybody said that Pierce was a crotchety old guy — and he was — but they also all said he was the dean of makeup artists, and that's all there was to it. Even some of the aspiring makeup men I sat in for were hoping to be able to meet Pierce someday.

So was I.

Jack talking to Karloff around the time of the original *Frankenstein.* The clay head sitting near Boris is the one Jack showed TV host Wayne Thomas in 1962.

My chance came several years later, in the summer of 1962, while I was working as a film editor at KNXT-TV (1313 North Vine Street in Hollywood). It all happened as a result of an appearance I made on *Panorama Pacific*, a live local morning show. Since *Panorama Pacific* came out of KNXT-TV, almost every Halloween I did some crazy thing on the show — play a monster or something. Wayne Thomas was the on-camera host of KHJ-TV's *Million Dollar Movie* and did his show in the same building; he saw me on *Panorama Pacific* and asked me to make an appearance on *Million Dollar Movie* with him. (Wayne was real interested in movies and effects stuff — and he was a great guy. KHJ also used him as their announcer. Wayne had a great voice and he looked good, and was the typical "jack of all trades" at the station.) The 1942 werewolf movie *The Undying Monster was* the featured presentation on *Million Dollar Movie* the night. I was a guest: I brought a werewolf head I had made, showed Wayne how I made masks from latex rubber (sculpting the original, making the mold and casting the finished mask) and plugged the magazine that Paul Blaisdell and I had going at that time, *Fantastic Monsters of the Films.*

Once in a while, Wayne had celebrity guests on *Million Dollar Movie*; for instance, the night they ran *King Kong*, I remember vividly, his guests were Merian C. Cooper and Fay Wray. Around July of that year, Wayne came up to me at work and said, "Bob, I've heard you mention Jack Pierce. He's going to be on the show. Would you like to come over and see him?" Jack had done the Humanoid makeup for *The Creation of the Humanoids* in 1960, about two years earlier; now the film was finally either playing theatrically or about to begin playing, and to help promote it, Jack was going to come in and recreate the Humanoid makeup on Wayne, live on the air. After Wayne said, "I'm going to have Jack Pierce here — would you like to come over?," and after I picked myself up off the floor, I told him that, yes, I would.

Although I'd never met Pierce at that point, I had talked about him a lot with Glenn Strange, who played the Monster (under Jack's makeup) in *House of Frankenstein* and *House*

On Wayne Thomas' TV show, I showed Wayne a werewolf mask and hands that I made. Later, Wayne donned the mask and hands and gave *me* an on-the-air "scare."

of Dracula. (Glenn was another one of the guys who told me, "Jack can be a crusty old guy once in a while.") I went to Wayne's studio that night and, of course, spotted Jack right away — I'd seen pictures of him. Even though he was now older than in those pictures, that distinguished-looking face was easy to recognize. I don't recall what film played on *Million Dollar Movie* that night but I'm sure it was a sci-fi or horror, to tie in with Jack's appearance. Before or after the commercial breaks, they'd keep coming back to Jack and Wayne, and every time you saw Wayne he was wearing more makeup and looking more like one of the Humanoids. Jack was expected to have Wayne fully made-up by the end of the film.

When I first met Jack, right at the beginning of the night, he was a little cold to me. Then I told him that I knew Glenn Strange real well, and that Glenn had asked me to say hello for him — at which point, Jack warmed up. Warmed up a *lot*. He said, "Oh, I loved Glenn Strange, he was one of my favorite people," and he proceeded to go into a big thing about Glenn — "I got him that Frankenstein part, you know!" Jack was very proud of having picked Glenn to take over as the Monster. After being a little standoffish with me at first, he was fine.

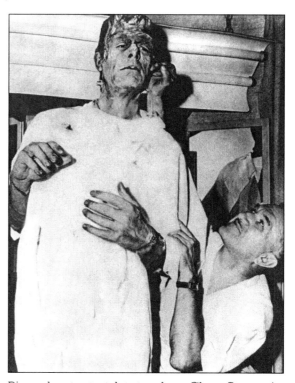

But the "cantankerous" side of Pierce that others had mentioned — I did see a little of it that night. With me, after I said Glenn's name, he became very warm and friendly. But with some of the other people there, he got just a bit testy a couple of times. He was trying to concentrate on the work he was doing, the Humanoid makeup on Wayne, but the producers were rushing him a little, telling him they wanted him to have it done by the end of the show. Well, Jack was the kind of guy you didn't rush, and he got a little bent out of shape: "Look, you can't push me, it's gonna take me time to do this…" — you could hear the annoyance in his voice. He had an "artist's temperament," I think — he didn't want to be pushed, and that was all there was to it.

Pierce has to stretch to touch up Glenn Strange's makeup during the filming of *House of Dracula.*

Wayne was seated in a barber chair and Jack stood the whole time he was making Wayne up. Next to Jack was a table with his makeup kit and supplies. Jack began by putting a bald cap on Wayne, and he used cotton and collodion to do the blend the old-fashioned way. It was the only time I ever got to see Jack work, and he did a great job — the guy hadn't lost it at *all.*

There was one mishap that night, one that was no fault of Jack's. To give Wayne silver-colored eyes like the Humanoids in the movie, Jack brought in scleral lenses — large contact lenses that covered most of the eye, similar I suppose to the ones Christopher Lee wore in *Horror of Dracula.* When Jack arrived, they were in little containers, the sort you would keep contact lenses in. I'm sure they had been made up by an optometrist — I don't think Jack had the facilities to make lenses up, or the capability to do it. Well, one of the contacts had a slight burr on it, and when Jack put it in Wayne's eye, Wayne said, "Boy, this one's pretty uncomfortable. The other one feels pretty good — but *this* one doesn't feel too comfortable…" Jack had no answer for that. Wayne didn't keep it in all that long, but I found out later, in talking to Wayne, that it had scratched his cornea. That was kind of serious for awhile — and a little bit scary — but it came out okay.

I brought a copy of *Fantastic Monsters* to the TV studio and gave it to Jack and asked him if possibly we could do an interview with him. The first thing he said was. "How much you gonna pay me to do it?" When I later told Paul Blaisdell what Jack's reaction was, he said, "Nah. Don't even bother with it," so of course we never got back to Jack on it.

Jack had brought with him his makeup kit, of course, but he also brought along some sort of gym bag — and in it he had one of the Kharis masks that he'd made up for *The Mummy's Curse*. I guess he brought it in order to show it on the air, but then never got the opportunity because he spent all his time doing the Humanoid makeup on Wayne. I was flabbergasted when, at the end of the night, while we were talking, he pulled it out and showed it to me. Some changes had been made since Lon Chaney wore it in '44. Jack used to loan it to his nephew to wear at Halloween; originally it was just a face, so Jack had glued a woman's bathing cap to it so that the kid could wear it. Jack had also cut the Mummy's

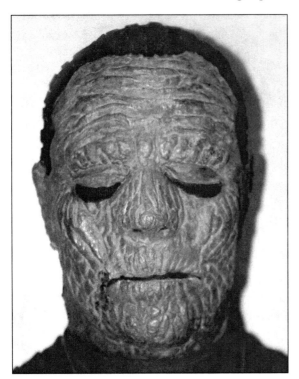

This is the Kharis mummy mask that Jack gave me in the early 1960s, as it looks today.

right eye open and slit the mouth so that the nephew could see and breathe better. I got the impression that the nephew had worn it several times, so it's a wonder it still existed at all.

I guess I was kind of oohing and aahing over the thing because, out of the blue, and to my great surprise, Jack said, "Would you *like* it?" I said, incredulously, "...Y-y-yeah. *Yeah*, I'd like it!" Jack seemed a little apologetic about the condition of the thing ("It's not much good any more...it's all kind of beat up..."), and he just *gave* it to me. It was as simple as that. He had no way of knowing how thrilled I was about this — it was like getting the wolf's head cane head from *The Wolf Man* all over again. As far as Rick Baker knows (Rick is a real Jack Pierce fan), this Kharis mask, which is still in my collection, is the only piece of Pierce's work that exists today. There's nothing else at all.

At the end of the evening, having met Jack and having been made a present of the Mummy face, I went home about as happy as I could ever be. Then, a couple of months later, I got a call from Wayne saying. "Jack Pierce is going to be back on the show, and this time I'm going to interview him and he's gonna have some stuff from *Frankenstein*. Would you like to come over?" You bet I did. So I met him again on that second occasion (September 17, 1962). The first time Jack appeared on Wayne's show, to do the makeup demo, he wore a smock, but this time he was very dapper in a suit and tie. I don't know if he really remembered me 'til I dropped Glenn Strange's name again, but then he said. "Oh. yes, I remember — you were here when we did the makeup demonstration." And again he was very pleasant to me.

Jack wasn't there from the beginning of the show that night, he came in about halfway through the movie and started talking with Wayne before and after a commercial break. (Wayne was a real movie buff, so I'm sure he made up the questions himself.) Whereas on the first show, Jack mainly spoke about the Humanoid makeup, this second show was an interview where he actually talked about *Frankenstein*, the "look" of the Monster, Karloff's padding, how the Monster's walk was done...some really fascinating stuff. I liked the fact that he gave Karloff. a lot of credit. Jack was a generous guy in his own way, he really was. Jack was a colorful interviewee who really loved reminiscing about this stuff.

On this occasion, Jack brought a clay head of the Monster that he'd made for *Frankenstein* — I think he sculpted it to show the folks in the Universal front office how (sort of) the Monster would look. The sculpture looked kind of crude, I have to say. Jack wasn't the best sculptor in the world. He was great at doing makeup on people — his talent was in building up on a human face. But he wasn't good at sculpting stuff. That's why Ellis Burman sculpted the Frankenstein Monster headpieces for *The Ghost of Frankenstein*, *Frankenstein Meets the Wolf Man* and both *House* films — because Pierce just wasn't that good at doing it. I've always had a sneaking suspicion that Ellis also sculpted up Lon Chaney's werewolf nose for all the Wolf Man films that Jack worked on. If Ellis did the Monster headpieces, why wouldn't he do the Wolf Man nose? It just adds up. (Ellis could have even sculpted the *Mummy's Curse* face that I own, although Jack told me that he did that piece and I have no reason to doubt him. It does look a little crude.)

In the interview, Jack described the color of the Monster makeup — he called it "sky gray." Interestingly, Wayne said, "Well, that's the same color makeup you used for *The Creation of the Humanoids*" and Jack didn't correct him, so maybe that was correct: The color of the Monster's makeup may have been pretty close to the blue-gray of the Humanoids. I thought it was kind of a cool thing, that Jack actually revealed in that interview the color of the Monster.

Besides the head, Jack brought along and showed a Wolf Man fur "neck piece" and a pair of the Wolf Man gloves. To me they looked like the hands from *Frankenstein Meets the Wolf Man*, because the fingers were pointy. They were in bad shape, all pretty much rotted away by then. Jack also said in the interview that he never used a mask, when of course he did; in *The Mummy's Ghost* and *The Mummy's Curse*, there were masks.

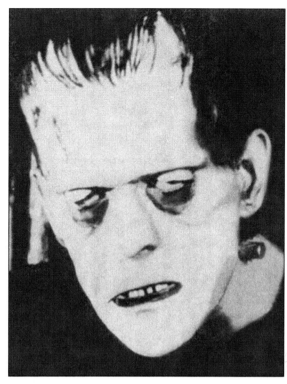

Jack described the color of the Frankenstein Monster makeup as "sky gray."

The two times he was there, Jack brought his scrapbook. It was a great scrapbook because the pictures were 11x14, big shots of all the key makeups that he had done, and some of his early stuff too. He had it with him both times and they actually showed pictures from it this second time. It was gorgeous "studio portrait" stuff. They were pretty much the same stills we've all seen, but they were beautiful blow-ups that the studio did for him. You could see every hair, everything. I got to see that, and it was really interesting.

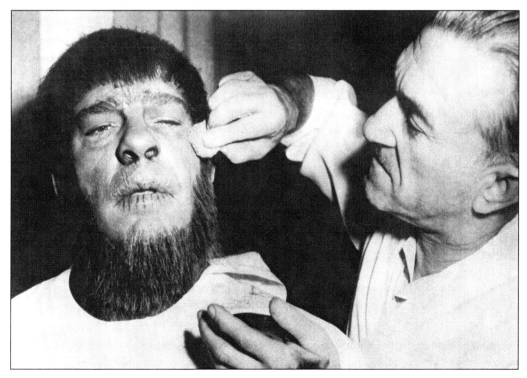

On his second *Million Dollar Movie* appearance, Jack brought along some souvenirs from the days when he made-up Lon Chaney Jr. as the Wolf Man.

The funny part about this second Pierce show is that the film on *Million Dollar Movie* that night on was *It! The Terror from Beyond Space* — a 1958 film that *I* worked on, assisting Paul Blaisdell, who made the Martian costume that "Crash" Corrigan wore! How ironic is *that*? There was a monitor there where we could see the movie when it was playing, and Jack did say, "That's a pretty interesting monster suit...that's not bad..." Of course I told Paul about it the next day. I thought it was pretty cool that Jack scrutinized the suit and said he thought it looked kind of neat.

On that second occasion, I believe that Jack was really there to plug *Mister Ed*, the "talk-

A gag shot of Jack and sitcom star Mister Ed.

ing horse" TV sitcom he was working on at the time; the show was then starting its second season. (I think all Jack did on that series was just paint the actors up to look good. He was reduced to doing "regular" makeup stuff, but I'm sure he was glad to be able to work.) As the interview was wrapping up, a grip brought out an off-camera cue card for him to read, and you could see Jack's whole demeanor change. He robotically said, "*Mister...Ed... stars...Alan...Young...and...it's...on...Thursday...nights...on...*" — that kind of thing. He sounded like he was reading it — and he *was*. Jack was kind of nervous that second time; I don't think he really liked being on camera that much. When he was doing the Humanoid makeup, being on TV didn't bother him, because he was doing his job. But sitting there, taking part in an interview, he was a little bit uneasy, and you could see that he didn't care too much for the camera being on him. He got a little flustered and tongue-tied once in a while.

On both occasions, I sat over to one side. They had like a little area where people could sit and watch, the producer and people like that, and I just stayed there. I was always so afraid I was going to mess up something, I usually stayed *way* to the side!

By this time (1962), I believe that Jack's last movie was already behind him. It wasn't a question of his health, he seemed to be fine health-wise; he had a lot of energy on this inter-view, and he sure had all his faculties. I think it was just simply that nobody was using him any more. His reputation wasn't the best, of course — he could get crotchety. Also, he either wouldn't or couldn't adapt to the more modem makeup techniques. He was an old-fashioned guy who loved the cotton and the collodion and all that stuff, and I think he was a little "afraid" of the new foam rubber stuff. When Jack was working at Universal in the mid-1940s, supposedly the studio got after him to keep up with the times and begin using foam rubber and so on, and he wanted to continue doing things the old way. Universal felt they didn't have the time to do that any more.

In the years after *Million Dollar Movie*, I thought about trying to hook up with Jack again, but never did. It was one of those things: You think about it, and just never do it. It was my own fault. I could have easy enough, and I'm sure he'd have probably talked to me. In fact, he gave me the telephone number of the *Mister Ed* set and said, "Give me a call some time if you want to see me." I have nobody to blame but myself, I just didn't follow up on it. I've kicked myself all around the block for that.

I was working at CBS on Sunset and Gower the day in 1968 when I heard that Jack Pierce died. One of my makeup friends called me and told me about it. It hadn't been on the news, of course — it wasn't even newsworthy in those days.

A closer look at the clay head Jack sculpted for *Frankenstein.*

The guy told me that Jack had died the night before. I felt so bad about it. Even though I barely even knew Jack, I felt like I lost an old friend. When I got home from work, I called Glenn Strange and broke the news to him; Glenn felt really awful too.

Neither Glenn nor I got any advance word about Jack's funeral. Then I heard, later on, that just 24 people showed up for it. I didn't know when the funeral was — I had no idea.

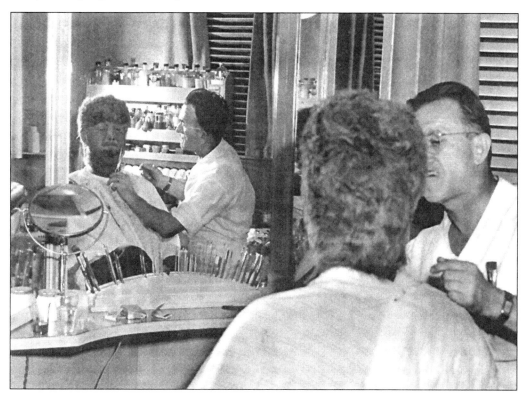

During the painstaking makeup process, Lon Chaney Jr. warily watches the mirror as Jack singes the Wolf Man's facial hair.

Glenn and I would have gone had we known, but we didn't know. Only two dozen people came to pay their respects, and just three were makeup artists. It was very sad, from what I hear.

When I was told that Jack was going to be interviewed on that second *Million Dollar Movie* appearance, I asked a friend to stay home that night and audio-tape it off TV for me, which he did, using one of the old reel-to-reel tape recorders. I still have that original tape. Owning what might be the only existing tape of a Jack Pierce interview means a lot to me now. At the time I didn't think anything much about it, but when Jack died, I suddenly

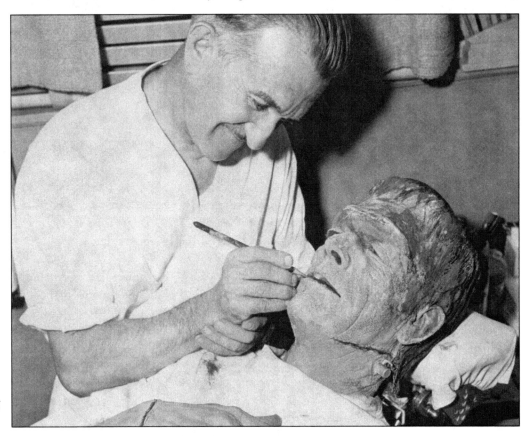

An unusually jovial-looking Pierce prepares Glenn Strange for the *House of Dracula* cave scene where the Monster is found in a deposit of quicksand.

realized, "My God, how precious *is* this thing?" Most of Jack's fans have only heard him speak on the *This Is Your Life* episode with Boris Karloff (1957), so this *Million Dollar Movie* interview is a gem of a tape. Even though it's only ten minutes, it's just so great hearing him talk about his work. I listened to it again recently and got a great kick out of it. He was a great character. And really funny — but not meaning to be! It's hilarious how half the time he really isn't listening to what Wayne Thomas is saying — Wayne asks a question, Jack starts to say something else, and Wayne has to get him back on track. But I think people will get some interesting information out of this, and it's a pleasure to share it...

The Jack P. Pierce Interview

The following is a transcript of Wayne Thomas' live September 17, 1962, KHJ-TV *Million Dollar Movie* interview with Jack P. Pierce. Some (but not all) meaningless partial sentences, etc., have been eliminated for the sake of clarity. The photos shown by Thomas throughout the interview were black-and-white 11x14s from Pierce's scrapbook. The segment began with a shot of Pierce's bust of the Frankenstein Monster, underscored with eerie *One Step Beyond* music.

WAYNE THOMAS: There you have the original head, sculpted 32 years ago, by Jack Pierce, back in 1930, for *Frankenstein*. And it looks as fantastic now as it did at that time. Jack, it's a great pleasure and honor to have you with us this evening on *Million Dollar Movie*. We had a science fiction thriller [*It! The Terror from Beyond Space*] with a monster in it tonight, played by "Crash" Corrigan. And now we have you here, and you created perhaps…well, most assuredly!… the most famous monster of all time, the Frankenstein Monster.

JACK P. PIERCE: Well, I believe that this character has been the greatest of *all* monstrossis [*sic*] men, or any…*anything* they've portrayed in motion pictures.

WT: In 1930, you started to work on this.

JPP: That's right.

WT: How did it come about? How did they decide to make the movie and how did they happen to have the Monster look the way it does?

JPP: Well, Junior Laemmle brought me the book, and I read the book three times. And from that, I did research work, for six months, before I created the Frankenstein Monster. And it was a lot of hard work. Tried to find ways and means…what can you *do* —

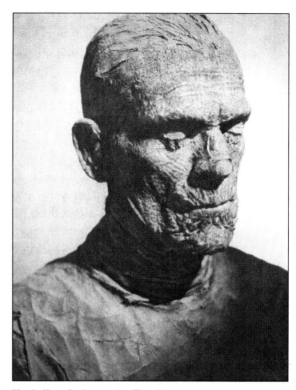

Karloff as Imhotep in *The Mummy*.

WT: Because in the book, there was no picture, no drawing of the Monster.

JPP: Not a thing! It just spoke of monstrossis man — that's all. And from there, I started out to find the ways and means. Because Frankenstein wasn't [a] doctor. He was a scientist. So to create that, he had to take the head, and *open* it. And then, he had to work from that. So he took the head and put another head on the top. So, instead of sewing it up,

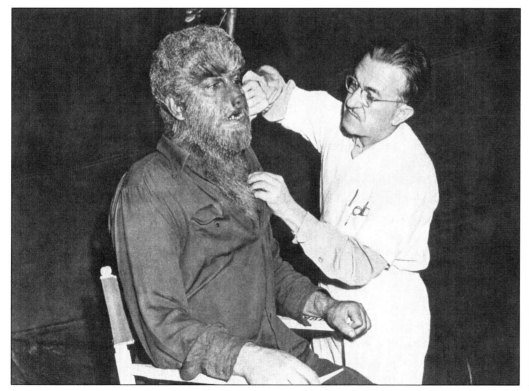

Lon Chaney Jr. looks stoic as Pierce applies his makeup for one of the *Wolf Man* sequels.

he took wires and put it as you see right here [*Pierce indicates the bust*]. All of these rivets, to rivet the head. Now, the *next* thing is to find out, from electricity, how the man was created through electricity. To bring him to life. So I had to bring the [electrodes] right in here to connect the electricity.

WT: That's what these are?

JPP: These are right here. On the neck.

WT: What is this head made out of? The one that you first made?

JPP: This is a wig, [this] was made. *This* [*he indicates the rest of the head*] is built, new, every day.

WT: On the character. Boris Karloff.

JPP: On Boris Karloff.

WT: Now, when you worked this head out, made it out of clay and put the hair on it and took it into his office, then what happened? What did he say to you?

JPP: Well, he was very much surprised. "You mean to tell me that you can do this on [a] human being?" I said, "Positively." So he says, "All right, we go the limit." And from there on, the story was written, continuity was written, and then we went to work.

WT: What happened when the picture first opened? Was it in Santa Barbara?

JPP: Well, that was previewed [in] Santa Barbara. During the picture, [people] were rushing out of the theater. They got so scared that they rushed out of the theater. So after we got through, everybody, all the officials of the studio and all like that, says, "What we *got* here? People gettin' scares, nothin'…" So I told Junior and a few others [who] were there, "Now, don't worry 'bout it. You gonna *see* somethin'." And two weeks later, after the picture opened back East, they received telegrams, suing Universal. For broken arms and broken legs and all like that.

WT: I want to show them Boris Karloff in the original makeup job. [*He shows a photo from the 1931* Frankenstein.] And isn't this a fantastic picture. Now, is this the first of the Frankensteins?

JPP: That's the first one.

WT: This was the first Frankenstein movie. Now, describe what went on up in here. What was the top of the head built up from? Is that cotton or, uh, plastic up there?

JPP: This is a wig…this is a wig that was made with a cotton roll on the top to get the flatness and the circle that protrudes out from the head [*Pierce is pointing to the Monster's forehead in the photo*]. Instead of givin' him a round head, you give him a different edge around the sides. That's the *first* one [the first Frankenstein movie].

WT: All right, let's progress to this one [*he shows a photo from* Bride of Frankenstein], this was after —

JPP: Now this is after the fire.

WT: A lot of the hair had been burned off in this picture.…What is this large gash on the top of the forehead?

JPP: …You open it to put the brains in there, with the brains…the artificial brain.

WT: This was the hardest part of the makeup, wasn't it, Jack? Building up the head? How long did it take you, with Boris Karloff, each morning, to put this on?

JPP: Three hours.

WT: The electrodes were just fastened onto the neck.

JPP: That's right, put on his neck.

WT: The makeup was a rather…because we don't have color, we can't show it…a rather ghastly gray color, wasn't it?

JPP: Yeah. Sky gray. That was originated by me, through Max Factor's organization.

WT: Now this [*showing a photo from* Son of Frankenstein] was still *another* Frankenstein movie here —

JPP: That's the third one.

WT: How many Frankenstein movies have been made to date?

JPP: Twelve [*sic*].

WT: And how much money have they grossed, up to this point?

JPP: The last time I heard, they grossed over 90 million.

WT: $90 million. And they're still running all over the world.

JPP: All over. You see in television, every so often, they're showin' the Frankenstein.

WT: And you, as one of the…well, the dean of Hollywood makeup men, Jack, the one that originally created the Frankenstein Monster and made him look the way he did…

JPP: That's right. Exactly.

WT: You tell an interesting story, I want you to tell it now, of how the Monster walks. And why he walked that way, and how you taught Boris. Tell it, and then we have to stop for —

JPP: Well, the tricks of that…Boris and myself and James Whale, the director, we got together. Instead of trying to be human being, this man was made of electricity. [*Unintelligible*] The walk — he had to balance himself, because the boots…supposed to have been weighted down, so when he walked from one foot to the other, he'd balance himself. And then…a long story about the coat…it was cut down, way up here, so the length of the arms, the fingers, so they'd look *long*, see? And everything in black, so they give him the heighth [*sic*]. And also the padding. The padding…to look eight feet…

WT: And you used to practice with Boris Karloff, particularly in how to walk properly.

JPP: [*tongue-tied*] Through…Together…I mean, I didn't…I taught him…We just simply talked. And the man is so wonderful. I think he's the greatest of them *all*, as far as playing these parts.

WT: Jack's gonna be back in just one second, to tell you about a makeup job that didn't take three hours as Frankenstein did, but took…*eight* hours. We'll show you *that* picture in just one moment…

[*After the break, the interview resumes.*]

WT: You know, there are sort of *two* ways, Jack, I suppose, of applying makeup. The way that you do it, using cotton materials, so forth, and then putting the makeup over it —

JPP: That's right.

WT: And then the *other* way they have of…Let me show this picture here…of one that my good friend, and yours too, Bill Tuttle did. [*Thomas shows a photo of himself being made-up as Abraham Lincoln.*] Where they apply pieces of plastic that are already made, and just glue them onto the skin. They had done it here to the nose and to the cheeks. They're building up the nose and cheeks, and the final product was *this*, where they made me to look like Abraham Lincoln. Then there's the way that *you* do it, and on *another* program… Well, let's show them the tape, I think the boys have it ready. Where you made me up to look like the Humanoid, and used cotton and a skullcap, and the same color makeup that was used on the Frankenstein Monster. Watch *this*…[*Part of a tape of Pierce's "Humanoid makeup demo" is shown, with* One Step Beyond *music playing.*]

WT: On this one, Jack, you put a skullcap on, to hide my hair, as I recall. And then covered the whole face with makeup. And then we put those silver contact lenses in.

JPP: That's correct.

WT: [*groan*] That was a spooky experience to go through!

JPP: [*laughs*]

WT: Let's show some of these other pictures, including this one [*a photo from* The Mummy]. And for this one, Jack was the only makeup man to ever receive an Oscar for his work. [*Pierce received a "Hollywood Filmograph award," not an Oscar, for* The Mummy.] This is *The Mummy*. When did you do that one, Jack?

JPP: That was 1933.

WT: How long did it take to put him into that makeup?

JPP: Complete makeup, from top of his head to bottom of his feet, eight hours.

WT: Eight hours. Because you had to wrap the body from top to bottom —

JPP: The bandages on the body had to be put on. And then, after it was put on, the *first* ones, then I had to seal 'em first, with tape, so they wouldn't unravel. And then, after that, I had to put the bandages that…they were burned…and put it on. And then, after that, I put the clay on. [So] that when he gets out of the sarcophagus, and starts to walk, this bandages will break and the dust will fallin' off exactly as a mummy who's been buried for 3500 years.

WT: Eight hours every morning.

JPP: And an hour and a half to take it off.

WT: Here is the after-picture [*he shows a shot of Karloff as Ardath Bey*], after the Mummy has come to life.

JPP: That's the live Mummy.

WT: Now, here is another famous Jack Pierce makeup job, the Wolf Man. In fact, we have part of it back here — this is the chest piece that he wore…

JPP: The chest piece in there, and the hands…

WT: And the hands of the Wolf Man. Again, this was…Not Boris Karloff that played this, was it?

JPP: No, that's…uh…Lon Chaney Jr.

WT: Lon Chaney Jr. How long did it take to apply that makeup?

JPP: That's two hours and a half.

WT: Put all this hair on, maybe just a little row at a time, is that right, Jack?

JPP: That's right. And, after the hair's on, you curl it, and then singe it, burn it, to *look* like an animal that has been out in the woods and rubbing and everything like that.

WT: And this had to be done…every morning?

JPP: Every day. Every morning.

WT: This wasn't just a mask that you slipped on over his head.

JPP: [*emphatic*] I don't use masks, I don't use any appliances whatsoever. The only appliances I use, it's right here. The nose that…looks like wolf.

WT: That was the only appliance you used. The rest of it is actually built up from the face.

JPP: New every day.

WT: How come you use a rubber nose?

JPP: Either you had to put a rubber nose or…model the nose every day. And that would [have] taken too long.

WT: Jack, I wish we had time to show some of these other things, the wigs and the other pictures. We'll have to have you back again some time, our time has run out. I want to ask you what you're doing now.

JPP: I am working with *Mister Ed*…Filmways.

WT: On the Alan Young show.

JPP: Yes. You know, Filmways TV…Productions…will open…their new season…1962-63… with *Mister Ed*…"Ed…Gets…Amnesia"…Arthur Lubin, producer-director…and starring…Alan Young, Connie Hines…and co-starring…Larry Keating and Edna Skinner.

WT: Very good.

JPP: It will show every day on…Thursday…

WT: [*interrupting frantically*] On another station, so don't say that word. Or we're all in trouble!

JPP: All right!

WT: Jack Pierce, creator of Frankenstein, the Wolf Man, the Mummy and many other fantastic makeup jobs —

JPP: Thank you very much.

WT: And the only makeup man in the business to receive an Oscar —

JPP: That's right. Maybe we can bring it next time.

WT: Thank you for coming on this evening, we've enjoyed it very, very much.

JPP: Thank you very much.

WT: We'll be back shortly. Thank you again.

Above: Behind the scenes on *The Mummy*, makeup magician Pierce works on Karloff's hands; Henry Hull's WereWolf of London as he looked in an early makeup test.

On the set of the 1931 *Frankenstein*, Pierce and an assistant work on Karloff's Monster makeup as Dear Boris derives some pleasure from a cup of tea (and probably even *more* pleasure from the electric fan in foreground).

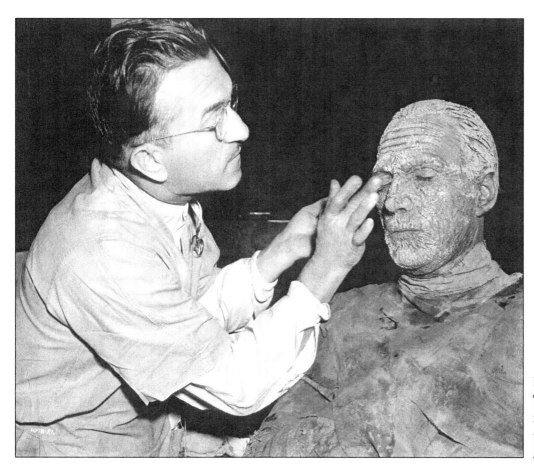

B-Western star
Tom Tyler gets
mummified by
the master for *The
Mummy's Hand.*

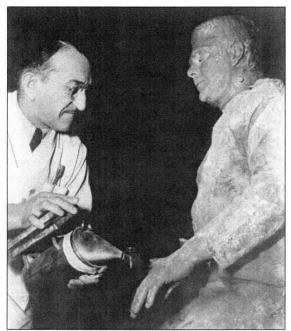

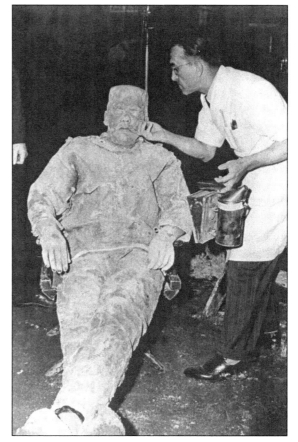

Pierce makes up Lon Chaney Jr. as the Monster
for his "risen from the sulfur pit" scenes in *The
Ghost of Frankenstein.* Notice that in both shots,
Pierce is holding a bee-smoker; it's filled with
Fuller's earth (fine clay) which he sprayed onto
the actor.

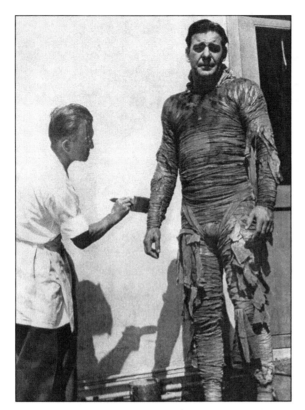

Above: Pierce applies Fuller's earth in liquid form to Lon Chaney Jr. for scenes in *The Mummy's Ghost.* The stuff stinks — and, in the second shot, Lon lets you know it!

In the best scene in *The Mummy's Curse,* Princess Ananka (Virginia Christine) fights her way up out of swamp mud. In this makeup-in-progress shot, Pierce has applied makeup from her chest to her chin and is now working on her hands and arms.

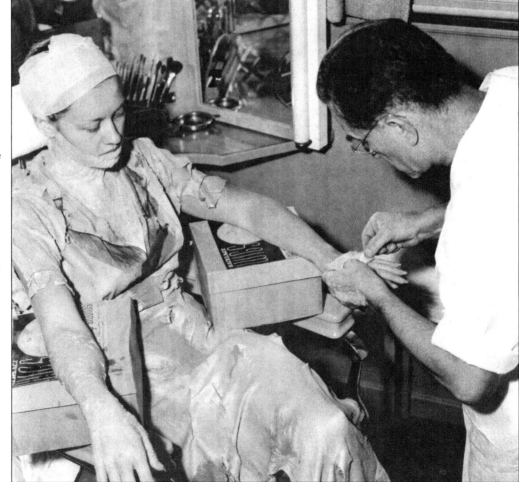

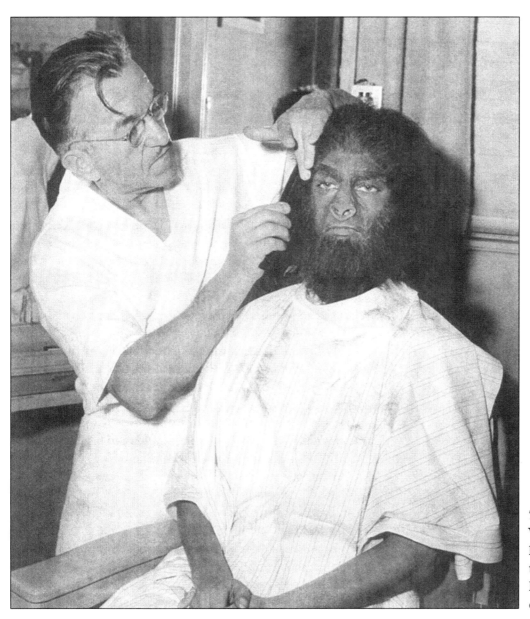

The Jungle Captive's Vicky Lane becomes Paula the Ape Woman in Pierce's makeup chair.

Castle of Frankensteins

Boris Karloff in a costume test shot for AIP's *The Comedy of Terrors* in the summer of 1963. On the set of that movie, I met him for the first time.

Several times in my Monster Kid life, I've had what I call "I've died and gone to Heaven!" moments. The first one was when I was ten years old in 1945 and got to watch the filming of one of the now-legendary Republic battle royals (from *The Purple Monster Strikes*); another came just three years later, when I witnessed the shooting of the dinosaur scenes on *Unknown Island*'s Palmdale location. I felt like I was halfway to Heaven when I stepped onto the *Destination Moon* lunarscape set in 1949. Then in my adult life came one of the biggest and best of 'em all.

On Franklin Avenue in Hollywood is a Victorian mansion (built in 1908) which for decades now has been a private club for magicians and lovers of magic. It's called the Magic Castle but I sometimes think of it as the Castle of Frankensteins because that's where I got to spend a never-to-be-forgotten day with the original Monster, his Bride and his Ghost: Boris Karloff, Elsa Lanchester and Lon Chaney Jr.

Back in 1962 or '63, I became a charter member of the Magic Castle, which was started by magician Bill Larson and his brother Milt. I knew Milt better than I knew Bill because Milt was one of the writers of the TV game show *Truth or Consequences* with Bob Barker, and I frequently played a gorilla on that show back in those days. When the Castle opened, Milt told me about it and I became one of the charter members — I think I was #46. There was the bar downstairs and the restaurant upstairs, and magicians would come to your table and do close-up magic for you. The neat thing about it was that it was spontaneous: They would just walk up to your table and sit down and do their tricks. There was also a theater where these guys would perform their more elaborate magic tricks and illusions. Kathy and I used to go there quite often, and it was always great fun.

One time when I was talking to Milt about the Castle, I said, "If you want me to, I'll be glad to do some stuff with the Kogar gorilla suit for you." He liked the idea, and so we did that. I'd also do a wolf man once in a while for him, running around and scaring the hell out of the people. No wonder Milt thought of me when, one day in 1965, he dreamed up a new way to publicize the Castle.

Milt got the bright idea of having *Look* or *Collier's* — I cannot remember now which of those two magazines it was — do a story on the Magic Castle. And, for the purposes of the story, he arranged to have Boris Karloff, Elsa Lanchester, Lon Chaney Jr. and Vincent Price come up to the Castle and pose for a photo shoot, to give the story some color: "Hey, look at all these important people who come here!" I don't recall now if Milt knew all these people personally but I wouldn't be surprised if he did; between the Magic Castle and the Mayfair Music Hall in L.A., a little theater where Milt used to put on vaudeville shows, he knew almost everybody in town. Milt called me and said, "These horror stars are gonna be coming up here for a photo shoot, and I'd like to have you for back-

The Magic Castle.

ground stuff. You're sort of our mascot gorilla guy." I wasn't about to pass that up!

The photo shoot was scheduled for a weekday morning, so I look the day off from work, packed the Kogar suit in the car and headed up to the Magic Castle (which we'd have all to ourselves — it wasn't open to its members until 5 P.M.). The horror guys (and gal) and I were asked to get there between 9:30 and 10; I got there at about ten and I was the last to show up, because there were Boris, Elsa and Lon when I arrived. (Vincent Price didn't come after all; I never did find out why.)

Coming in through the door of the Magic Castle, you find yourself in the main lobby: then you get into the bar area by passing through a big bookcase (part of it opens up for you like one of those great old hidden passages in "old dark house" movies). Off to the left of the bar is an area where you'll find tables and chairs, a place where customers can sit down and have their drinks. And that's where we all congregated, waiting for the arrival of the magazine photographer: Boris and Lon, both very dapper in suits and ties, Elsa in a one-piece, loose-fitting dress, and me.

My first encounter with Elsa Lanchester, "menacing" her in the Magic Castle restaurant.

Fortunately for me, I didn't have to climb into my gorilla suit right away because Milt told me, "No, no, let's wait, we got time. Wait 'til the photographer gets here and starts to set up." (The photographer was supposed to show up at 10:30.) This, of course, gave me an opportunity to sit down with these three horror greats.

We were at a big round table that would probably seat six. At first I did a lot of listening as they talked back and forth. They weren't saying anything really interesting, they were just palavering, and yet it was still a magical moment. Elsa was the first one I engaged in conversation because she was the one of the three I had already worked with: She was a guest

Elsa gets carried away by yours truly as Kogar on the set of *Panorama Pacific.*

on a segment of the *Panorama Pacific* morning TV show in which I appeared as Kogar and as the Mad Mummy. She remembered the experience (and me) as soon as I started talking to her about it, and she said she loved it: "Oh, my gosh," she laughed, "that was a real fun day." I had brought with me to the Magic Castle a picture that was taken on the *Panorama Pacific* set, me as the Mad Mummy going after her, and she signed it, "To Bob — Help Help — Mummy Mummy — All The Best Tho! — Elsa Lanchester." And then a couple of times later that day at the Castle, while we were all just sitting there, she would look over at me and, out of the blue, go, "Mummy! Mummy!" She was very zany, a real kick to meet and talk to. I treasure my memories of Elsa Lanchester.

By this point, 10:30 had come and gone but still no sign of the magazine photographer, but that was okay with me because it meant I'd have a bit more "face time" with these three superstars of the horror film. Karloff was also very nice, but unfortunately I don't think he was at all well at the time. In fact, I recall that the original idea was that the photo shoot would take place upstairs, but the plan was changed when Boris said he didn't feel up to the task of climbing the stairs; that's when it was decided to have the shoot downstairs instead.

Boris was just sitting there, very quiet. I guess he was quiet most of the time on sets and at events — he was certainly quiet the whole time he was at the Castle that day. It seemed to me that he was a little bit better health-wise the first time I saw him, which was at Producers

Elsa Flashback

The photo shoot day at the Magic Castle actually marked the third time that I encountered Elsa Lanchester. The first time was in 1963 — also at the Magic Castle. Milt had me running around the upstairs restaurant in my Kogar gorilla suit, and it just so happened that she was dining there that night. Milt told me, "Elsa Lanchester's here — go and scare her!," and so I did. I did the typical "menace"-type thing, growling and reaching out toward her with her big gorilla hands (I didn't actually touch her). The Magic Castle photographer got a great shot of me accosting her.

The second and best of the three times was when she made an April Fool's Day (1964) appearance on *Panorama Pacific*, KCBS's live, two-and-a-half-hour morning show. *Panorama Pacific* was one of the first "magazine shows," sort of like *The Today Show* except that it was strictly a local thing. I was working at KCBS and it became a tradition that I was the guy who did the Halloween show with them every year (either playing a monster or talking about Halloween). Well, I was also pressed into service this April Fool's Day after the producer of the show told me that Elsa was scheduled to appear. He asked me to bring in my gorilla suit or my mummy suit and do some fun stuff with her. Playing it safe, I brought 'em both.

When Elsa came on, the co-host of the show, Red Rowe, interviewed her and talked (of course) about *Bride of Frankenstein* and other topics. Then Red said, "Well, here's an old friend of yours..." and I came out as the Mad Mummy, doing the slow Lon Chaney-Kharis walk and dragging one foot. She had not been told this would happen because they wanted to see her real reaction, and it was great: Being the pro that she was, she screamed and did all of the fun stuff that a damsel in distress would do in that situation. I started chasing her around the set and then she finally ran off stage (with me still in slow pursuit) to end the bit.

The Mad Mummy (me) grabs Elsa on the KCBS morning show *Panorama Pacific* on April Fool's Day, 1964.

Elsa had done her interview and was all through there, but during the break the producer asked her if she wanted to stick around and do a second bit, this one with me as Kogar the gorilla. She said that that sounded like fun. She waited for me to get into my Kogar suit (it took me about a half an hour to get out of the mummy suit and into Kogar) and then she went out to talk with Red Rowe a second time. "So, you've come back, you've gotten away from the mummy?" he said kiddingly, and then they talked a bit more about this and that. Then all of a sudden I came out (very fast) as Kogar and chased her all around the set as Red yelled at me, "Kogar, will you quit monkeying around?!" This time she didn't get away: I caught up to her and picked her up and ran off-stage with her. It was very funny. How I wish I had a kinescope of it, but they weren't doing that in those days.

Elsa was a great, gracious and very funny lady.

Studio on the set of the AIP horror spoof *The Comedy of Terrors* about two years earlier. But even then, he was quiet, just sitting off in a chair most of the time if he wasn't needed for anything.

Boris and Lon talked, but just a little bit — I didn't overhear that much of what they said, but I could tell it was about "the old days." I had with me that classic shot of Karloff, Chaney and Peter Lorre on their Halloween episode of the TV series *Route 66*, an original 13x17 I'd already had Peter sign when I met him on the *Comedy of Terrors* set a short time before he died, and now I was hoping to get Boris and Lon to sign it as well. When I showed it to Boris, he looked it over and saw that Peter had signed it in a very shaky hand. Boris

Boris Karloff exactly as I remember him from my days on the set of *The Comedy of Terrors*: sitting quietly in his chair, keeping to himself.

got this very sad look on his face and said, "Ohhh, poor Peter...he was a lovely man. Such a lovely man..." You could tell that Peter's passing had hurt him — he evidently liked Peter a lot. "He had a great sense of humor, you know," he told me — that was something I didn't know at the time. Evidently Peter was a real prankster, pulling all kinds of practical jokes on people when they were shooting movies. I had no idea!

So I didn't talk to Boris that much, about *anything*. Just about that (Peter Lorre and *Route 66*), in fact. He didn't seem to want to talk a whole lot. He sat most of the time; didn't talk much; I remember one of the Castle waitresses bringing him some tea. But that was sort of *it*. It was a tremendous thrill to be in the same room with him but I was so sorry that he was obviously unwell.

It was long past 10:30 now, and the photographer was still nowhere to be seen. It was getting on toward lunchtime, and the fellow had neither come nor called. Milt was in and out of the bar area now and then, always with a "Hey, folks, hang in there, he should be here any time" — but I wonder if at that point he really believed that. I think he was just trying to keep the peace!

The wonderful surprise of the day was Lon Chaney Jr. The first thing that struck me about him was that he actually looked pretty darn good that day, very nicely cleaned up. By that time I'd heard enough stories about Lon to expect something quite different — but to my

Boris Flash-Forward

The third and last time I met Boris Karloff was on the set of TV's *The Wild Wild West*, during a reunion with Glenn Strange which I'm very happy to say I helped arrange.

When somebody over at Studio Center told me that Karloff was going to be guest-starring in an episode of *Wild Wild West*, it occurred to me that the first and last of the Frankenstein Monsters, Boris and Glenn Strange, would be working on the same lot (Glenn was there every week appearing as Sam the bartender on *Gunsmoke*). I mentioned this to my friend Art Ronnie, a writer for *The Los Angeles Examiner*, and he said, "Gee, it'd be great to do an article on this." He decided to try and pitch the idea of a little write-up on the two Frankensteins for the *Examiner*'s TV section, and he got the go-ahead.

I told Glenn about it and he loved the idea, and it all came together very nicely. The four of us, Boris and Glenn and Art Ronnie and I, spent a good two hours there on the *Wild West* set, which was a lot of fun. Karloff definitely wasn't feeling well then; this was a year after the Magic Castle experience, it was now 1966, and he looked drawn and thin. He was also in a wheelchair by that time. He could still walk, I saw him walk…but he wouldn't walk far. Most of the time when he had to go from one place to another, they'd wheel him around in his wheelchair.

Boris spotted and recognized Glenn as soon as we walked in — "Glenn, how *are* you?" he called out. They talked about *House of Frankenstein*, and of course Glenn thanked Boris yet again for helping him; Boris used to stay late on the *House* set and tutor him, show him how to move as the Monster and so on. Glenn didn't end up moving much like Karloff in the finished film but still — the gesture was there, which was real nice. Glenn always remembered that and always appreciated it. And Karloff said of *House of Frankenstein*, "It was nice for a change not to have to be buried under makeup." In that picture, all's he had was a wig and a mustache.

Listening to Glenn and Boris talk about the old days in general, and *House of Frankenstein* in particular, was wonderful. They also talked about J. Carrol Naish, who played the hunchback in *House of Frankenstein*. In one lab scene toward the end of the picture, Glenn had to grab Naish and pick him up, and he was afraid he might injure him. ("I didn't wanna hurt him," Glenn told me. "He's a little fella, y'know!") But Naish said, "Aw, come on, I'm a tough old Irishman. You can't hurt me!" Glenn described that moment and remembered how much he liked J. Carrol Naish, and Boris also said that he was a very, very nice man.

Monsters reunited! On the set of *The Wild Wild West*, Glenn, in his *Gunsmoke* Sam the Bartender wardrobe, poses with Karloff, in his costume for the episode "The Night of the Golden Cobra."

pleasant surprise, he looked to be in pretty good shape and was obviously sober. Except for a Coke, I didn't see him have a drink of any kind all day. It really looked like he was on the wagon. At first he didn't say a whole lot. At one point he and Boris talked a little bit, but mostly he was pretty much just kinda sitting there, waiting for something to happen. I had used *Panorama Pacific* as an icebreaker with Elsa, and I was able to do sort of the same thing with Lon: About a year earlier, when the Hal Roach Studios were going out of business, I had a chance to go over there and I managed to get a whole batch of pictures from *Of Mice and Men* — great original stuff. I had doubles on about 20 shots of Lon as Lennie, and so

This is the *Of Mice and Men* shot that Lon Chaney Jr. signed for me after I sent him a batch of photos from the movie.

I sent him this whole set of doubles — at that time, he was living on top of Cahuenga, up in the hills. I also sent an extra one, and in a note I asked him to please autograph it for me. Well, Lon was thrilled to get these photos because he didn't have any of 'em, and that's why the autograph on the photo he mailed back to me was so special. Almost invariably, he signed everything "Luck, Lon Chaney," using the same big L for both "Luck" and "Lon" — that was his standard. But on the *Of Mice and Men* shot he sent back to me, he wrote, "With Gratitude To Bob, Lon Chaney." It was very unusual for him to do that, but he was evidently touched that I had made him a present of the pictures.

When I introduced myself as the guy who had sent him the *Of Mice and Men* stuff, he remembered it right away: "Oh my God, you sent me all those great pictures!" He lightened up immediately. Later, when I mentioned that Glenn Strange was like a father to me, he *really* warmed up — Lon loved Glenn, and hadn't seen him in a long time. "How *is* that ol' Pee Wee son of a bitch?" he asked me. "I gotta call him. We gotta go out and fish." (Lon loved fishing, that was his passion. Lake-fish, ocean-fish, he didn't care what it was, he loved it.) Once I mentioned Glenn, the door was wide open at that point. He lit up and we started talking about some of his films, *Of Mice and Men* for one. Boris and Elsa, off on the side there, were talking a little, but they were also doing a lot of listening to Lon and me, I think. And occasionally Milt would come in and talk to Boris and Elsa too ("I'm really sorry that the photographer hasn't shown up, but if you can wait just a little bit longer…?"). Everybody had been okay with the delay at first, but now you could see that Boris was getting a little irritated, saying things like, "Well, I hope we can *do* this…"

At one point I told Lon, "One of my absolute favorite things you ever did, one that I really loved, was a TV thing called 'The Golden Junkman.'" I was completely sincere about that. It was a 1956 episode of a minor TV anthology series called *Telephone Time* which probably very few people remembered in 1965 (and even fewer people remember now!), hut Lon gave an excellent performance as an immigrant junk peddler who wants the best for his sons (Corey Allen and Robert Arthur) — both of whom receive a fancy education at their dad's expense, and now look down on their junkman father. When I told him how much I loved it, he looked at me and he asked, almost in a whisper, "You remember that?"

"I sure do," I said.

"Oh, my God," Lon muttered — and he actually started to tear up. "You know, outside of *Of Mice and Men*, that's my favorite thing I ever did. And the family — they all think that's one of the best jobs I ever did. I loved that." And with that, he stood up and started toward me. So I stood up too — because I didn't know what he was going to do! Well, what he did was give me a hug — a big ol' bearhug! (Believe me, Lon was a strong guy!) Out of the corner of my eye I could see that Boris and Elsa were watching what was going on, and they were both smiling. It was an amazing moment. In my interaction with Lon, things had gone from good (when I mentioned the *Of Mice and Men* stills) to better (when I mentioned Glenn) to...unbelievable.

"Thank you for telling me that," he said, still a little emotional, the tears still in his eyes. "That makes me feel so good. Everybody always wants to talk about that damn *Wolf Man*. It's such a pleasure to have somebody talk about something else that I've done." If the door was open before, it was off its hinges now. "Well, I thought you were great in *High Noon* too," I said, and then we also talked about a Western called *Only the Valiant* in which he played a great character called Trooper Kebussyan, a mad bearded *A*-rab (that's how everybody in the picture pronounces it) consumed with hatred for his commander officer Gregory Peck. I might have mentioned *The Wolf Man* at some point but I sure didn't dwell on it, because I could tell that it meant a lot to him that I was talking to him about his mainstream movies and leaning away from the horror stuff a little. But I'll never forget how totally thrilled he was when I mentioned "The Golden Junkman." ("That is so nice to hear...I can't wait to tell my wife...") Lon was the most fun of the three of them that day, he really warmed up to me and it was just super-great.

By this point it was getting late and Milt, when he reappeared again, finally had to bluntly admit, "Y'know, we've called the guy's number, we can't get a-hold of him, we don't know where he is." Boris said, "Well, I'm getting very tired. I'm really getting very tired" — it was obvious that he'd just finally had it. And Elsa reminded us that she had something else she needed to do that afternoon — by now it was probably like two o'clock. Chaney probably would have been content to stick around longer, I don't think he had anything else going and it didn't seem to bother him at all. He was in a very, very good frame of mind that day.

But Boris was tired and Elsa had somewhere else to be, so that was it. After waiting for the photographer for almost four hours, it was decided that the whole thing had to be called off, and everybody went their separate ways. Even though you could tell they were a little steamed about having been stood up, the goodbyes were all very nice. I thanked everybody, including Lon, who put his hand on my shoulder and said, "Thanks again for talkin' about that show. I loved that show..." And off he went. Hindsight, of course, is always 20-20: Milt later said to me, "Damn. Why didn't I think of just getting a camera, and have you get dressed up, and get shots with all these guys myself? I didn't even think about it." The funny part was, I hadn't thought of that either! Sometimes when you plan to do something a certain way, and things don't come together just like you planned, you call it off...and it's only afterwards, when it's too late, that you realize you could have very easily come up with a Plan B and done it anyway.

It was a real neat thing to be able to sit in the bar of the Magic Castle with these icons and talk to 'em, just the four of us (five counting Milt, but he was gone more than he was there). It wasn't a fan-based thing, it wasn't like one of these autograph shows they do today. This was one-on-one, quality time — hours of it! — with three of my absolute favorite horror heroes. And getting all three to sign pictures was really neat. I thanked Milt over and over again for giving me that opportunity.

And I'm also grateful to one other individual. In fact, of all the people I've never met, he is perhaps the one I'm most grateful to: The photographer who didn't show. I'm very indebted to that guy, because it wouldn't have happened otherwise. He's a hero in my eyes!

The Ghost Busters

It was one of the kookiest kid shows of the 1970s: A Saturday morning comedy series about a trio of professional "ghost busters" who operate out of a small office, and get their monster-exterminating assignments from an unseen boss who speaks to them via inanimate hardware store objects. This ghost-busting team was comprised of the irascible Jake Kong, the bossiest of the bunch; the slightly dimwitted, zoot suit-wearing Eddie Spenser; and Tracy, the brains of the operation. The funny thing was…Tracy just happened to be a gorilla.

Well, the fact that Tracy was a gorilla was just one of the many funny things about *The Ghost Busters*, the 1975-76 half-hour series that became one of the highlights of my career as a performer. The show's brand of humor was a cross between Abbott and Costello, Laurel

Tracy (me), Kong (Forrest Tucker) and Spenser (Larry Storch), known collectively as the Ghost Busters.

and Hardy and the Three Stooges — pure slapstick. It also included lots of puns, funny rickyticky music and, again, the outrageous premise that the smartest of the three was a propeller beanie-wearing gorilla who understood English, drove their car, and was usually the one who cracked the cases. I got to play Tracy, which was one of the great experiences of my life.

The Ghost Busters was a show that creator-co-producer Marc Richards had wanted to do for years. I didn't know a thing about it until the day I found myself right in the thick of things. I was in the KCBS film department one day in 1975 when I heard someone running like crazy up the stairs toward the room where I was working. It was Anne, an assistant

On the left is the gorilla head I'd always used when portraying Kogar; it was built by Don Post. It was replaced by a Rick Baker gorilla head (right) before I began work on *The Ghost Busters.*

director on the KCBS news shows. "Bob, you gotta call a guy named Lou Scheimer," she panted. "It might be a gorilla thing for you!" Well, *that* got my attention right away, needless to say, and I asked her to tell me what it was all about.

Anne was then attending some sort of class in TV production and she said that, at the school the night before, there had been a talk by Lou Scheimer. Lou was the head of Filmation, a company that produced a number of kid shows of the 1970s — a lot of cartoons, but also live-action shows like *Shazam!* and *Isis.* At some point in the evening there was a break so that the folks could have some refreshments, and during this break she saw Lou sitting with his head in his hands, looking like it was the worst day he'd ever had in his life. She asked him what was wrong.

"Oh, man…" he said, like he didn't even know where to start. "Filmation's got this show we want to do, starring Forrest Tucker and Larry Storch. But one of the characters in the thing is a gorilla. It's gotta be played by somebody who knows how to do a gorilla, but he has to know how to do *comedy* as well. We *had* a guy to do the gorilla, but at the last minute his agent called and wanted *triple* the money. If I don't find a replacement in a couple of days, I'm probably gonna have to cancel the show. I really don't want to, but we're not gonna use a gorilla guy who isn't able to give us what we want. It's got to *work.*"

"Well, gee," Anne said, "I work with a guy that has his own gorilla suit, and he does comedy stuff all the time. Bob Burns."

Lou stammered out, "W-w-where is he? I've never seen him!" (Lou had gone through all the casting agents' books looking for gorilla guys, but I'd stopped advertising myself years before. I didn't have an agent, I was strictly word-of-mouth.) Lou asked her, "Is there any way we can see this guy tomorrow morning? Please, have him call me the minute you see him. It's make or break!"

Right away I phoned Lou, and after I introduced myself, the first thing he said was, "When can we see you? In the next couple of hours, we have to make a decision. The producer's sitting here, the writer, we're all sitting here, and we've got to know!" I said, "I'll see what I can do."

I called Kathy, who was then working at Universal, told her what was going on and asked her if she could take a long lunch in order to come home and help me suit up. (I

This is the cross-legged pose that I struck in my first meeting with the Filmation producers, helping me land the role of Tracy.

wanted to show up at Filmation already in the gorilla outfit.) The suit was the one that Kathy and I had made in 1962 but the head was a 1974 Rick Baker creation. After I was inside the costume, Kathy drove me out to Sherman Oaks, where Filmation had their two-story building. We went directly to Lou Scheimer's office, and he then took us to the office of Marc Richards.

I try to stay in character when I'm in the gorilla suit. I don't talk — "snort, snort," that's about all I do. (Call me crazy, but I believe in the "mystique" of the thing!) In Marc's office, Kathy and I found Marc, the director Norman Abbott (the nephew of Bud Abbott of Abbott and Costello) and a couple other people I don't now remember. I went in doing my best "comedy walk" and I could see right away that they liked the look of the gorilla. They all introduced themselves to me but I would not speak — I wanted to come across as "pure gorilla." Then Marc painted for me a word picture of what the show and the Tracy character were supposed to be about: "Tracy is a real gorilla but he tries to imitate humans as much as he can. He can't talk. He can motion, he can draw, he can pantomime, but he can't talk." And then Marc kind of put me on the spot: "If you were that gorilla," he asked, "what would you do?"

I stood there probably a full 45 seconds thinking, "Gosh, what can I do? How can I get all that across?" But the answer came to me when I spotted an empty chair and some other potential "props" nearby. I went over to the chair, sat down in it, picked up a copy of *Variety* that was lying on a table within arm's reach, crossed my legs and started reading. I did all this very casually because I "undersell" him — I didn't want to do anything in an animated fashion until I was doing schtick. I wanted to show them the gorilla could be subtle as well.

"Good God," Marc said. "There's Tracy the Gorilla." And I was signed right there all the spot.

Of course, nothing should be that easy — and it wasn't. I already had a full-time job at KCBS that had to be taken into consideration. I had five weeks vacation coming to me, because I hadn't yet taken any time off that year — but *The Ghost Busters* was scheduled to be a nine-week shoot. I had to have four more weeks, which meant that I would need to take a leave of absence. I went to my boss and told him the situation, and he said, "If you can work it out with the other three guys in your crew, it's okay with me." The other guys had no problem with it. But then I had to go to Fred, the station's program director. And Fred said, "Naw. No, no, we can't let you go that long."

My heart sank. "You won't even miss me. And you won't be payin' me…!" I babbled.

"No…I just don't want this happening," he said.

Fred (who looked like a thin Basil Rathbone) was, I believe, a little jealous of me as I was always involved in the local KCBS shows, wearing costumes and doing crazy things. I think he was a frustrated actor and it bugged him that they always wanted to use *me*. He told me that my primary job was a TV film editor and that if I wanted to be an actor, I would have to pursue that on my own and not try and stick to my film editor job as well. It seemed like that was the end of it.

I was so depressed that my dream job had been pulled out from under my gorilla feet. It looked like there was no way to make it work; the program director was, after all, my top boss.

In this sequence of shots, Tracy and Spenser listen to Zero's voice as played on a fire hose...

...the message self-destructs (notice crew member with fog machine)...

I called Lou Scheimer and told him I'd run into a brick wall with the KCBS program director, and to my great relief he said, "Wait a minute — *Ghost Busters* is gonna be *a CBS show*!" The Lord was smiling down on me that day: Filmation provided a big chunk of the network's Saturday morning kiddie lineup, and *The Ghost Busters* was going to be their new addition to it. If *Ghost Busters* had been earmarked for NBC or ABC, I'd have been sunk, but since it was going to be a CBS show, all of a sudden there was new hope. "I'll call you back in a few minutes," Lou told me as he hung up, and he then proceeded to phone somebody at the network. Well, the network then called the KCBS program director and reamed him out but good.

...and Tracy is tangled up in hose in the aftermath of the blast.

The program director then called me up singing an entirely different tune: "It's fine. You wanna go? Take all the time you need! Not a problem. Go right ahead. Fine! Glad to see you doin' it!" He did a complete 180, and that problem was solved.

The plan was to do 15 episodes in nine weeks; the series was going into production very late, mainly because of the lengthy search for the right gorilla guy. For each episode, we would read it one day and then rehearse and shoot it the next day, and that was *it*. It was going to be breakneck, but I had high hopes that it was also going to be fun.

The very first thing we did was to shoot all the exteriors outside the little hardware store where the Ghost Busters got their assignments. Marc Richards had previously worked as a writer for Soupy Sales, and you can see that way-out Soupy Sales humor in these hardware store scenes: In every episode, Spenser (Larry) and Tracy would get into our old car, the Ghost Buggy, and drive out to the store, where Larry would stay with the car while I hurried inside. After a few moments I'd come out carrying some crazy item — a fire hose, a bicycle, a French horn, whatever. Then I'd do something that would "activate" it, and we would hear the voice of our boss: "This is Zero, Ghost Busters. Your assignment today is…" and he would give us our instructions. Then, just like on *Mission: Impossible*, the voice would always finish up by saying. "This message will self-destruct in five seconds." Upon hearing that, Larry

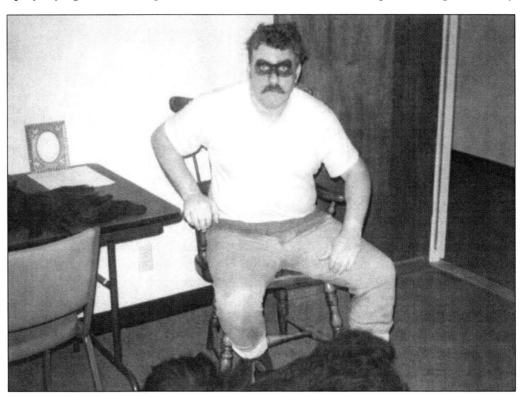

The "raccoon" eye makeup, which flakes off and gets in your eyes, was one tough part of the job.

would run off, but Tracy continued to stand there holding the item, looking into the camera and doing a "5…4…3…2…1…" countdown on his gorilla fingers. The "explosion" would go off (flash powder) and then there I'd be, all disheveled and my beanie torn up.

The store was a real, open-for-business hardware store in a funny little place called Lake Piru, where Larry and I spent two days doing these "getting the assignment" scenes for all 15 episodes. Lake Piru is a one-block town and it's been seen in countless TV series, always as "a lonely little town," "a strange small town," that kind of thing. Unfortunately, a lot of drunks lived up there at the time — a *lot* of 'em — and, to make things even stranger, there was also some kind of rest home up there, and some of its residents were wandering around the town too! It wasn't an easy two days of shooting: For one thing, it was about 110 degrees when we were there. I'd never been that hot in the gorilla suit before. Then there was the Ghost Buggy, which was actually a 1928 car called a Whippet which they outfitted with a *GHOST BUSTERS* sign. I was asked. "Can you drive this car?" Drive it? I'd never even *heard* of it! But I said, "I dunno. I'll try…" It was all mechanical — no power anything. On top of which, of course, I had to drive it wearing my gorilla hands (which made it hard to turn the wheel) and gorilla feet (which kept slipping off the pedals). I asked the director Norm Abbott if I could wear gloves and sneakers — I knew that viewers wouldn't be able to see them — but he said, "No, no. There'll be scenes where you get out of the car, so you've got to be fully dressed." Luckily, I could see — my peripheral vision was cut off a *little*, but I could see *enough*.

The Lake Piru drunks kept showing up, loud and boisterous — "Hey (*hic*!), what are you guys (*hic*!) doin'?" Eventually Norm or one of the crew guys figured out that the best and fastest way to get rid of them was to give 'em ten dollars and point 'em back in the direction of the bar! It became the job of one of the crew guys to keep an eye out for the drunks and give them a few bucks if they promised to go back in the bar and *stay* in the bar. He was our "drunk wrangler," and he took care of the problem! Then, too, there was a big fire on a nearby hill, and throughout the day there were four-engine planes, possibly bombers, flying over dropping water and fire repellent on it. These planes were flying maybe 500 feet away

Norm Abbott (with hat) stands by as Larry and I rehearse a scene at the Lake Piru storefront.

Filming Larry and Tracy as they stroll the streets of Lake Piru.

from us, very close, and making so much noise that we had to stop time and again because the sound of their engines would have been picked up by the sound recorder.

This was probably the first time that most of the crew guys had ever worked with a guy in a gorilla suit, so when the heat finally started to get me down, they didn't know what was wrong. Finally someone asked what was the matter, and I had to say, "Well, I've got 60 pounds worth of suit on me here, and it gets a little bit warm!" There was one moment that day when I did get so overheated that I almost passed out. After that happened, they gave me a little break and I was all right again.

Bernie Kopell (right) as Dr. Frankenstein and Bill Engesser as his Monster in the episode "Dr. What's His Name," the first one we taped.

At one point, I went from "fire" to "flood": In one of the episodes, the object I carried out of the hardware store was a bathroom sink which, after giving us our assignment, blew up. When the smoke cleared and you could see me again, the faucet was sticking out of my mouth. To make the bit even funnier, Larry was then supposed to turn the spigot and the water would come on. To make this happen, they ran a hose up inside my suit to the base of the faucet. But when they turned on the water, the water pressure made the hose pop off the faucet inside my mask, and the whole head filled up with water! The sight of a gorilla with water shooting out of his eyes, nose and mouth must have been hilarious from the outside, but unfortunately for me I was on the *in*side, damn near drowning!

We got all those scenes finished in the two days, and now it was time to report to Filmation and start work on the first episode. At that point, I needlessly created a problem for myself: nervousness about working with Forrest Tucker and Larry Storch. I'd just worked with Larry for two days at Lake Piru and he'd seemed nice enough, but I didn't really know him. And Tuck I hadn't met yet at all: I would be meeting him for the first time at the readings for the first episode, which was going to be a Frankenstein story. I was about as nervous as a whore in church — I didn't know what would happen.

Standard operating procedure for each *Ghost Busters* episode was for us to come in one day and get the script for the first time and, in a conference room, do a reading and familiarize ourselves with the plot; then the next day we would rehearse and block the episode just before we began to shoot it. I went in for the first reading (without my gorilla suit, as instructed) and there were that episode's guest star Bernie Kopell (Dr. Frankenstein), Bill Engesser (a big, tall, nice guy who was going to be playing the Monster), Tuck and Larry. When Norm

Tuck was unconcerned that Tracy might steal some scenes, giving me free rein to mug and do schtick to my heart's content.

Abbott introduced me to Tuck, Tuck said, out of the corner of his mouth. "Hiya, kid, how you doin'…?" Not over-friendly, I thought.

We read through that first script, and of course my dialogue was "the hardest" — "snort snort," that's all it was! That was the day I found out that they didn't know I could do my own gorilla-like snorting sounds. When we got to a scene where Tracy got excited and I went "snort snort," Norm Abbott did a little bit of a double-take and said, "Holy shit, you can do your own gorilla noises?!" The sound guy apparently liked what he heard, too, because he said, "That saves us some dough right there!" They thought they were going to have to go into their sound effects library and find some animal growls and dub them over whatever noises I made, but now they realized that that would not be necessary; it was decided right then and there that I'd be allowed to also "voice" Tracy. It was a neat moment.

The next day was the dress rehearsal of this Frankenstein episode, to be followed by the actual shooting. That was the first time I saw the interior sets that would be used in all the episodes: the Ghost Busters' office, the graveyard and the old castle. At one point during the dress rehearsal, just before we were going to start shooting, I looked at Tuck and he gave me what I thought was "a bad look." I had the gorilla suit on and I was doing all my schtick — and then I saw That Look. And I thought to myself, "Oh-oh. If I'm upstaging these guys, they're gonna kill me." When we started shooting, that was still in my mind, and so I pulled back — I didn't do all the stuff that Norm wanted me to do. After two or three takes, he said, "Bob…c'mere, I wanna talk to you, man." He got me off to one side and he said, "In rehearsals, you were doin' all this wild stuff that you need to do. But on-camera, you're kinda just…standin' there."

"Norm, I'm sorry I gotta tell ya this, but…I got a problem."

"A *problem*? We got 15 shows to do! If you got a problem, you better work it out quick."

I said, "It's with Tuck and Larry."

He said, "Well, you better go talk to 'em."

During this break, Tuck and Larry were sitting in their canvasback director's chairs. I

Two things I love to do are: do the gorilla, and do comedy. On *The Ghost Busters,* I got to do both.

walked over to them and I said, "Guys, I'm real sorry, but…can I talk to you for a minute?"

Tuck looked up at me and said, "Yeah, sure,"

And I said. "I got a problem."

Tuck looked at me with a look of puzzlement and he said, sternly, "What could possibly be your 'problem'?"

I wanted to turn around and leave. But I could see Norm out of the corner of my eye and he was giving me a look that said, "Don't chicken out! You better talk to them!"

I got up my nerve and continued. "All right, here's the thing: I'm the new kid on the block here. I realize that. And the last thing I want to do is upstage you guys. I loved you guys in *F Troop*…Tuck, I've loved you in the Westerns…I gotta tell you right now, I'm in awe of you guys, I'm so thrilled to even *be* here. So the last thing I want to do is cause any friction or any trouble."

Tuck gave me this big, long look, and I braced myself for whatever it was he was about to say.

"Is *that* your problem?" he asked, a note of amazement in his voice.

"Yeah," I said sheepishly.

Tuck rolled his eyes, "Oh, my *God*," he said. "Look, I'm too old for that ego crap. I've *long* since passed that phase. You're gonna walk off with this show, we *know* you are. I'm not worried about that. And Larry's just too dumb." I looked over at Larry, and (in a dumb-guy voice) he went, "Yup. Mm-hmm. Yup." (Tuck could say things like that to him — they were *real* good friends on- and off-camera.) Tuck continued, "If you can stand behind me and do crazy stuff and get a laugh, do it. We're here to make people laugh, that's the whole reason for this show. You don't worry about us, we'll take care of ourselves. You just do your thing. Give it your all, do anything you feel like doing."

"Okay," I said, "if you're sure."

He said, "I'm ab-so-lute-ly sure." And from then on, I had no problem. I went heavier into my schtick than ever, because of Tuck's encouragement. People have asked me, "What is the most fun thing you've ever done?," and that had to be *it*.

Another great thing: Since it was being shot on tape, we sometimes came up with stuff funnier than what was written. Something would happen in the show that would give one of us an idea for a gag of some kind, and we'd say to Marc Richards, "Wait a minute — what if we tried *this*?" And he was always so great about it: "It's just tape, for cryin' out loud — sure, try it, absolutely. If we don't like it, we won't use it, that's all." Half the time, the stuff we came up with did make its way into the show.

Phew! Thanks to Tuck's intervention, Tracy got to take some much-needed breathers during *Ghost Busters* shooting.

Tuck became the father figure to me on the show. When he first met me, he called me Bob, but after that, it was "the kid," "Trace" or "Tracy" from then on. One day, probably about the third show in, I fainted. I'd kept the suit on too long because I didn't want to cause any delays and I wasn't taking breaks like I should have. I was so happy to be doing what I was doing, I pushed myself too far, and that day, on the office set, I got overheated and fell over. Tuck was the first guy over to me, asking me what had happened. When I told him that I got a little overheated, he said, "Wait a minute. Aren't you supposed to get breaks in this suit?" Hesitantly I said, "Yeeeah…but I don't want to cause any trouble…"

"'Cause trouble,' my ass!" he ranted. "Man, if you die, we don't have a show!"

He called everybody over, Norm and everybody else who was there that day, and he said, "All right, I'm gonna set up some new ground rules. We don't want this happening again. So whenever he's tired—" With that, he turned and looked at me and asked, "You're gonna *tell* me, right?"

"Oh, you bet. Yes, sir! I'll do it!" Six-foot-five, I'm telling him anything he wants to hear!

Tuck went back to addressing Norm and the crew: "Here's what we're gonna do: After we do a shot and he's tired, you pull the head off of him, give him some water, put a fan on him, whatever you have to do. I'm gonna go to my trailer and have a little drink. I'll be back in about 15 minutes, and if I feel he's okay, then we'll continue." Everybody agreed with that. And that's exactly what happened. On a regular basis, Tuck began asking me if I was tired, and if I told him that I was tired, even just a *little* tired, he'd say, "Okay, fine. That's it. We're takin' a break." I'd rest up while he went off to his trailer and had a little drink — maybe more than one!…he'd come back…he'd make sure I was okay…and only after I told him I was okay would we go back to work. He did this through the whole rest of the run of the show, all the time. "Want anything? You just let me know. I'll boom it out if you want anything at all!" — he had that big booming voice. One day between takes, he belted out the whole

"Trouble in River City" song from *The Music Man* for us, and he was brilliant. In addition to his Western roles and tough guy roles and *F Troop*, Tuck was also a singer and a dancer, and he toured with *The Music Man* for years. In fact, all four of Tuck's wives were dancers.

Speaking of dancing, we did an episode called "The Dummy's Revenge" where Tuck, Larry and I had to dance. I don't dance. Don't ask me. End of discussion! But we had to learn these "simple" dance steps in the episode, so they got Larry and me a tutor. (I wasn't wearing the gorilla suit when the tutor was working with us.) About a third of the way through the rehearsal, the tutor just looked at me and, very flatly, said, "This guy ain't never gonna get it."

Tuck could put a whole fifth of Jack Daniels away and still leap into action the moment it was time to shoot.

Norm, undeterred, told me, "Bob, just vamp it, do the best you can do. You're a gorilla, you don't have to do it well." Now, here's what's funny: There's a psychological thing that goes on in me when I put on the gorilla suit, and I can do things I can't do as me. When the cameras rolled, I did the dance steps perfectly, I think because I now had the gorilla suit on. I didn't miss a step, I was right on. But when the tutor was there and I was "me," I couldn't do it at all.

We did one episode that involved some bananas, and I made a joke about them: "Hey, everybody got bananas except Tracy. Good God, he's the guy who should have the bananas!" The next day when I went over to the neighboring stage and opened the door to my little trailer dressing room, I found that I couldn't get in. There blocking the opening were two full stalks of bananas, probably 50 bananas on each stalk, and a little note that read, "Are you happy now? Love, Tuck." We all had bananas for a week after that!

Another thing: At the end of many of the episodes, we did a "rimshot," a closing gag that involved a final closeup on somebody. A lot of times, they wanted to end the episode with a closeup on Tuck, and they did sometimes, but half the time he'd say, "No, no, no, no. Go out on Tracy. He's got a funnier face than me. Give him the closeup. I don't need it." He gave me his closeup a lot of times. He had to be one of the most generous guys in the world that way.

Tuck had a photographic memory. I never saw him with a script. He'd read the script at night; come in the next day (he never brought the script with him); and he never blew a take. Larry was just the opposite: In rehearsals, he couldn't remember one line. (He'd be constantly calling out to the script girl, "Jody — what's the line? What's the line?") But, funnily enough, when the camera went on, something clicked in him, and he never, never blew a line. He was perfect, absolutely perfect in the shows whereas in rehearsals he was a nightmare, and we never thought we were going to get through it.

As I mentioned earlier, Tuck did drink a little bit. Actually, more than just "a little bit": He could put a whole fifth of Jack Daniels away. But I never saw the man drunk. Not one time. Ever. He had such a capacity! He used to hang out with actors like Bruce Cabot and Errol Flynn and other guys who were heavy drinkers, and his tolerance for the stuff was

Most of the drive-by footage featured Larry and me simply driving past the camera, sometimes with a double for Tuck in the back.

Larry and I once took the Ghost Buggy for a high-speed spin down Mulholland Drive — with no brakes!

incredible. He'd be sitting in his director's chair some afternoons after polishing off a fifth and it looked like he was in a daze. "Oh, man, we're finished now!" I'd think to myself. But when they'd call out, "Okay. On set!," he'd go right into action. He would get out on the set…do everything he had to do…never blow a line. Then he'd return to his chair and go back to looking like he was in a drunken stupor!

About two weeks into the schedule, Larry and I went out on location again, this time to shoot all the drive-by footage; Filmation got the necessary permits to close off part of Mulholland. Driving that old Whippet up and down those hills was not the most fun I've

I never wanted to drive the Ghost Buggy again after the hair-raising day the brakes gave out.

ever had. I maintained that, in order to drive the car on those Mulholland roads, I was going to need gloves and sneakers instead of the gorilla hands and feet, but again I was told, "No, we might want you to get out of the car. You've got to be fully dressed as Tracy."

Long shots were all we were doing; Larry was in the car with me, in the back seat, and occasionally there was a double for Tuck. Most of what we did were shots of Larry and me simply driving past the camera, and that was no problem. But they wanted one shot of the car racing down a hill, looking a little like it's out of control. Norm told me to drive the car up a fire road, come back down again and, when I got to the bottom where the camera and the crew were, to make the car fishtail a little, right in front of the camera.

"Wait a minute," I said. "I'm not a stunt guy. I'm very restricted in this gorilla suit." Norm told me to do the best I could.

The camera and crew were positioned near the bottom of that hill, and about 12 feet behind them was a drop-off that looked like it had to be 60 feet. When I got to the bottom, I'd be heading for that drop-off. With Larry in the back seat of the car, I did the scene once but I didn't make the car fishtail, I just kind of swerved a bit. Norm said, "That was okay, but I want you a little bit more frantic when you come by." So again I drove to the top of the hill and started coming down. That was when I noticed that the car was starting to pick up a lot of speed. I stepped on the brake…and it went right down to the floor. I pulled the emergency brake and, again, nothing happened. The car was picking up more and more speed.

"Larry, there's no brakes in this car," I said. "I don't even know if the steering's gonna work. If I tell you to jump, jump." Upon hearing this, Larry started flailing his arms — that's what he was supposed to be doing in the shot, but this time it was for real, and he was yelling, "Oh shit! Oh shit!" I was holding onto the steering wheel for dear life. I knew that, if we crashed, the big shoulder pads in the gorilla suit would protect me a bit — but how much?

By this time I was getting close to the bottom of the hill — close enough to hear Norm yelling, "That's great, guys! That's really great!" — and I was terrified. I didn't think I'd be able to turn the car and avoid the drop-off. At the bottom, I gave the wheel a big turn and the car fishtailed and almost hit the camera guy.

It felt so good just to be on the road at the bottom again. *But* — I still had no brakes, and couldn't stop. Even the road at the bottom of the hill was a slight decline, and there was nothing I could do to make the car stop. Larry asked me, "Why aren't you stopping?," and I said, "Larry, I *can't* stop the car. There's no brakes, no nothing. I don't know how far we're gonna go." We coasted half a mile, maybe a mile, probably at around 25 or 30 MPH — fast enough that we couldn't jump out of the car without getting hurt. (Larry certainly would have gotten hurt — he had a plastic hip.) After a while I could see up ahead the two motorcycle cops who were stationed at that end of the road to prevent other cars from coming along and interfering with our shooting. Naturally they didn't know that anything was wrong and they begin waving at us. I told Larry, "Tell 'em to get out of the way!," so he started yelling, "Get out of the way! Get out of the way!" But the cops kept happily waving back to him — they had no idea what Larry was saying!

Werewolf Lennie Weinrib threatens Tracy in the episode "Who's Afraid of the Big Bad Wolf?"

We got closer and closer and all of a sudden the cops realized what was happening and they peeled off on their motorcycles. I went right over the spot where they had been stationed and, of course, kept on going. I thought we were gonna go 'til we got into New Mexico — I didn't know where we would end up. Finally I did the only thing I could think of to do: I ran the car into a ditch, and finally it stopped. Neither Larry nor I had gotten hurt, we'd just been bounced around a bit, but I was shaking like a leaf when I got out of the car. I was shook-up enough that when Norm came down to us in one of the studio vans and said, "I'd kinda like to do the thing one more time," I told him, "No way…!" (Norm didn't yet know that the brakes had gone out, he just thought it had taken me a while to stop.)

The next day I was at Filmation when Tuck came in, red in the face. I said to myself, "Oooh. He's not happy. He's not at *all* happy." I assumed that, on the ride in to work that morning, Larry had told him what happened the day before. (Larry didn't drive, so Tuck would bring him in in the mornings and I would take him home at night — that was the deal we worked out.) Tuck came over to me and looked me up and down and he asked, "You okay?"

"Yeah, I'm all right."

"You didn't get hurt?" I told him I had not. "I'm still kinda shook," I said, "but no bruises or anything."

Norm happened to come walking over at this point and Tuck sternly grabbed him by the shirt and said, "If you *ever* send those guys out in that car again without me checkin' it first, I'll bust your butt!" Boy, he was mad! And poor Norm was shaking a little bit, because he could tell that Tuck wasn't kidding. It was the only time I ever saw Tuck mad. Then he turned again to me and he barked, "And *you*. Don't *ever* let them talk you into driving that car again, until you talk to me about it first."

"You don't have to worry about that," I said, "I never even want to be *in* that car again — ever!"

That Mulholland incident was the one scary moment on the show, but — one was enough. It was truly scary, because Larry and I knew we could have been very badly hurt. In the opening credits of every episode of the show, you can see the first take of that shot where I'm driving down that Mulholland fire road and see how steep it is.

Ted Knight and Kathy Garver appeared in the *Ghost Busters* episode "The Canterville Ghost."

Outside of that, the rest of all of the 15 episodes was shot at Filmation and it went off without a hitch. And we had some great guest stars. The same thing happened on *The Ghost Busters* as happened on *Batman* about ten years earlier: We had stars calling up, asking to have cameos in it. But unfortunately the episodes were already written and already cast. Redd Foxx got upset that he couldn't do it, and Jack Carter also wanted to be in one, very badly.

Not that I'm complaining about the guest stars we did have on the show. I had the most fun with Huntz Hall, who did two episodes with us, one about a witch and the other with Merlin the Magician. He was a *funny* man. We did a couple of things that weren't in the script;

Norm Abbott was great. This guy really knew comedy. Here he is, surrounded by his Ghost Busters.

for instance, in a scene where we were leaving the office, as we headed for the door he started ad libbing, babbling out a lot of nonsense exactly the way he used to do when he was Sach in the Bowery Boys movies: "Oh, that's a nice fur coat you got, that's a *really* good coat. Do you know some girls we could go out with?" I snorted, he said, "Oh, that's good!," and we walked out together — Huntz started it and I went with it. Norm laughed and told us, "Oh, God, that was funny — that was really funny." Lennie Weinrib, who played a werewolf, was another great guy to work with. He gave me the greatest compliment I ever got on the show: "I've seen a lot of mimes, I've seen a lot of guys work in suits," he said. "But you have the best body English I've ever seen in a gorilla suit. You make that thing totally live." I really appreciated that.

Richie Balin, the brother of actress Ina Balin, was a great guy who played the Abominable Snowman and the Mummy. Now *there's* a fellow who had great body English: He really made that Snowman work. He and I had so much fun because we could work together well, miming back and forth. The late Billy Holmes, who played Dracula, was another guest star I really enjoyed. He was actually a young guy but, like Walter Brennan, he could play an old guy. A funny, funny, delightful man.

Howard Morris was originally supposed to direct the whole *Ghost Busters* series, but he was directing commercials and couldn't get away, so Filmation brought Norm Abbott in on it. But Howard said, "I'd like to be *in* at least one show," and he was, as the ghost of the Red Baron. He was a madman — I had trouble doing the scenes with him, because I was breaking up all the time. Jim Backus was very funny doing Eric the Red, and Ted Knight did a great job as the Canterville Ghost. We were all so happy to work with him, and thought he was a cool actor to get for the show, because he was then on *The Mary Tyler Moore Show*, a hot series. But — it was weird — Ted was so nervous…probably the most uptight actor we ever worked with! He was nervous about not getting his lines right. He was so nervous, he started to make *us* nervous!

On the stage next to ours, Filmation shot *Shazam!* and *Isis*, and JoAnna Cameron came over to our set a couple of times in her Isis outfit. We were shooting one day in an actual

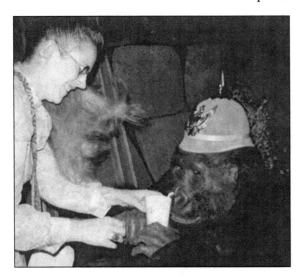

Filmation hallway when she came up to me and said, "Take me away from all this. Please. Take me away." I grabbed her and picked her up and ran her all the way down the hall, and everybody was laughing like crazy. I'd have kept running if I could have — she was very pretty and had a great sense of humor. Les Tremayne, the great radio actor, was a regular on *Shazam!* and sometimes he'd visit our set as well. He was a terrific guy with whom I talked about George Pal's *The War of the Worlds* (Les played General Mann) and his radio series *Mr. First Nighter* and so on, In addition to JoAnna and Les, other TV stars would occasionally visit, and sometimes even kids. When I heard that kids were coming over, I would make sure to keep the gorilla head on, because, I felt, "It's got to be 'real' for them."

I can't tell you how much fun I had on that show. It was the best of all the worlds I ever had. Every day, I'd be in by six in the morning — Tuck and Larry would come in about eight, but I'd come in early because I was just so excited and I wanted to get in early. The people could not have been nicer. Norm Abbott was great. This guy knew comedy: He'd directed *The Munsters* and *McHale's Navy* and *Get Smart*, a lot of series, and he really knew the stuff. The makeup artist Frank Griffin. the brother of Debra Paget, was a terrific makeup artist and really a good guy. He made-up the Frankenstein Monster, Dracula, the Abominable Snowman, all those guys. Black makeup around my eyes (the "raccoon look") was all he had to do for me as Tracy. The black-around-the-eyes is the worst part of the gorilla suit — that's so uncomfortable, because the stuff flakes off and gets your eyes all red and hurts like crazy. Also, I would sweat a lot, and Frank was always having to touch it

The only way to drink water without removing the head of the costume was to insert a straw through a nostril (my mouth was right behind the snout), as Leanetta, the *Ghost Busters* costume gal, is doing here. Below: Leanetta adjusts Tracy's head.

up. One day we were having a particularly bad time with it and he said, "I've got an answer for this. One of these nights, let's go out after the show, let's go to a bar and get you *really* drunk. Then I'll take you to a tattoo parlor and get your eyes *tattooed* black. *That'll* take care of it!" Well, by episode number eight, I was about ready to do it. "Frank, where is that tattoo place, man?" — that was a running joke we had from then on.

Frank never got me drunk — but there was one day that Tuck did. In a warehouse-type building right next door to Filmation, there was what we called The Hot Stage, where we did all the chases in the castle hallway with all the doors. It was always really hot in there — there was no air conditioning, no nothing. So, it figures, that had to be the stage where we did all the running and the chasing and the Three Stooges-like physical stuff, right? Well, one day I fell over — I was out like a light. I was so "out" that it took them a while to bring me back around. I had some ice water and little by little I was beginning to feel better, but we had a lot more to shoot. Finally Tuck said, "I know what he needs…" He went and got an iced tea glass, filled it with bourbon and ice, handed it to me and said, "Take this. This'll fix ya." Because I was so hot and dehydrated, I just chug-a-lugged it…and after that, I don't remember doing the end of that episode! A studio driver had to take me home that night, there was no way I could get home by myself, I was so wiped. He drove me home and deposited a drunken gorilla on my doorstep!

Tracy looks puzzled as Norm Abbott runs through the next office scene.

When Tuck learned I was working for scale (the Screen Actors Guild minimum), he was shocked. (George Barrows, another gorilla guy probably best-remembered as Robot Monster, called me "an idiot" when he found out!) One day about halfway through the shooting, Tuck said to me, "If you don't mind…how much do you get for doin' this? You're working your ass off in that suit." When I told him I was getting scale, he went, "*Scale*? That's *all* you're getting? Nothing for the suit?"

I said, "No…nuthin' for the suit."

"Oh, my God…" Tuck sighed. "Well, if we go another season, *I'm* negotiating for you, *I'll* take care of it. *You* don't worry about it. *I'll* take care of it for you." And I'm sure he would have, too!

But I didn't mind getting scale, I loved the work so much and I was treated so well. The craft service guy found out that I loved jelly doughnuts, so he made sure I had jelly doughnuts every single morning — he'd even put a note on 'em:

TRACY'S JELLY DOUGHNUTS — STAY OUT!

I've worked as a gorilla on a lot of shows where they treat you like crap — they don't give a damn if you live or die. But this was totally different. I never felt so accepted on a show in my whole life. About seven episodes into the shooting, suddenly there was talk of doing *The Ghost Busters* as a movie, a piece of news that made me very happy.

Throughout the shooting of the series, one thorn in our side were the CBS censors, who were very worried about any type or level of violence. There was a scene in one episode where at the end I had to throw pies in the faces of Tuck and Larry. The censor said, "The pies can't be shown being thrown and hitting Tuck and Larry in the same shot. *That* would look violent. In one shot, you can show Tracy throwing the pies out of frame, and then in the *next* shot the pies can fly into frame and hit Tuck and Larry." Frustrated, Norm asked, "What's the *difference?*" and explained to the censor that he wanted to do it in one shot, shooting over the shoulder of Tracy. But the censor said, "No way. You can't do that. But if you do it

Tuck, Tracy and Larry take their places on the *Ghost Busters* office set.

in two different shots, *then* it's all right, then it's not a violent act." Huh?? What does that even *mean*? When we did an episode with Marty Ingels as Billy the Kid, he couldn't have guns. Not even a cap gun. Not even a *water* gun. No gun of any kind. I asked, "Can he have bananas in his holsters? Tracy could come up behind him and steal the bananas and eat 'em." The censor said no, not even a banana — Billy the Kid couldn't have *anything* in his holsters! In fact, I'm not sure now whether the *holsters*, even though they were empty, were allowed!*

A lot of my fondest *Ghost Busters* memories are of Tuck, but I want to make sure I'm not giving the impression that I thought any less highly of Larry Storch, a great, funny, wonderful guy who, I remember, introduced me to sushi. I used to bring Larry home from the studio every night, and one time he mentioned a Japanese restaurant on Ventura Boulevard and asked me if I'd ever had sushi. In 1975, I didn't even know what it was. When he told me it was raw fish, and asked me if I'd like to try it, I said, "Whoa, whoa — I don't think so!"

"C'mon, c'mon. Let's go to that restaurant," Larry said. "If you don't like it, I'll eat it." So we went to the Japanese place and ordered sushi and I found I really liked it a lot; in fact, we stopped in there four or five more times in the weeks ahead. Sometimes, just to pass the

---

* John Davey, who played Captain Marvel in Filmation's *Shazam!*, told me that that show even had worse censor problems: Captain Marvel could never hit or grab or even touch the bad guys, If a bad guy was trying to get away, all Captain Marvel was allowed to do was tell him to stop, and then lecture him: "You're a bad man! You're going to jail!" CBS had a censor there all the time, making sure Captain Marvel didn't touch anybody. The restrictions in those days were ridiculous.

time as I was driving him home, he would start doing these crazy voices which had me responding to him in *my* crazy voices. We did these character things back and forth on the way to his home, which was a beautiful gated place in the hills up above Studio City. I liked Larry a lot.

We finished shooting the last episode a very short time before the first episode aired; I remember that at the end of the last day's shooting, they had me do some "wild track" snorts and growls so they would have some extra stuff if they needed to "sweeten the track." Tuck gave the wrap party at his home in Toluca Lake. He had trees in his backyard, and on at least three of them he had stalks of bananas and signs reading TRACY'S BANANA TREE. Tuck loved the show and he was counting on it going into a second season and beyond. It was easy for him and he thought that we would be doing the show until he retired.

At first, CBS wasn't sure where they wanted to slot *The Ghost Busters*, and there was a chance that it would become a nighttime show if they found themselves with an opening at 7:30; they thought that it was as much an adult show as it was a kid show, because adults would also enjoy the Laurel and Hardy-like slapstick stuff. Eventually, though, it aired at 11 o'clock on Saturday mornings.

I have very fond memories of both Tuck and Larry.

The show went over big with its audience. and Tracy started getting fan letters. I'd never before in my life gotten a fan letter, but now to my great surprise I was getting *lots* of them. Quite a bit of the mail, of course, came from kids; they would send them to CBS, and CBS would forward them over to me. "Tracy, I really like you, you're really cool"; "I want you to come and stay with me, but my mom says you can't," letters like

Tracy always wore a hat, *(a)* to kinda humanize him, and *(b)* because it just looked funny! A sailor hat, a cowboy hat, an Air Force hat, etc., but usually the beanie.

that. In the opening credits of the show, when Tracy was shown, the superimposed title read **TRACY TRAINED BY BOB BURNS**, so one question I got a lot was, "Is Tracy real?" Other letter writers just assumed that Tracy was real, and asked me how I trained him to do all his tricks and got him to act so human. I used to write 'em back and tell 'em the truth — I didn't *want* to, but I did!

One weird lady wrote to me saying that she knew that the streets of Hollywood were paved with gold, that she had three kids to support now that her husband had walked out on her — a long sob story. "You have so much and I have nothing. You could at least give my

Kids loved Tracy! The idea behind the beastie was to make kids realize that Tracy was there for fun and was not scary.

children shoes." The lady wanted a gorilla to send her shoes! CBS gave me a copy of the letter but they kept the original on file, because it was so strange that they were a little concerned about it. But that was the only bizarre thing that ever happened.

Once the show was on the air, it became the subject of several newspaper articles. We even got a bit of free publicity courtesy of the USC football team: One day in the newspaper, it said that during their Saturday practices, they would always take a half-hour out to watch the show! "Nothing can stop these players," the article said, "except *The Ghost Busters!*"

I even got to do a couple personal appearances as Tracy, one in Illinois that was a bit of a disaster. Kathy and I were sent to the Old Chicago amusement park-shopping center in Bolingbrook, where I had to suit up as Tracy in a boiler room that had to be 140 degrees! Kathy nearly melted too. Just getting the suit on was terrible, and the event hadn't even started yet! Then there was a magician who was probably the worst I've ever seen in my whole life. He wasn't doing schtick, he wasn't *pretending* to be a magician who couldn't do it right — he just couldn't do it right! I felt so sorry for the poor guy, especially when he started getting boos!

All that Tracy was supposed to do was sit down and sign autographs, but when I came out I did a little bit of schtick, chasing a few of the kids around a little. One guy standing there had this smug "Awww, it's just a guy in a suit" grin on his face, so I started walking over to him, reeeal slow, and once I got close, I gave him a big snort — my gorilla snorts work really well when I'm in the suit, because it amplifies in the muzzle. That guy started running, and that was the last I saw of him! There were probably 500 kids there wanting Tracy's autograph — when you've got gorilla hands on, that ain't real easy to do! But I signed their *Ghost Busters* flyers ("Beast Wishes, Tracy and the Gang") and had a good time even though the event wasn't organized at all.

But the event of events, the time of my life was riding as Tracy in the 1975 Hollywood Christmas Parade, a big annual event that began in 1928 as the Santa Claus Lane Parade.

The 1984 movie *Ghostbusters* had many similarities to our series (starting with the title!). One night the movie's star Dan Aykroyd was on TV saying that he watched our show and loved it, and admitting that the two were very much alike. "But if the *Ghost Busters* people do anything, we've made so much money, we'll be able to pay 'em off," he added. Lou Scheimer heard about this and made a few calls — and the *Ghostbusters* folks made a settlement payoff of around a million bucks. It never even had to go to court.

It's a nighttime parade that includes a lot of movie and TV celebrities riding in open antique automobiles, and that year Larry, his wife Norma, Kathy and I got to be part of it. (Tuck wasn't there — he'd already gone back East to star in a play at the Drury Lane North in Chicago. Theater and golf were Tuck's passions.) The parade was before the Bolingbrook event and before a lot of the fan mail came in on the show, so going into it, I didn't know if the people there would even know what the show *was*. Well, to my great surprise, kids began running out from the sidewalks to this old classic car of ours yelling, "Tracy! Tracy! Tracy!" Kathy said she'd never seen anything like this in her life. These kids were everywhere — it was like the Pied Piper was in the car! Larry got completely carried away, shouting, "Ooh, man, this is great!" and pounding on me with his fists (it's a good thing the suit was padded!). And I was just as drunk with excitement as he was. It was one of the biggest thrills and the most fun and the greatest nights I've ever had. I was euphoric.

It came as such a shock to hear that Filmation cancelled the show. *The Ghost Busters* was one of the top kid shows in the nation, right behind Filmation's *Shazam!* and *Isis*, which I thought was a sure sign we'd be renewed. But *Shazam!* and *Isis* were more expensive shows for Filmation — they were shot on 16mm and they involved a lot of location work, and Filmation decided to drop *The Ghost Busters* and put that money into their superhero shows.

I got the bad news from Frank Griffin the makeup man, who phoned me and said he'd just heard that Filmation was dropping *Ghost Busters*. I called over to Filmation and got a-hold of Lou Scheimer's secretary and told her I'd "heard a rumor." and she said, "Yeah, it's true, Bob. We had to cancel the show." I phoned Tuck to tell him, but he had already heard. "Those bastards," he grumbled. "I'm really ticked…" About two months later, when Filmation again started considering doing *The Ghost Busters* as a movie, Tuck told 'em to shove it. His feeling was, "You guys screwed us over. We're not coming back."

Later on, talking to Lou Scheimer about the cancellation, I made an analogy: "Say there's two horses in a race and one comes in first and one comes in second. You don't kill the one that came in second, 'cause he's liable to win the *next* race!" Lou agreed, and admitted that the cancellation of *Ghost Busters* had been a bad judgment call: "*Shazam!* and *Isis* seemed to be the more popular shows and we went with that…and we were wrong."

CBS loved the show a lot (and, obviously, loved the ratings it got), and they kept running those 15 episodes over and over until the fall of 1976. But that was the end of it, pretty much. There were only 15 episodes, which wasn't enough for it to go into syndication. If it had gone another season, there would have had plenty, and the reruns might still be on the air today, on Nick at Nite or one of the other nostalgia channels. But back in the 1970s, you had to have at least 26 episodes of a shows or it was dead syndication-wise.

I had a few favorites: I loved the Dracula show because I loved Billy Holmes; Dena Dietrich, "Mother Nature" in the old TV margarine commercials, was in it too, and she was great. I also have a special fondness for the Frankenstein episode, even though it was the very first one and you can see that we hadn't totally developed the characters or found our footing yet. The last show we did, the one with the Abominable Snowman, might be my very favorite of the bunch, just because it was so bizarre. But they were all fun for one reason or another.

The more I think about *The Ghost Busters*, the more I think it was the greatest professional experience I've ever had. I'd never had so much fun in my life, never worked with a crew or with actors who were more fun. It was a near-perfect thing. I'll probably never get to do it again, or anything even close to it. But at least I got to do it once. A lot of people never get that close to their dreams. I feel so fortunate that I had that chance.

And I do still have the beanie.

Above: A personal appearance with Jim MacGeorge and Chuck McCann as Laurel and Hardy; Tracy in a tutu, getting his first (and last) ballet lesson.

Publicity shot with Ronald McDonald.

The *Ghost Busters* episode "The Maltese Monkey" was a takeoff on *The Maltese Falcon* with Johnny Brown (pictured) as the Fat Man — and Billy Barty as the Peter Lorre character equivalent!

Left: Tracy dressed warm (including ear muffs) for "The Abominable Snowman," the last episode we did. The snow was actually Styrofoam peanuts ground up into little bitty pieces. It stuck to my hairy suit like cactus thorns and it took a couple of weeks to comb it all out. Right: Tracy watches as Kong aims the Ghost Dematerializer.

A publicity shot of Tuck and Larry giving me the royal treatment.

Richie Balin (with Abominable Snowman costume head off), me and my dresser Leanetta entertain some kids on the *Ghost Busters* set. Kids frequently visited and when they did, I never removed the Tracy head because I didn't want to spoil the illusion of Tracy. I also didn't talk when kids were around, I only did the snort.

Haunted Halloweens

This is one of my very favorite photographs that captures the spirit of Halloween. I was shooting a promo film for a friend when a kid in a homemade mummy costume showed up and I gladly posed for this shot. (Note that he's holding the Mummy and Creature toy figures.)

It was 1967 and Kathy and I had just recently moved into our present home in Burbank when Halloween decorations and costumes began appearing in the local stores and I realized our favorite holiday was about to come around again. But for some reason, the idea of simply answering the door and dropping some candy into the kids' bags just didn't seem like enough any more. It occurred to me, "Wouldn't it be neat if, when they came to our house, the kids could actually *see* something?" I wasn't thinking at all of doing a Halloween show, but just some kind of a tableau that they might enjoy looking at.

Neither Kathy nor I had any idea that that little germ of an idea would eventually grow, like the Blob, the Magnetic Monster, the Amazing Colossal Man, to the point where it would change our lives.

The Halloween shows that Kathy and I and our friends have staged in my Burbank house and backyard were popular for decades, but it wasn't until recently that someone asked me why Halloween meant so much to me that I started all of this. I actually sat up that night thinking about it. And do you know where I think it came from? The old serials. As a boy, I always liked to dress up like one of the serial hero guys that I admired so much. The first one I ever did was Spy Smasher, when I was a little teeny kid — and I loved it. I was a fan of the comic book *Spy Smasher*, and then when the Republic serial starring Kane Richmond started playing in 1942, I just had to have a costume. In Muskogee, Oklahoma, my folks took me to one store when we found goggles and a cap, and then to another where we found a jacket that resembled Spy Smasher's. I already had a toy gun and holster set and that became part of the costume too. *(See photo on page 13.)*

All the dressing-up was partly an escape mechanism, I'm sure. After the family moved to California and I started going to grade school here, I used to get beat up a lot because I had a very thick Oklahoma accent that the other kids didn't like. I was called an Okie all the time, and I got beat up by the school bullies regularly. I was a little guy, and pretty thin, so I guess it was easy to pick on me. I was shy in school as a result — because I didn't like getting beat up!

Then one Halloween my mom and dad got me a Mickey Mouse costume, with a mask made out of stiffened cheese-cloth and the pants with the tail and the two big buttons on the front. It wasn't anything special, it was just something my folks found in a store. Before I wore it for Halloween, though, the teachers had all the kids come to school dressed in our Halloween costumes and we had a parade around the school-yard to show them off. I came as Mickey Mouse, and what happened was really weird: For that one day, I was the Pied Piper of the school. In the schoolyard, everybody followed me all over the place. I think I could have led 'em off a cliff, if I wanted to. (And there were a few I wanted to!) But it was very odd: Dressed as Mickey Mouse that day, I felt like I was somebody different, totally different, and everybody not only accepted me, they thought I was cool. And of course, after

As you can see, I have this Thing for Halloween.

Halloween, things went right back to "normal" and I started getting beat up again! Why the Mickey Mouse was so popular, I still can't say, but that one day in the schoolyard, it was like I was the King Mouse and everybody treated me really well. That, I now believe, set me to subconsciously thinking, "Hey, this is how I can escape into something else and not be laughed at, not be put upon."

Then, too, of course, Halloween was always fun for me for the same reasons it was fun for every other kid: It was a very exciting time when you would dress up and go door to door and get candy.

A group of friends that I made up for a party. The Frankenstein Monster is Lionel Comport and I'm the Son of Dracula.

Most kids eventually outgrow Halloween but it remained a big deal for me. By the time I was a teenager, I had begun playing around with makeup. Cutting up my mom's wig and gluing it to my face *(see story on page 136)* had made me aware that I could change my face without putting a mask on. Once I figured out a few of the basics by playing around with makeup and nose putty and mortician's wax, I began making up myself and my friends for Halloween. One Halloween, 1950 I think, I made up my buddy Lionel Comport as the Frankenstein Monster (because he was the tallest guy of all of us) and another fellow as the Hunchback and another as the Wolf Man. I was the Son of Dracula that year. We

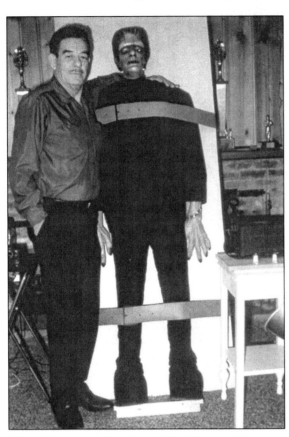

Glenn Strange, who played the Monster three times, stopped by to see himself brought back to life for one of our shows.

went around trick or treating and then we all went to a party, which was a lot of fun. Most of the people at the party had regular store-bought costumes, not one of them was made up, so we were the "belles of the ball." As crude as the makeups were — and, believe me, they *were* crude! — at least they were makeups, and nobody else was doing that at that time. On the first Halloween after I saw the movie *The Thing from Another World*, I made up Lionel as the Thing. There were no photographs of the Thing available then so I had to do it from memory. Later, when photographs of James Arness in makeup as the Thing did start to surface, I was very pleased to see that I got very close with the makeup job I'd done on Lionel. And it just kept going from there.

1967: "The Frankenstein Monster"

Our first Halloween show was a very simple tableau, a Frankenstein "mad lab" set in my living room, just inside the front door of my house. My inspiration was a Frankenstein mask that I'd made up over at Don Post Studios from an original *Abbott and Costello Meet Frankenstein* mold.* Thinking it would be fun to use that mask, I decided my "Halloween tableau" would be the Frankenstein Monster on a lab table.

I also had the Monster boots that Glenn Strange gave me, so now I had head and feet — but nothing in between! So I made up a dummy by stuffing a dark coat and dark pants with newspapers. Then, using wire coat hangers, I attached to the dummy the mask and the boots and a pair of Don Post Frankenstein hands. To dress up the living room a bit, I tinkered together a Jacob's Ladder, the prop you see in so many "mad doctor" movies — it's the lab gizmo with the arc of electricity that rises up, up, up between the two wires, vanishes and then reappears at the bottom again. I made it out of a neon transformer, and probably could have gotten killed in the process. I didn't know it at the time, but those things are pretty powerful.

On Halloween night, when the kids came to the door, either Kathy or I stood out of sight and opened the door reeeeal slow, like it had opened by itself, and they would see the Monster dummy on a long table we had propped up in an upright (diagonal) position, just

---

* In 1966, when Don Post got a license from Universal to make masks of some of their old monster characters, they also got from them the mold that was used to make the head for the Frankenstein dummy that falls through the burning pier at the end of *A&C Meet Frankenstein*. I was working at Post's nights and weekends at that time and, with Don Sr.'s permission, I made a mask up for myself.

like the Monster-on-the-table scenes in *House of Frankenstein*. The Monster was facing the trick-or-treaters, fastened to the table with leather straps I'd made. It looked very much like a real person. Of course it didn't move, but that didn't matter: The kids had never seen anything like this before, *anywhere*. And the Jacob's Ladder, sitting on a second table (to the left of the Monster), was on, making that familiar "zzzzzip…zzzzzip…zzzzzip" noise we've all heard in a hundred movies. One room light was on, others were blinking, and I also had an audio tape running — electrical sounds from *House of Frankenstein*. That was about all there was to it; it didn't scare anybody, but at that point we weren't *out* to scare anybody. It went over very well. We let the kids look at it from the doorway for 15 or 20 seconds and then either Kathy or I, whichever one of us had opened the door, stepped into sight with the dish of candy and said, "Happy Halloween!"

Well, the kids must have liked it, because word-of-mouth spread fast. The kids who saw it told other kids, and we started getting big bunches of trick-or-treaters coming to the door to see this thing. My friend Gene had come by just to hang out, but when things started to get a little out of hand (kids hanging out all over my porch and front yard and driveway, waiting their turn), he got 'em organized single file and then he "headed the line" (let them come to the door six at a time) to see the tableau.

But the best part of the evening was when Glenn Strange showed up. I'd called him a couple days earlier and told him what Kathy and I were doing ("Pappy, we're doing *you*!"), and he said, "Oh, I gotta see that." He came over the night before Halloween to see the set-up, and then on Halloween night itself he came again and stayed almost the whole evening — that's how much he loved seeing the kids' reactions and meeting and talking to them. Gene would tell the trick-or-treaters, "Here's Glenn Strange, the Frankenstein Monster from *Abbott and Costello Meet Frankenstein*," and these kids would swarm over to see him. Glenn was talking to the kids and signing autographs all night — signing anything they gave him to sign, or signing pieces of paper out of a notepad for kids who had nothing he could sign. The kids were more excited to see him than they were the show! Glenn stuck around and had a great time, which was really neat. He was very flattered that I did him as the Monster.

That was our very first "Halloween show," and the first time I became aware that I always had to expect the unexpected where these shows were concerned: I was very pleased with myself making up that working Jacob's Ladder, but what I didn't realize was that it sent out a signal: For maybe a hundred feet around, it messed up my neighbors' television sets all night long. None of them could figure out why their sets were going crazy. I'd turn off the Jacob's Ladder between trick-or-treaters, and their sets would go back to normal; then I'd turn it back on and everybody's set would go on the fritz again! In all my neighbors' houses up and down my block, I'm sure there was a lot of angry pounding on snowy TV sets that night!

1968: "Haunted House"

For the first five years of our Halloween shows, the tableau would be inside the house, in the living room, and the trick-or-treaters would just look through the door — we didn't get grandiose 'til much later! There wasn't much to our second Halloween tableau, the "Haunted House" show. When you came to the door and it opened, you saw a painting of Bela Lugosi as Dracula over the mantel and you saw a "ghost." For the "ghost" I draped a white sheet over a small light stand to which I had already attached a rubber ball the size of a human head up top (to give our ghost a head shape) and, sticking out from the side, a coat hanger wire (to give it a hand). A fan, positioned out of sight of the trick-or-treaters, was blowing on the sheet, making it look like the "ghost" was moving. The whole scene was lit with candles.

Then after a few seconds, I'd suddenly appear from behind the door for the first time, wearing a monster mask, and let out a big growl — and the kids would jump halfway off the porch!

Actually, the outside of the house was a lot more interesting than the inside. A friend of ours, Tommy Scherman, a prop and model maker, did a marvelous painting of the winged demon Chernobog from the "Night on Bald Mountain" sequence in the animation classic *Fantasia*. It was a great big painting on cardboard, probably eight by eight, that we hung on the porch. We also made a bunch of cardboard tombstones (one said **FRANKENSTEIN**, one said **DRACULA** — one even said **BURNS!**) that we stood up in the front yard, like a cemetery.

For our 1968 "Haunted House" show, Tom Scherman painted the demon from *Fantasia* as a backdrop and made the tombstones out of cardboard.

As I said, there wasn't much to that show, but that was the first show where something happened: I popped out from behind the door as a monster and scared the trick-or-treaters. It was still a tableau thing, but a monster came into play for the first time. And I could tell that the kids really got a kick out of that.

1969: "The Mutant"

In 1969, with the encouragement of Tommy Scherman and my friend Dennis Muren, we decided to get a little more ambitious with the Halloween show. That year, because I had a mask of the Metaluna Mutant from *This Island Earth*, we did a show we called "The Mutant" and built an actual set in my living room.

Using wood and cardboard, Tommy and Dennis constructed the set (an interior room of a spaceship). Dennis did the lighting, devising some really creepy effects. Trick-or-treaters knocked on the door and it opened "by itself" (Kathy was behind it), and they saw this little room-within-a-room lit by blinking lights. Then, through an interior door, I came onto the set as the Mutant. I wore a silver lamé suit that Kathy had made, plus of course the Metaluna Mutant mask and hands, both courtesy of Don Post Studios, and some generic "monster feet" that I'd made. The neat thing about my Mutant mask was that it was full-size, made from the original mold the Universal makeup guys created in 1954. Don Post Studios had the loan of the mold from Universal but never manufactured a full-size Mutant mask — it would have taken too much rubber, and no kid could have afforded it. So one of the Post employees, a gal, sculpted up a smaller version of it that became part of Don's "Universal Monsters" collection. But Don told me I could make a full-size one out of the original mold for myself, which I did — I poured it up and painted it, and it came out pretty neat.

Back to Halloween night: Wearing the mask, hands and silver suit, I came onto the set and spent about a minute playing with dials on the spaceship wall and looking through a big, weird-shaped porthole at a Tommy Scherman painting of the war-ravaged Metalunan city. Then, menacingly, I headed for the front door and the kids who were standing there. A lot of kids hightailed it off the porch right away, because with that big Mutant head sticking up as high as it did, I was darn near seven feet tall, and pretty scary-looking. Once I got to a certain point, Kathy stepped into sight wearing a red *Destination Moon*-type spacesuit that my Aunt Ruth had made for me — Kathy didn't wear a helmet, just the costume, boots and gloves. With a "Happy Halloween!," she dished out candy to all the trick-or-treaters. Well, to however many were left.

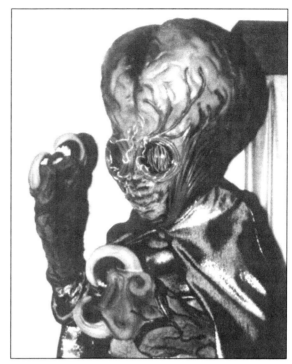

That's me as the *This Island Earth* Mutant. Acting never gave me a swelled head...

The line this year was longer than ever: Kids who saw the show would tell other kids, and a lot of kids who already saw it once came back to see it again. At one point, there was a line of probably 70 or 80 kids. It took Kathy and me by surprise — in fact, we even ran out of candy, something we tried to make sure never happened again.

Dennis Muren (left) and Tom Scherman built the sets for our "Mutant" show right in my living room. Yours truly is the Mutant at right.

1970: "Goombah"

When I first met Mike Minor in 1960, he had just graduated from college. We met because he'd heard through the grapevine that I was a big fan and friend of George Pal, whom he idolized. He phoned me and then came over to my house to show me many paintings and drawings he had done based on the Pal films. We hit it off right away. As Mike was leaving after that first visit, he gave me all of the art that he brought, saying that he could

We glued tissue paper to Goombah for a wrinkled texture. Here, Tom Scherman paints on the finishing touches.

redo them any time. He did a lot of his drawings with colored pencils which I always called his "magic pencils" as he worked real magic with them on black paper. Mike later got into the movie and TV world and worked as a production illustrator on the original *Star Trek* TV series and many movies. He started working on our Halloween shows starting in 1970 with one we called "Goombah," and worked on all of them up through 1982. Mike became the hub of our shows, a real dynamo. Everyone loved to work with Mike as they learned so much from him. He was one of our closest friends until the day he died.

"Goombah" was our most elaborate show to date at that time. Goombah was a big, blue-gray, one-eyed monster, an octopoid thing four feet tall, seven feet wide and five feet deep. The tentacles were eight feet long, We sat it up on the roof of my house, just back of the porch roof. Tommy Scherman had come up with the idea for Goombah and designed it, and it was a pretty original monster.

We got big crowds with "Goombah," partly because at night, when the thing was lit up with black light, you could see it from all the way down the street. That was the first time we had a lot of people show up — close to eight or nine hundred, I'd guess.

Two guys operated Goombah from the inside, one of them Jon Berg the movie special effects artist. As a group gathered below, the Goombah operators wouldn't move it at first, and the audience thought it was just a static thing. Then the operators would make the whole thing pulsate a little, and rise up and down. (Goombah was pretty flexible, so they could do all that with just their hands.) Goombah's big orange eye was directed down toward the people — the guys inside Goombah could see *out* through the wire mesh of the eye, but the audience couldn't see *in*. The operators would spot somebody in the crowd who was really looking at it very closely, and they'd suddenly pop the eyeball out at the guy — it went out about five inches. The guy would say, "Oh, my God, the thing just looked at me!" — it was startling! The guys inside Goombah would keep that eye moving after that, in and out as well as "around," like a real eye. It really got to people. Sitting up there on the roof, glowing blue, with the eye moving around, making a weird metallic breathing noise, Goombah looked and sounded *very* unearthly. PHOTO 9 — The finished Goombah sits atop the roof of our peaceful suburban home. It really shook up the crowd whenever his eye moved to focus on a "victim."

When people came on the porch and we opened the door so they could look inside, what they saw was a "wrecked" room. Again we made a room-within-a-room, using a fake wall that included a door that had been partly knocked off its hinges, A lamp on the floor looked like it was broken, flashing on and off like a shorted-out lamp would do. A fake piece of "ceiling" hung down, as though the ceiling had partially caved in, and two tentacles dangled into the room through this "opening" in the ceiling, (Outside, up on the roof, Goombah was directly above the fake hole in the ceiling,) Using a wire, we made one of the dangling tentacles move around; the other was wrapped around a dummy which was also on a wire, wiggling around like the guy was trying to get away. David Allen, my stop-motion animator friend, was behind the wall providing the voice of this victim: "It's eating my *brains*! *It's eating my brains*!" We had cut a hole in the wall and attached a cone to it, sort of like a megaphone, that Dave could yell into. It came out quite loud!

It was a pretty neat set — I think we did a good job of making it look like the house had really been hit hard by something and the living room wrecked.

1971: "The Return Of Mr. Hyde"

In the movies, as far back as Paramount's 1931 *Dr. Jekyll and Mr. Hyde* with Fredric March and even before that, moviemakers would use special makeup and special light filters to create the impression that an actor's face was changing, The actor would wear (say) red makeup, and the moviemakers would light him using a filter that was exactly the same shade of red as the makeup. When the actor was bathed in red light, you couldn't see the red makeup. Then when the filter was changed to a blue-green, the red facial makeup now began to show up to the naked eye of onlookers — and to the camera — as dark gray or black. A facial transformation seemed to begin because the makeup had begun to appear, and without the use of lap dissolves or any of the other trickery that moviemakers sometimes employ.

In 1951, when Columbia made *The Son of Dr. Jekyll* with Louis Hayward, they did the same thing with Hayward that Paramount had done with Fredric March. *Life* magazine ran an article (on color pages) on the process, showing all the different colors that were used. Once I read that article, it was in the back of my mind from then on. Twenty years after *Life* ran that article, it became the inspiration for our show "The Return of Mr. Hyde."

Dennis Muren, once again a key member of our fabulous Halloween crew, hooked up two lights: One had a red gel and the other a blue-green gel, and he made a "cross-fader" so that one light would go down as the other came up. This would make the Mr. Hyde makeup on the face of the actor (me) appear — but only if I could figure out how to do my job. My job was to prepare a red makeup that would be exactly the same density as the red light. I got some red greasepaint and, on a palette almost like one that a painter would use, I started making up different shades of red. I put streaks of the various reds on my face and, looking at myself in my bathroom mirror (with the red light shining on me), I squinted to see if I could still detect the red streaks under the red light. It took a lot of mixing and lightening and darkening of the greasepaint, but finally I hit upon a shade that I could not see on my face under the red light. My face was covered with this red makeup, but in the red glow of the light, it looked like there was *nothing* on my face. I had finally done it—but not before making myself look like an Indian chief!

This year we were back in the living room, where we put together a "mad doctor"-type lab set — I borrowed a bunch of lab equipment from a prop man friend and we also made

Here I am standing on the laboratory set for our "Return of Mr. Hyde" show. The crowd saw me transform before their eyes.

some electronic-looking gadgets. Then, inspired by something I'd seen on a recent visit to the Haunted Mansion at Disneyland, I decided I also wanted to have Kathy's severed head sitting on a little table, with her heart beating below. I thought I could do the "severed head" part by putting a wig form on the table and projecting Kathy's face onto it.

After making up Kathy in shades of grays, with highlights and shadows, I shot some 8mm footage of her against a black background. I told her to be sure not to move her head. She could move her eyes and open her mouth, but she couldn't move her head at all. I shot that, had the film developed and then made about eight feet of the film into a loop that would run through the projector over and over (avoiding the hassle of constant rewinding and re-threading). I set the projector in a hiding place beside the door and I projected the image of Kathy's face onto this wig form on the table. It looked a little flat at first, so I put a wig on top of the wig form. Then I made a slight protrusion on the "face" of the wig form, a nose-shaped blob of putty right where a nose would be. It was just enough of a three-dimensional thing that it now looked great: The projected image of'Kathy's nose now landed on the putty "nose" and it looked extremely realistic.

As for the heart, I wanted it hanging under the table, about where Kathy's heart would be if the rest of her body was still under her head. I got a little red rubber balloon-type thing in the shape of a heart and I put it in a cylinder made of clear plastic. A friend of mine rigged up a little pump, similar to one you might use in a fish tank, that pushed air into the balloon and then sucked it back out again. This made the thing look like it was beating. There was also a beating-heart sound effect and a little light shining on it, just enough to show it off.

Halloween night, the door would slowly swing open and there'd be Dr. Jekyll (me), bathed in red light, mixing up a potion. (For atmosphere, there was also a bit of flashing light and the sound of bubbling chemicals.) I'd go over to Kathy's head and pat the top of it in a comforting, "everything's okay" kind of way, I had it timed so that I patted the head at the same time that, on the film, Kathy's eyes looked up in my direction. That freaked the people out!

I crossed back to the lab table and picked up the beaker with the potion and I drank it. Then I faced the audience — I made sure not to turn my head or cover my face at all. I looked right at the audience and started to grab my throat and do the typical Jekyll-turning-into-Hyde thing, making sure they saw my face the whole time. Dennis Muren, who was operating the cross-fader from behind the door, slowly took the red light out and brought the blue one up…the red makeup on my face was seen for the first time…I parted my lips and opened my mouth to reveal fake fangs that I'd been wearing all along…and there I was as Mr. Hyde. Then, menacingly, I would start toward the audience. I'd get just about to the door and *bam*, Dennis would slam it shut. At that point, a guy outside handed out candy to the people as they came off the porch.

Once again, we got a good turnout. To entertain the people as they waited to see the show, Jon Berg and another fellow were made-up as Dracula and the Frankenstein Monster and they staged a mock fight. But as it turned out, the most interesting thing about the show wasn't the Dracula-Frankenstein battle, or even my Jekyll-Hyde transformation; it was Kathy's head on the table that freaked everybody out. Something we'd tossed in as a macabre bit of icing on the cake turned out to be the hit of that particular show.

It's funny to look back on some of the older Halloween shows and know that Dennis Muren, the multi-multi-Oscar winner for special effects (*E.T.*, *Innerspace*, *Terminator 2*, *Jurassic Park*, more) worked on them, sometimes doing the most mundane jobs! For instance, on "Mr. Hyde" he had the boring job of being the one opening and closing the door! He was also working the cross-fader, which was positioned behind the door, so it just seemed logical for him to do the door too. ("Mr. Hyde" became one of his favorite shows because of the transformation illusion.) Dennis is the type of guy who doesn't mind doing "grunt" work, and it was a pleasure and an honor to have him involved in so many of our shows.

It was after the "Mr. Hyde" show that Kathy finally kicked us out into the backyard — at least, that's what I always say when I tell the story of our Halloween shows. After five years, she finally got tired of the living room being all messed up all the time. But moving the show out to the backyard was the best thing we ever did, because we could have more of an audience and we could do more. It was a blessing in disguise.

1972: "Kogar Escapes"

When the Magic Mountain amusement park opened in Valencia, California, in 1971, it was as much a park as it was an amusement park and it employed 500 people. It's still there and bigger than ever, now called Six Flags Magic Mountain, and today there are over 3000 employees and rides spread out over the whole property, a full-fledged Disneyland-type place. That's progress I guess, but I remember fondly the early days of Magic Mountain, and particularly the "Kogar Escapes" show we did out there.

I had a friend named Larry Sands who worked at Magic Mountain, booking acts for the park's Showcase Theater. Larry had once seen a Las Vegas act where a gal turned into a gorilla — or maybe it was vice versa, I don't remember now. It was done with mirrors but Larry was impressed nevertheless, and he used to tell me, "Boy, if I can ever find a way to incorporate you and your Kogar gorilla suit into a stroller act, that'd be cool." ("Stroller acts" roamed the park, putting on shows to entertain people standing in long lines.)

I knew a fellow named Art Laing, a field reporter for radio station KFWB. Art was the guy who went out in the field talking to people about "light" news stuff. When Larry showed an interest in an act involving Kogar, I talked to Art about it and we came up with this idea: Art would play a gorilla trainer, a "great white hunter" type, and he'd ride around the park in a truck with a caged Kogar (me) in the back. Whenever he came across a line of waiting people, he would stop and show off Kogar, try and make Kogar do tricks — but then Kogar

A sneering Art Laing as Kogar's trainer taunts the unruly ape.

would go a little wild and start to break out of his cage. That was what we came up with, and Larry loved the idea. I had Tommy Scherman build me a cage with a big KOGAR sign on it, and we were ready to go. It was a lot of fun. On Saturdays and Sundays, a driver took us around the park in a battery-operated truck, and when we came upon a lined-up crowd, we stopped and Art began his spiel. Art put on this English Cockney accent and did a great job. He was the one who really "sold" the show.

I was in the back in the cage, and Art pointed me out to the people and told them he was going to make me do a few tricks. Art had a piece of rubber hose about two and a half feet long that he called an "authority stick." He stuck it in my cage and I ran to the back of the cage as if I were scared of the "stick." He told the crowd that he would show them again how afraid I was of the "stick" — but this time, I grabbed hold of the stick and went nuts and charged toward the cage door. We had it rigged so that when I pushed on the side of the cage, the door would suddenly pop open. I never got all the way out, but...almost. Art would slam the cage door shut again and yell to the driver, "Kogar's gone crazy! Get him back to the compound!," and we'd drive off real fast. But you could always tell where we'd been by the half-eaten hot dogs and spilled Cokes all over the ground. It was amazing how those crowds reacted. Grown men would run like crazy. Women would take off and leave their *babies* in their strollers. The baby would be there in the stroller, and the mother would be *gone*. We had one guy whose girlfriend fell down, and he dragged her about 20 feet. Another guy jumped in the pool of a fountain because he said he had heard that gorillas were afraid of water! It worked every time, and the reaction was great. This was the first summer Magic Mountain was open, and "Kogar Escapes" was the hit of the park.

After a while, I just didn't feel like doing it any more — it was the middle of the summer, so it was really hot work. But then I thought, "Boy, that'd be the perfect thing to do for Halloween." And there wasn't all that much work involved. I of course already had the gorilla suit, complete with a brand-new head that Rick Baker had made for me, and I still had the cage from the Magic Mountain show. So it just became a matter of Tommy Scherman and Mike Minor and the rest of the guys creating in the backyard a jungle compound complete with crates, bamboo fences with native spears attached to them, etc. By then, our shows were beginning to get media coverage pretty regular. Newspaper and TV reporters would come over on the night of our dress rehearsal, when we had an audience made up of people from our block, and their stories would appear on our opening day.

A crowd of kids lines up to walk through the giant gorilla head entrance to the "Kogar Escapes" show.

The people who came to our show walked halfway down the driveway, where there was a giant gorilla head cut-out (painted by Mike Minor); they had to pass through the open mouth to get to the backyard to see "Kogar Escapes." Once again Art Laing played the great white hunter and I played Kogar. Rick Baker spelled me from time to time, wearing a gorilla suit he had made — Rick's first-ever complete gorilla suit. In shows where Rick took over for me as Kogar, my buddy Charlie Dugdale the KCBS announcer took over for Art so that he could take a breather too, Art and I would do maybe eight or nine five-minute shows, and then Charlie and Rick would step in.

After "Kogar Escapes," I felt that our Halloween show was totally established within our community — we were now something that everybody knew would happen every year. From that point on, we would have people coming by the house starting in September to ask, "What are you guys doin' this year…?!"

1973: "Forbidden Planet"

It was Mike Minor who came up with the idea for a show based on the movie *Forbidden Planet*. He simply said, "Why don't we get back to a science fiction kind of thing, and do something really cool?" That was fine with me — especially since I knew that our friend Bill Malone had a Robby the Robot recreation he himself had made. Bill said, "Sure, we can use my Robby. Not a problem!," and we were halfway home.

For the Altair-4 set we built in my backyard, Mike did an incredible backdrop-cyclorama, a painting of the planet surface, the blue-green sky and (in relief) the touched-down spaceship. The thing was probably about 12 feet tall and 30 feet long, with a slight curve to it. It ran across the length of my backyard and was free-standing. Then we built a cave opening, a "proscenium arch"-type thing that the audience would look through to see the set and the show.

Charlie Dugdale, last seen battling Kogar in "Kogar Escapes," played the head of the spaceship crew. The show started in darkness, and then the lights came up and there was Charlie and two of his crew guys on the surface of Altair-4. The two crewmen wore original uniforms from the film, loaned to us by Bill Malone. Charlie said, "Good evening, ladies and gentlemen. Our images are being transmitted via holograph from Altair-4 to Bob Burns' backyard…" Charlie was a great showman, a guy who really knew how to handle an audience. I used Charlie in a lot of shows.

Continuing to address the audience, Charlie said, "We have found a person…I guess you'd call it 'a person'…on this planet," and then, calling off-stage, he said, "Would you come out here, sir?" And out came Robby. Every audience went berserk when they saw this — apparently everybody knows *Forbidden Planet* and Robby the Robot! Robby (Bill Malone inside) lumbered stiff-legged out onto the set and in that familiar robotic voice he identified himself as Robby and stood there for a bit, talking with Charlie.

Robby and Charlie Dugdale flash the victory sign in front of Mike Minor's terrific "Forbidden Planet" backdrop.

Then all of a sudden Robby started looking around in a way that conveyed, "Oh-oh. Something's wrong."

"W-w-what's a-matter, Robby?" Charlie stammered. "What's wrong?"

"Some-thing is com-ing from the south-west, sir…ver-y close," Robby reported.

Off to the right, we'd built another cave entrance (up against the wall of my garage), and this one had a rear-projection screen inside it. And at that point in the show, we projected the *Forbidden Planet* Id Monster onto that screen, so it looked like the Id Monster was in the cave. Not only did it look great, it also *sounded* great. I had a speaker blasting a recording of those weird electronic "screams" that the Monster lets out in the movie. As the Monster was standing there, stomping and roaring, Charlie called out to his men, "Fire your blasters! Fire your blasters at it!" Bill Malone had made up ray guns that looked just like the ones in the movie, and they lit up when you pulled the trigger. Charlie and the other crewmen began blasting away at the Id Monster, and finally it disappeared.

"Well," Charlie panted, "it's okay, it's over" — and then at that point, big monster tentacles started falling down from above the tops of the cave walls, trying to grab him. And then, because we always liked to end our shows with a big "Boo!," our friend Robert Alvarez, the cartoon animator who did the Id Monster animation for the show, suddenly burst onto the scene wearing a replica of the horrible rat-like "Pickman's Model" monster suit from the TV show *Night Gallery* and he came running at the audience. Boy, that scared the bejesus out of everybody — I wasn't sure we'd ever be able to top that scare.

But then came *The Exorcist*.

1974: "The Thing In The Attic"

"The Thing in the Attic," based on the then-new movie *The Exorcist*, came together the same way several of the shows did: I would come up with the idea, then sit down and have a brainstorming session with the key crew guys, Mike Minor, Tommy Scherman and so on. This time, however, I wanted to do something within the show that none of us could figure out how to manage. "It'd really be neat," I said, "if the possessed girl in our show could rise up in the air, float four feet above the bed, like Linda Blair does in the movie. Now…can we *do* it?" I had no idea if we could do it, and even Mike Minor was stumped.

But Kathy's boss at Universal, Al Jerumanis, came up with the answer.* "Oh, that's easy!" he scoffed. "We'll just do a cantilever thing…," and he went on to explain a very simple way it could be done. He devised the solution right away, and what he suggested worked perfectly. Al was a genius, a guy with a degree in engineering who could figure out *any*thing. With him around, I could dream up almost any crazy idea and I just knew that he could get it to work.

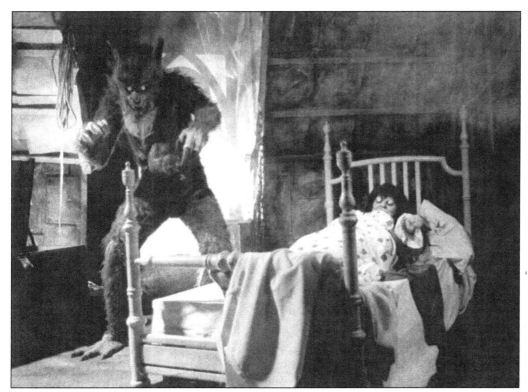

In our 1974 show "The Thing in the Attic," the possessed girl (Kathy Burns) calls forth her demon (Rick Baker) to terrify the audience.

What Al suggested was a cantilever device, a teeter-totter-type thing that the girl would lie on. When off-stage crew guys pushed down on one end of the teeter-totter, the girl rose up off of the bed atop the *other* end. But the girl would be wearing a nightgown which, as she "levitated," draped down over the teeter-totter so that it was impossible for the audience to see. A lot of people who saw the show thought we used wires. But there were no wires at all, it was Problem Solver Al's cantilever device.

Kathy and Elaine Baker, Rick's then-wife, agreed to take turns playing the girl. While Al was getting his cantilever device ready, Kathy did a test on it. She laid down on her end of it and Al and his friend Morey Winegart pushed down on the other end. But they pushed it down so fast, Kathy shot up in the air like she'd be shot out of a catapult. She went about

---

* Jerumanis was vice-president and chief information officer for the MCA corporate entity overseeing the data processing for all divisions of the company, including Universal Pictures, Universal Television and MCA Records. The department had a staff of 180 people for which he was responsible. Kathy wore two hats. Wearing one, "Manager of Administration," she prepared and monitored the department's budget, prepared proposals for computer system implementations and supervised clerical support personnel. Wearing the other hat, she installed the first IBM computer system that allowed word processing throughout the studio, specifically for scripts. The system started with one mainframe and just six work stations and three printers in the script department. It grew to ten systems with 220 work stations and 180 printers networked between Miami, New York, Hawaii and Los Angeles. As an interesting point of information, the IBM personal computer was born from the technology of this system. In a voluntary capacity, Kathy was also the lead writer for *MCA Ink,* the company newspaper, distributed to over 8000 employees.

six feet up and came down in the driveway! Since she didn't get hurt, it was very, very funny. After that, we took the precaution of strapping the girls to the thing with a belt, just to make sure that didn't happen again!

I came up the idea that the girls should have blood-red, glowing eyes. I got some little Grain of Wheat bulbs, the kind you can buy in any train shop, and we figured out a way to tape them to the girls' brows right over their eyes. Rick Baker, who did the makeup on Kathy and Elaine, made up rubber piece brows to cover the wires leading to the bulbs, (We also painted the back of the bulbs black so they wouldn't blind the girls.) The rest of their makeups,

The completed "Thing in the Attic" set was impressive. This was one of the scariest shows we ever did.

he did just with highlights and shadows. (Rick had worked on *The Exorcist*, the movie itself, with Dick Smith, so he knew the face pretty well.) Rick also made up a demon head and a devil head for a scene toward the end of the show. The demon suit was actually the ape suit that Rick had built for John Landis' *Schlock*, and the hands were the baby hands he had made for the mutant baby in *It's Alive!* The demon suit was made up of quite a few different things!

The set for the show was an attic room which Dennis Muren helped build and then lit. The show began with Charlie Dugdale walking out onto the set and, referring to the girl in the bed, saying, "Ladies and gentlemen, we don't know what's the matter with this girl, but she seems possessed." Then, as he lectured about the deities of the underworld, the girl started to talk. This scared Charlie, and he told the audience, in a shaky voice, "W-w-we better get out of here. This wasn't planned. This wasn't supposed to happen in the show" — and he turned tail and got off the set. That was the point at which the girl took over, going into her spooky dialogue. To light up the Grain of Wheat bulbs in their eyes, the girls had contact points on their forefinger and thumb, and when they touched 'em together, the eyes glowed. They could make 'em flicker, they could make 'em do anything they wanted. That blew *every*body's mind.

But the best was yet to come, the rising-up from the bed. You could hear the intake of breath from the audience when this happened, along with a lot of whispered comments like, "Oh, my God!" and "Look at that…!" The girl lifted up four feet but it looked like she levitated even more than that because we'd "raked" the set slightly down, built it on a slight decline, to heighten the effect. Then, still up in the air, she conjured up the demon, which was played by Rick Baker. At a fast pace, Rick came out to the very edge of the attic set and started down a flight of stairs toward the audience — just as we turned the lights out. (Our shows were "big" on blackouts!) Then, from the side of the set but on the ground level where the audience was standing, I ran out in front of the crowd, wearing the devil mask! That was our "Boo!," and it scared 'em real good.

The funny thing about Rick's demon and devil masks was that, a few years later, when Rick was working on *Star Wars*, he borrowed both of them back from me to use in the film's cantina sequences — he needed all the monster heads he could get! (While most of *Star Wars* was shot in England, the cantina scene shots that Rick did were filmed here in the States, in the San Fernando Valley.) So two of the masks that appeared in *Star Wars* were built for this show.

Rick strikes a threatening pose as the demon.

"The Thing in the Attic" was at that point in time probably the scariest show we ever did, because it was moody, and because the levitation bit freaked some of the people out. Again, that was thanks to our resident genius Al Jerumanis. One of the unsung heroes of our Halloween shows, he also came up with gags for "Forbidden Planet," "The War of the Worlds" and "Return of the Time Machine." Al is a shy man, a very humble guy, and never boasts about anything, so I'll say it because he won't: He was responsible for making "The Thing in the Attic" work. Without him, we wouldn't have had a show.

On a personal note, "Thing in the Attic" was certainly the scariest Halloween show for *me* — nothing to do with the presentation itself, but because of something that happened one night during its run. I was in the backyard between performances when one of the guys heading the line came back and he said, "Bob, you better come out here. We have some potential

Elaine Baker as the possessed girl floats above her bed on the levitation device created by Al Jerumanis.

problems." What had happened was, a motorcycle gang showed up. A bona fide motorcycle gang of about 12 guys who had parked their 'cycles all across the street, completely blocking the street off. Real Hell's Angels types — leather, chains, the works. I thought, "Oh-oh…"

Thinking up a way of maybe getting them out of there fairly quickly, I walked up to the group. As I approached, I was trying to figure out which one of them was "the head guy," but they *all* looked like "head guys" — this was a rough-looking bunch! I said, "Hey, fellas, since there's a whole bunch of you, would you like to go ahead of the line? We'll put you in like a special group." And to my surprise (and relief), one of the guys said, almost sweetly,

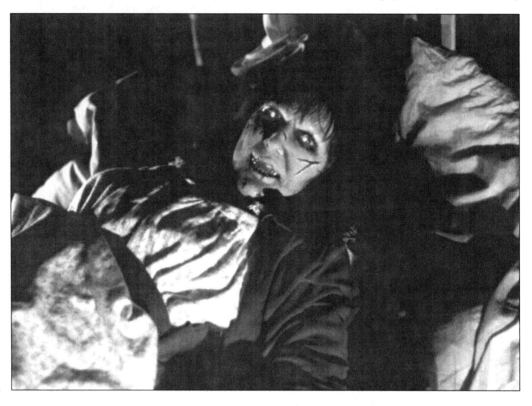

A great shot of Elaine in gruesome makeup as the possessed girl with her eyes literally glowing with hatred.

"Oh, no, man. We'll stand in the line. No problem!" They went to the back of the line, which was probably two-thirds of the way down the block, and they gave nobody any problems at all. I thought they might start hassling people, but they didn't; in fact, they began joking with other people in the line, and they were great. Nevertheless, after they saw the show, I went out front to make sure they got out of there without incident, and now all of a sudden I realized that they were looking for "the head guy" of the show — in other words, me. One of 'em was going around asking people, "Who's headin' this show? Who's in charge here?" With a gulp, I told him, "I guess that'd be me."

The guy came over to me and he said, "Man, that was incredible. It is *so* cool, what you're doin' for the kids and for the other people. You don't even *charge*." (We never charged for any show.) He said, "Listen, man: If anybody ever gives you a hassle about this, you let us know and we'll come and bust some heads!" And with that, they got on their 'cycles and roared off into the night.

1975: ''The War Of The Worlds''

Halloween 1975, I thought I had let myself in for a lot of trouble: For our show "The War of the Worlds," we built a spaceship in back of my house that stood 30 feet tall. And the night before the show was scheduled to start, a severe windstorm came up. We get a

ever happened in the past was
to rebuild the whole thing the
was coming right through the

Jerumanis who had engineered
hip is so large, how are we going
nd he figured out how it should
didn't even move. In fact, about

The 30-foot
spaceship that
"crashed" into the
Burns home for our
"War of the Worlds"
show.

a week later, after the show had closed, we went to dismantle the spaceship and we found
that we had to use *sledgehammers* to knock it down! I think that son of a gun would still be
there today if we hadn't — it was engineered that well. That was the genius of Al Jerumanis.

The spaceship was gigantic, and very impressive — the "look" of it had been designed by
Mike Minor. We also built a fake wall that looked very much like the wall of our house (we
even put a window in it and stuccoed it to make it look identical to the existing walls) and
had the spaceship jutting up out of a hole in that wall, as though the spaceship had crashed
right into the back of our house. Funnily enough, it looked so totally realistic that a few of
my neighbors thought I'd gone a little too far and actually crashed my own house in!

We were starting to get real rambunctious when we decided to be a big-scale show like
"The War of the Worlds." (Once again, it was Mike Minor who came up with the idea.) We
knew we couldn't "do the movie"; even with the large, fabulous crew we had by that time, we
couldn't make a Martian war machine big enough. So we decided to do a combination of
the original H.G. Wells novel and the Orson Welles radio show. Tommy Scherman made
three great-looking Martians, octopoid-looking things with four tentacles (two in the front
and two in the back). two glowing eyes, a semi-nose and a lip-less mouth. Tom made them
almost exactly from the description in the book.

Once again our old buddy Charlie Dugdale was the star, playing a radio reporter standing
in the crater created by the crash-landed alien spaceship. To get across that this was a "period

piece" (set in 1938, like the Orson Welles radio show), I borrowed from CBS Radio a 1938-39 microphone that Charlie spoke into as he surveyed the weird scene. "Ladies and gentlemen, I don't know exactly what this ship is, but there are three state troopers here now and we're trying to figure out what's going on…" he announced. An off-stage light blinked the way the light on top of a police car would, adding to the excitement of the piece. Then Charlie gasped, "Wait a minute! Now we're starting to hear strange noises coming out of this ship…!"

As Charlie continued to broadcast, a hatch cover in the side of the spaceship started to rotate and then fell open, and one of Tommy Scherman's Martians appeared in the

Reporter Charlie Dugdale (on left with microphone) "broadcasts" about the horrible Martian that has just crawled out through the spacecraft hatch.

opening, its tentacles reaching out toward the audience. "Oh, my God," Charlie gasped, proceeding then to describe to his "radio audience" how hideous this thing looked. At this point, one trooper got brave and decided to try to communicate with the alien. He came toward it waving a handkerchief like a white flag and, of course, the Martian zapped him.

What the audience saw and heard were a big flash that momentarily blinded them; a ray gun-type sound that was like nothing they'd ever heard in their lives; and white fog that rose up around the screaming trooper and then became red. By the time the fog cleared, just seconds later, the trooper was gone.

It took a lot of very innovative people to create this effect. My friend Craig Newswanger, a genius electrical guy, created the blinding light. The ray gun sound was created by my friend Ben Burtt, a sound effects expert who was then working on *Star Wars* — and had created that sound for use in the movie!*

Making the trooper disappear involved a fog machine that was on the set under the lip of the crater where the audience couldn't see them. When the trooper got zapped, our fog machine operator Jim started this fog coming out, covering him with fog as he screamed and sank to his knees. Jim also operated a red light on a dimmer; a twist of a switch and suddenly the fog was glowing a god-awful blood red. And by the time the fog began to settle

---

* Ben is now the biggest sound effects guy in the world, with I-don't-know-how-many Academy Awards and Special Achievement Awards to show for all his work.

and the audience could see the set again, the trooper had slipped unseen under the crater lip, hiding alongside Jim. It was a simple trick, but sometimes the simplest tricks work best.

The "Boo!" this time: A fake wall (complete with window) had been built across the front of my nearby garage…and, behind this wall, the garage door was up and a second Martian was hidden inside. Every performance, we tried to position a lady from the audience near that window, and at the end of the presentation, after the trooper disintegrated, the tentacles would come out of the garage and grab her (or who*ever* was out there). *Nobody* was ready for that!

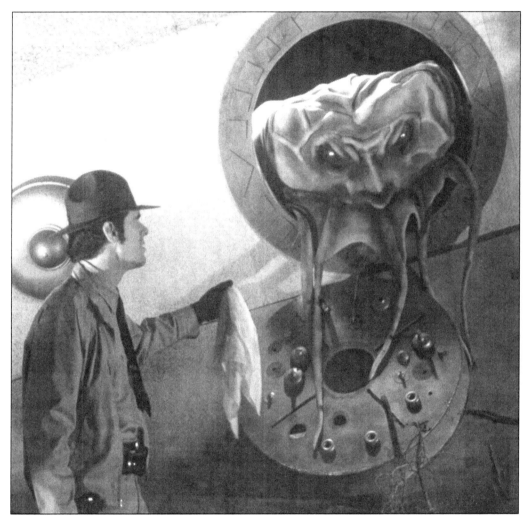

A brave trooper attempts to communicate with the Martian emerging from the spacecraft.

One last note about that show: Once again, one of the guys heading the line came and found me and said, "Bob, you better come out here." I thought, "Here we go again," remembering the motorcycle gang from the "Thing in the Attic" show, but this time what was being brought to my attention was the arrival of a Gray Line tour bus, packed with people who'd come all the way up from Orange County — maybe 40 miles! They'd seen a story about our show on the local CBS news, chartered a bus and there they were, over three dozen of 'em. Because they had come so far, we asked the people who were already in line if it would be was okay to let them go in right away, and everybody said sure, fine. The bus driver, a big burly guy, saw the show twice, and I think he got more of a kick out of it than anybody. "That was worth the trip!" he told me.

Nothing like that had ever happened before, and we started to get an idea of how well-established, and far-reaching, our Halloween shows had become.

1976: "Return Of The Time Machine"

Some of the behind-the-scenes things that happened on our 1976 show "Return of the Time Machine" have already been mentioned in the George Pal chapter. David Gerrold wrote the script and also played the Time Traveler, alternating with Charlie Dugdale (the two of them spelled each other).

The show began with the Time Traveler on a lab set, getting into the Time Machine and

Dennis Muren shoots a scene for our coverage of the "Return of the Time Machine" show.

starting to work it. At that point, the background went dark. The audience never lost track of him, he was always there in front of them in the Time Machine, but in darkness. There was the effect of shooting stars streaking past as he hit the "explosion in time," and then after a few more moments the lights came back up real fast and there he was in the cave of the Morlocks. Here again, perhaps needless to say at this point, Al Jerumanis was the one who engineered how to change the background from the lab to the Morlocks' cave: There were walls that we could spin around in the dark; on one side was the lab and on the other side were three-dimensional cave walls. Al engineered it so that we could do this whole change in two and a half seconds.

Throughout the show, the Time Traveler's thoughts were heard as narration, pre-recorded and played over a speaker in the top middle of the set (Charlie was the voice of the Time Traveler). The Time Traveler went through time, reappeared in the cave and realized where he was ("I found myself in the cave of the Morlocks…"). He got out of the Time Machine and took a long look at "The Sphinx" in the distance (actually a Mike Minor painting). Then he saw a skull on the ground, picked it up and examined it. Now he knew that the Morlocks were cannibals. All of a sudden the Morlocks appeared, six or seven of them, and they began closing in on him. "No, no," the Time Traveler pleaded (his only "live lines" in the show). "No! No, no, no…!" — and then, as they went in for the kill, *bam*, lights out!

Then, for our "Boo!," we had two Morlocks run right through the audience. We had to get mops for that one — it really shook 'em up!

At that same time (the fall of '76), we did something that we would never do again: We did a Magic Mountain show simultaneously. At Magic Mountain, there used to be a train (open on both sides) that went around the whole perimeter of the park. Our job was to scare the passengers who didn't know they were going to *be* scared. These were people who had gotten on the train just to get from one side of the park to the other.

In the back of the park was a place they called the North Forty, where people on the train could see cows and horses and some buffalo. At night, after the animals were locked away, we did our show, "Heap Valley," out there. I created the Heaps, which were weird-looking,

One of Mike Minor's wonderful backdrop paintings for "Return of the Time Machine."

Dennis Muren (his hand in the air) and crew working on the sets for "Return of the Time Machine." Dennis also created the show's lighting effects.

mutated trees — pretty scary-looking. We put seven of them in a gully in the North Forty that the train had to pass through, and waited for our "audience."

Before the people saw the Heaps, a "storm" would begin. We had a Ritter fan, which is a giant wind machine with six or seven blades on it. I believe it's run by a plane engine, and you can use it to produce hurricane-like winds. (I think that's what they used in the silent comedy *Steamboat Bill, Jr.,* with Buster Keaton, in the scene where the whole town blows away!) We had that, we set up some strobe lights as lightning, and I made up a thunderclaps-and-wind soundtrack to enhance the experience.

The train would get into this middle-of-nowhere section of the park where it was darker than pitch, and the "storm" would begin, complete with the cold wind. (And it *was* cold wind — it chilled you to the bone!) Then the people saw these tree-type things, the Heaps, on both sides of the train. They were all "posed," they just looked like a bunch of really ugly, gnarly trees, but as the train went by, they came alive and their big arms reached out for the people! (Inside the Heaps were guys I had taught what to do.) It scared the hell out of the people on the train — it happened very fast, and they just weren't ready for it. One of the funniest things about Heap Valley was the sight of the train as it pulled into a station just a few seconds after their encounter with the Heaps: Everyone on the train was bunched up in the middles of the long seats that ran from one side of the train to the other!

We — me, Tom, Mike, most of the "Halloween crew" — did that at the same time we did "Return of the Time Machine," and it was a real hassle working the two things simultaneously. In 1977 and '78, two years when Kathy and I did not put on our Halloween show, we worked out at Magic Mountain again. In '77, they hired us to come out and restage the Heap Valley show, and they also rented my Jekyll-and-Hyde idea. I went out and taught them how to make-up the guys who'd be playing Jekyll and Hyde and I gave them the red makeups and the gels and everything else they needed. Then in '78, Magic Mountain did not only "Heap Valley" and "Dr. Jekyll and Mr. Hyde," but they added "Alien Invasion," an adaptation of our "War of the Worlds" show. Magic Mountain built a spaceship, different from what we had, but they rented our Martians and we ran the show. I lined up some of my crew and we went out there, Mike and Tom and a lot of the crew. (And we all got paid too!) "Alien Invasion" became a yearly thing at Magic Mountain, slightly different every year and culminating in 1981 with a show now called "Nightmare Express" that involved not just the spaceship and the Martians but a bunch of actors playing an army unit that commandeered the train for a battle with six or seven Goombahs! Tommy and I built the new Goombahs, which had legs so they could stand up in the North Forty, and my pal Joe Viskocil did all kinds of flash pot stuff for us — the soldiers had fake bazookas and Joe was setting off big explosions all over the place, so it looked like the Army guys were firing at the Goombahs. There was even a repeat of the disintegration gag from our "War of the Worlds" show, with a soldier being zapped by a spaceship ray gun and disappearing from sight — right in the middle of an open field. Again it was a case of fog and red lights being used to keep the audience (the people on the train) from seeing the soldier drop into a pit — where Kathy was working the fog machine and our friend Dorothy Fontana was working the lights! It was a pretty elaborate show, and the last show we did.

Doing the Magic Mountain shows was fun because we reached a bigger audience than we could doing them at my house. But it didn't have the same feeling for all of us (the crew and Kathy and me) as doing it at the house. Our shows were completely under our control. At Magic Mountain, we had to compromise a lot with the people who ran the place. I'm still glad that we did them as we got paid and it was our first experience doing shows for a mass audience. I guess we were doing it right as they kept asking for us to come back year after year.

But, if I had my druthers I'd rather do it at home.

1979: "Alien"

I saw *Alien* when 20th Century-Fox released it in 1979, on the second day of its run, and I liked it, especially the sets and the effects stuff. I liked them enough that I thought, "This has got to be the Halloween show this year." And then, almost magically, things started coming together in an amazing way.

The KCBS morning show *Panorama Pacific* had two of the stars of *Alien*, Tom Skerritt

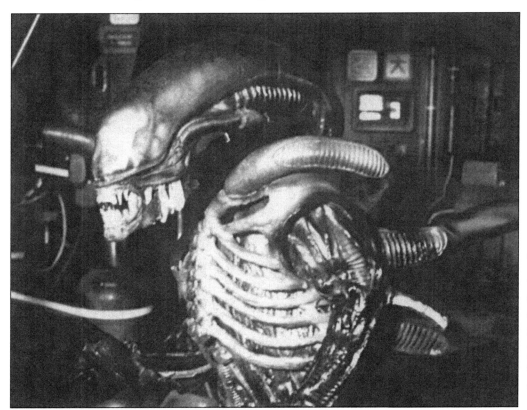

Tom De Veronica suited up to play the Alien. Three others guys, including me, took turns portraying the deadly creature in our show.

and (I think) Harry Dean Stanton, on as guests, and two publicity men from 20th Century-Fox were there too, backstage. I told them about the Halloween shows that we had done and said that I'd really love to do one on *Alien* if I could get permission. They had no idea what I was talking about. It occurred to me that if I sent them a copy of the recent *Starlog* magazine issue which featured an article on the history of our shows (we even made the cover), they'd know that I was legit. I got their address from them and the next day, fingers crossed, I put it in the mail to Tom (one of the two guys) care of the publicity department of 20th Century-Fox.

To my delight, Tom called me back three days later and said, "We read it, and it's pretty interesting. It's *very* interesting." A pause. "If you want to do it, go 'head." I felt like I was floating on air.

Tom imposed a few conditions on me: He said to make sure that 20th Century-Fox was mentioned in connection with the show, things like that, and I told him, "That's not a problem." Then, a day later, he called me again and said, "You know, we've got some of the props from *Alien* here at Fox — they've been shipped over from England. If you'd like to borrow some of them…" I was stunned! He told me to come out and take a look, and I did: In a warehouse area at 20th Century-Fox, in what's now called Century City, there was all these fantastic props from the movie — weapons, an alien detector, costumes, even the mechanical face hugger. I was allowed to borrow all kinds of stuff — I was amazed that this was even happening. Except for reading that *Starlog* article, they didn't know me from a hole in the mud! But Tom said, "Well, that article read real well, and you seem to be a trustworthy guy…" If that was good enough for him, it was good enough for me! One more condition was imposed on me: Audience members couldn't take pictures of the props. I said that would be fine. I brought a bunch of this stuff home and I called Tommy Scherman and several of the other key crew guys and I told them what had happened ("You're not gonna believe this…") and "We *gotta* do *Alien* now." And they all said, okay, we'll do it.

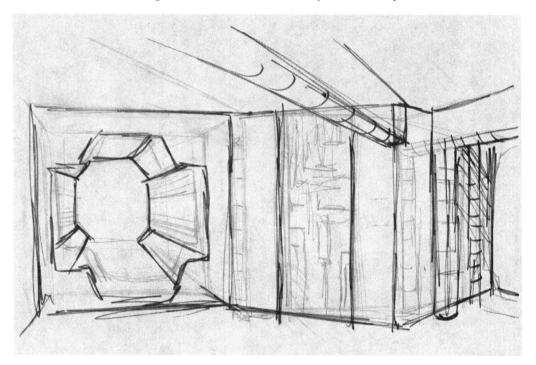

Mike Minor's sketches were used as the plans for constructing our "Alien" show sets.

The plot we worked up involved a space explorer menaced on a spooky spaceship set by the Alien. We were trying to figure out who to cast in the part — this was the only Halloween presentation we ever did that was really pretty much a one-actor show involving live dialogue. (I thought for a moment I might do it myself, but then I remembered I'm not that good of an actor!) One night I was talking about this to actor Walter Koenig, a buddy of mine,* telling him I was trying to find an actor, and he said, "Hey, *I'll* do it for you." *I* wasn't going to ask him to consider doing it, because that's his *profession* — you don't ask somebody a favor when it's their profession. But he volunteered and said he'd love to do it. (Then, of course, later on he said, "Never ask me again! *Never ask me again!*," after doing like 50 performances a night!

Mike's crew paid attention to every little detail when building the "Alien" sets.

Bob and Denny Skotak and Dorothy Fontana were the key people making the Alien costume for our show. The actual head used in the movie was over at Don Post Studios; they were planning to make a mask of it at one time, but the deal fell through. We got the use of the real head but had to make the rest of the costume.

The set that was built for the "Alien" show was amazing: An enclosed spaceship corridor ran down our driveway and into my backyard; it looked very "busy" with pipes, valves, equipment and gadgets everywhere. The audience walked down that corridor until they got to a larger area that we had dressed as close to the movie as possible. Walter, playing an Alien-hunting spaceman, appeared through an open hatchway, guided to this section of the spaceship by the alien detector he's carrying and by two female voices (Kathy and Dorothy Fontana playing other crew members) heard over an intercom. Talking to the intercom women, Walter described what he was doing: "My detector's registering…I think the Alien is on Level One. I'm going to go up and see…" He climbed a ladder (the intercom women were saying things like, "Be careful… be careful…!") and got to the top, and then you heard him scream. And when he came down, he had got a face hugger hooked to him!

Fortunately the spaceman was able to pull the face hugger off of him and throw it to one side. (We used a Don Post face hugger prototype, never marketed.) He regained his composure and the suspense began to mount again, and then there was a loud screech — but all that had happened was, Walter had (supposedly) stepped on the spaceship's cat.

Then we did one or our "misdirection" things: A big crash was heard, and Walter told the audience, "It's in the back corridor!" and cautiously started walking in that direction, away from the audience. Then, reacting to what he was seeing on his alien detector, he swung around to face the audience again, but looking up and behind them and crying out, "Oh, my God!" An instant later, there was a screech from above and behind the audience and they turned to see the Alien itself, just feet away and moving toward them. Then, of course — the blackout.

---

* It's funny: People who know I'm a friend of Walter's think it's because he was Chekov on *Star Trek*. But I'm no Trekker at all. The truth is that Walter is a toy figure collector like I am; we met at a party one night and started talking about collecting figures, and we became real friends.

The Alien was played by my next door neighbor Tom De Veronica. During one performance, his hand happened to touch a woman in the audience — and she fainted dead away! Two guys had to help her out of the place, and they heard her say she "never wanted to see anything like this again." I guess today we would have been sued.

Walter was great, a big asset to the show, and he was in almost every performance. Another guy did occasionally spell him — Walter was directing some acting classes at that time, and we had one of his own students play the part two or three times so that Walter could take potty breaks. At that time, my opinion was that it was the best show we ever did, and the most involved.

Walter Koenig, just below the Alien's jaw, surrounded by part of the crew responsible for our "Alien" show.

I invited some of the 20th Century-Fox execs to come see the show — I didn't think they would, but I thought, "I'd better make the gesture." To my delight, they showed up with their wives. I'll never forget, as we were walking down the main corridor, one of them said, "My God, this looks just like our set. And our set cost hundreds of thousands of dollars!" I said, "Well, you just didn't have the right crew. You needed the Bob Burns Crew!," and he said, "Gosh, I guess we did!" They enjoyed the show so much, they stayed and saw it twice.

The great offshoot of this experience was that, when the show was over and I called the Fox publicity department to make arrangements to bring the props back, Tom said, "Y'know, we're been talking it over here, and…would you like to keep that stuff?" I said yes as soon as I was able to lift my jaw up off the floor. I was flabbergasted! He said, "We normally don't do this, and we probably won't do it again, but you seem like a very trustworthy guy." They'd heard I was planning to one day have a museum of SF props in my house, and he said, "Keep 'em for that." Then he said, "We have some other props from *Alien* that we would like to send you if that's okay. We'll send a truck over." Once again I had to lift my jaw up off the floor.

I didn't realize what I was getting into. I took a day off from work and was expecting maybe a pickup truck when a truck with a crane on it pulled up in front of my house. Then, maybe 20 minutes later, a semi truck, an 18-wheeler, arrived. This truck brought a 2100-pound crate plus a lot of other crates and boxes of various sizes! I took pictures as the crane swung this stuff over the top of my house to deposit it in my backyard, because I didn't think anyone would ever believe me. One of the props turned out to be the miniature of the refinery seen at the beginning of the movie. Then that truck and the crane left, and *another* truck loaded with stuff showed up! I called Kathy at work and said, "You gotta come home. You gotta see this. You can't believe what's happening here…" Between the *Starlog* article and then the executives' visit to the show itself, the Fox guys were sure I was "okay" and I became the curator of all this great stuff, the 12-foot *Nostromo* model, the derelict spacecraft (about the same size), a staggering amount of stuff. To this day, I've got most of it.

The whole "Alien" show experience, before, during and after, was amazing.

1982: "Creature From The Black Lagoon"

Our "Alien" show was such a success, people were surprised that we didn't do shows in 1980 and '81. But the reason we had a few years off was that the movie careers of some of our key crew members were beginning to take off. Dennis Muren moved up north to work for Industrial Light & Magic, Mike Minor was involved with the *Star Trek* movies, Tommy Scherman was working on commercials — *every*body got too busy to do anything. (A lot of the people who worked on the shows became big people in the industry — Dennis, Rick Baker, Bob and Dennis Skotak, Doug Beswick, Bill Malone and so on.) We did manage to find a window of opportunity and do a show in 1982, "Creature from the Black Lagoon," but after that, this new problem of "Everybody's too busy" reared up again. "Creature" turned out to be our last show before a 20-year "hiatus."

For the "Creature" show, we built a whole cave (designed by Mike Minor) down my driveway and into the backyard. Just like the studios might make a cave on a soundstage, we used wooden flats and chicken wire, then covered it up with what's called industrial foil (thicker than the stuff you'd use in the kitchen). We used contact bond cement to glue the industrial foil to the chicken wire, and there was so much area to cover, we all had a buzz on after a while! It's a good thing we were working with it outside. *In*side, it would have

Bill Malone built this striking recreation of the Gill Man for our "Creature from the Black Lagoon" show.

probably killed us all! For the final texture, Mike sprayed the cave walls with a glue mixture he made up himself, then threw real fine sand and pebbles and stuff that adhered to it. The cave set was completely enclosed, ceiling and all.

There was one lucky accident during the preparations for the show. Walking around on the outside of the cave set, I accidentally ran into one of the walls — and suddenly there was this resonation, and also this weird feeling in my stomach. I'd started the chicken wire inside the walls vibrating, and it was like being in a big subwoofer! I went inside the cave and I had one of the crew guys pound on the outside, and again it hit me right in the stomach.

Our "Creature" show was dedicated to Chris Mueller (center), who sculpted the Creature head for the original film, seen here with Bill Malone. Right: The object of the original Creature's affection: Julie Adams on the set of our "Creature" show.

So now I put six or seven crew guys on one outside wall and six or seven on the opposite outside wall and had them start pounding — not with a cadence, but random.

My stomach felt like it feels during an earthquake. It was wild.

Denny Skotak and Dorothy Fontana (who had first met on our "Alien" show, and were now man and wife) hadn't arrived yet that day, so I told the crew, "Hey, I want to try this out when they come over…" When Denny and Dorothy arrived, I brought them into the cave and was talking to them and I used a cue word that the crew (hidden outside) was waiting for, a word that prompted them to start pounding. And when they did, Denny literally ran out of the place! Dorothy followed, but by the time she got outside, Denny had already made it to his car! They "bought" it — Denny especially. They thought it was a real earthquake.

In the show, a paleontologist carrying a battery-operated lantern took 25 people at a time, maybe 30, through the cave like he was just giving them an actual scientific tour. The paleontologist was an actor named John Stinson, and he was so good in the part that people thought he *was* a paleontologist. Bob Skotak used Styrofoam to make some "fossils" — trilobites, a crab-type creature and a couple other things that a paleontologist might actually find. These props were imbedded in the cave walls, and there were "field workers" dressed in tan uniforms and pith helmets examining them with flashlights and dusting them off with brushes, like real scientists would do. I was one of the field workers.

After John pointed out the field workers and the fossils to the audience, they proceeded downhill toward the main chamber of this cave. At that point, we simulated the earthquake, and it worked very well. There was the noise and the feeling of vibration, and even some Fuller's earth wafting down from the ceiling. It was very realistic and the people would get a little unsettled, because California *is* earthquake country. John would say, "Folks, it's all right, we have these tremors every day, this is nothing much…," alerting them that this was just part of the show, and then it would settle down.

In the main part of the cave, a roundish chamber we called "the grotto," was another field worker examining a fossil and also a cave pool. It was actually a Doughboy above-ground pool, three and a half or four feet high, but we made the sides look like rock so it would look like a natural formation. For atmosphere, there was a little fog drifting over the surface of the water.

"I want to show you the most interesting find so far," John told the audience, showing off a Gill Man-like fossil hand jutting out of the wall (just like at the beginning of the movie). "This looks sort of human, sort of amphibian…perhaps a cross of both. We don't know exactly what it is, but we're starting to study it…" Suddenly there was the sound of a big splash, as though somebody — or *something* — was in the pool. (When the audience wasn't looking, we had dropped a big bucket filled with rocks into the pool.) The water was rippling and the fog moving as a gal paleontologist working nearby babbled out, "Professor, what was that?" John brought the lantern over to the pool and looked down into it. Bubbles began to appear, like there was something just under the surface…

…And then, all of a sudden, the Creature came walking onto the set *behind* him, out of another tunnel. A pre-recorded Creature yell played on cue as he charged the audience. As usual, we had misdirected the audience, made them think the Creature would come out of the water. (That would be the natural assumption — why the heck would we go to the trouble of putting a pool in there if we weren't going to use it?) As the Creature came toward John and the audience, John used a kill switch on the top of the lantern to extinguish the light, so that now the audience would think the Creature was still coming at

Another impressive shot of Bill's terrific Creature costume.

them — but now in the dark! During the ten seconds or so of darkness that followed, there were cries and laughter — and usually a few blood-curdling screams. The Creature left the set unseen in the dark, and then John turned the light back on and said, "That's our show, folks. Happy Halloween." As always, the misdirection worked well. I watched a couple performances from the back of the group, and when the Creature appeared, the people backed up so fast and so hard that I got scrunched — it dang near left my imprint in the cave wall!

The Creature suit was made by Bill Malone. The head itself was a casting out of Universal's mold of the head of Ben Chapman, one of the men who played the Creature. I think that was the last-ever casting — Universal threw that mold away right after that. Bill sculpted the rest of the suit himself, and he did a beautiful job. Every scale was just like the one in the film. Bill and two other guys played the Creature in the show, which ran three nights: I think Bill worked the first night, and then a second guy the second night and a third guy the third.

Here again, I got a heads-up from one of the people in charge of the line that something was going on outside, making me flash back to the motorcycle gang and the tour bus incidents. But this time, it was a wonderful surprise: Julie Adams, star of the original *Creature from the Black Lagoon*, had heard about the show and was curious about it and, since she lived in the area, decided to show up. It was a total surprise to all of us. She saw the show and thought it was great, and said that being in our cave was very much like being in the cave Universal made for the movie. It was a thrill having her there, just as it was a thrill to have Glenn Strange show up for the Frankenstein tableau and George Pal for "Return of the Time Machine."

2002: ''The Thing''

After "Creature from the Black Lagoon," there were no more Halloween shows. Too many of the guys got really busy and just didn't have the time to do them any more. And without those guys, the rest of us were sunk. Then Tommy Scherman and Mike Minor both died, within several years of each other. They were both young guys, Tommy in his early 50s and Mike in his mid-40s, if I'm remembering right. Tommy died of lymphoma, Mike of AIDS. That just kind of broke my spirit, and now I became certain we'd never do a show again. They were our dynamos. Tommy and Mike were awesome together, a perfect team, and they'd become the hubs of our shows with their leadership.

So I just gave up. Dropped it. Some of the remainder of the old crew would occasionally call and get after me to do one last show, even Bob and Denny Skotak. But it just didn't seem like it would he possible. It certainly wouldn't be the same.

Capt. Hendry (Frank Dietz) and one of his soldiers discover the dead body of a scientist hanging in the greenhouse.

Then things started to move in that direction. A friend of mine, a Texan named Joe Riley, is a guy who does a lot of sculpting, and for Halloween 2000 he made a mask and hands of the Thing from the 1951 *The Thing from Another World*, just to wear to a Halloween party. I guess I'd mentioned to Joe at some point how much I'd always wanted to do a Halloween show around *The Thing*, and talking with him on the phone one day he said, "Well, I did a mask and hands. And if you ever decide you want to do a *Thing* show, I'll be glad to make up some masks and hands for you if you want." He e-mailed me some pictures of them, and I thought they looked pretty darn good. Good enough that, after 20 years, I now began

going back and forth in my own mind whether to do another show. When I threw the idea out to other people, including Bob and Denny Skotak and Dorothy Fontana, the response was always the same: "Oh, God, we'd *love* to do one again."

Well, that was no surprise coming from Dorothy: She always wanted to do a *Thing* show, because that's one of her favorite movies in the world. It was beginning to seem like it was the thing to do…to do "The Thing."

The thought was, do "The Thing" for Halloween 2001. Joe made and sent me two heads and two sets of hands and all systems were go — and then I got sick. I got sick and I *stayed* sick for six months with a severe sinus infection. I was in the hospital twice. All of a sudden, there was no way we could do it.

Then, finally, in 2002 I was feeling better and thinking about it again. But it was my friend Greg Nicotero who finally pushed it over the brink. He's a makeup artist and one of the three owners of KNB, the special effects and makeup company that has worked on such films as *From Dusk Till Dawn*, *Spy Kids*, *The Hulk* and many others. Greg said, "Bob, if you really want to do *The Thing*, I'll build all the props and stuff for you, the Thing costumes, whatever you want. I'll do it. I'll 'finance' that part of it." You just have to marvel at people like Greg. He is one of the nicest guys, in or out of the business, that I've ever known. He and his partners were doing two movies and a TV series at the same time and he still got all of the stuff done for our show. How cool is that?

The corridor set constructed for our "Thing" show.

Greg's beyond-generous offer was the little extra nudge that I needed: I officially made the *Thing* show a go. Dorothy wrote a script and I got together with what I considered the key personnel for our first show of the new millennium, among them Bob Skotak (who did the designs), Denny Skotak and Keith Myatt, my next-door neighbor, who was going to be our main set builder along with his sons Evan and John.

Our first unpleasant surprise came early this time: The world had changed quite a bit since Reagan was in the White House and we'd done our last show, "Creature." In the good old days, we usually started building sets and getting props together around the second week of September. This year, 2002, we found we had to have a lot of permits from the city of Burbank before we'd be allowed to do anything like what we were planning. Seven different permits, it turned out. That's just the way it is now. Twenty years ago there wasn't this problem, but nowadays with all the new safety rules and regulations and liability laws, there is. Especially after 9/11. We finally cleared all those hurdles, but by that time it was October 3 and we had like three weeks to do everything that remained to be done. Starting with the set!

I just started calling people and, sure enough, everyone who had offered to help came through. News of the show spread by word of mouth, and we wound up with a crew of like

50 people! And they were the most dedicated crew in the history of our Halloween shows…
the best crew we ever had. Some of them — quite a few of them — were teenagers. Our
last show, "Creature," was done before they were *born!*

A lot of the new crew people came in as novices. "I don't know how to hammer. I don't
even know how to paint. But just show me what to do and I'll do it." But, boy, by the time
we finished, they were all old pros. Sam Park, for instance — he wanted to work on the
show really bad. He said, "Bob, I don't know how to do any of this stuff, but I'll be a grunt.
I'll do anything." Well, Sam ended up being so good at the carpentry stuff that pretty soon

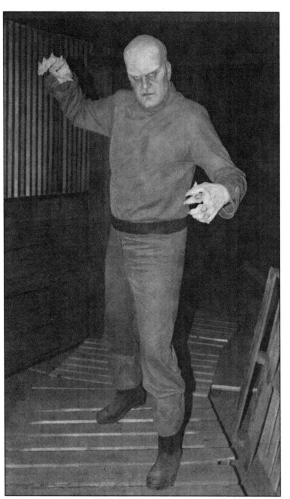

Jake Garber strikes a scary pose as The Thing.

he was teaching the other people how to do it! "I can have a
new career now," he told me! It was astonishing how these
people picked this stuff up. Some of 'em may have come in as
novices, but they all went out hardened veterans!

One of the things Kathy always loved about our shows
was the camaraderie of all the people. This group was laughing and giggling all the time, having a blast, even though we
were all under a lot of pressure trying to get it done in time.
We got everything done in the three weeks, which was just
a phenomenal accomplishment considering the size of the
project. If we didn't have this crew, the show would have never
got done. I wish I had room to mention all their names and
tell you about each and every one of 'em here, but I'd have to
write another whole chapter!

Our set this time was a replica of a corridor in the North
Pole experimental station where the movie *The Thing* took
place. L-shaped (and completely enclosed), it stretched
across my front yard and then turned down my driveway.
We even "dressed" the exterior of the set with fake snow
and icicles, to set the mood. The crew dubbed the place "Ice
Station Burns."

Next to the door through which the audience would enter,
14 to 18 people at a time, was a TV set playing a DVD of a
montage of black-and-white clips we had made up: footage
from the original movie plus new scenes designed by Bob and
Denny Skotak and shot by Patrick Myatt, Keith's other very
talented son. In one of the new scenes, the character of Capt.
Hendry tells the audience that he and his men are trapped in
this outpost with an alien that's trying to kill them.

When you entered, you were greeted by Capt. Hendry
(played by either Dan Roebuck or by Frank Dietz; they took turns), who tells more of the
backstory and points out a series of tableaux familiar to fans of the movie: a room with the
half-melted block of ice with the Thing-shaped impression in it; a window through which
you could see the Thing's severed but still-moving arm lying in the snow; a bin which, when
opened, spills out its contents, the mangled body of a sled dog. Opening another door causes
a dead human body to drop into sight head-first, a scientist killed and then suspended
upside-down by the Thing.

An urgent-sounding intercom voice (supplied by this book's co-author Tom Weaver, a
good friend with a great "radio voice") announces that the Thing is now in the building and
hunting them. Hendry hustles the audience to a spot in the corridor where they might be
safe. And now the Thing appears, moving ominously along a second corridor (the other part
of the L) toward the audience. But it turns out that Capt. Hendry has set up an electrical

trap — and the Thing walks right into it. After writhing in agony amidst flashing light and fog, the Thing dies and drops to the floor. Capt. Hendry walks over to the body, makes sure it is dead, and then, much relieved, begins making his goodbyes to the audience and leading them to an exit door. But opening it reveals a second Thing, who grabs the screaming Hendry and pulls him out through the door, which slams behind them.

Part of the reason "The Thing" was one of our best-ever shows was the fact that it had music from beginning to end. One day when I was in a small movie memorabilia store, telling the owners about our upcoming "Thing" show, a young fellow named Christopher Drake

Dan Roebuck as Capt. Hendry finds the body of a dog drained of blood. (Relax, folks. No animals were harmed in the making of this show.)

overheard and recognized me and introduced himself. He said, "Y'know, I'm a composer, and I'd love to do a score for your show." And then, only about two days later, he phoned me and he said, "I'd like to bring over some sample stuff I just did." He came and gave me the CD and I played it on the stereo in my living room, and it was fabulous! A terribly nice guy, Chris went on to compose music for the whole show, wall to wall, and it was just incredible. That music, as far as I'm concerned, was the frosting on the cake, the thing that made the show "complete." I consider that a milestone in the history of our Halloween shows, actually having a score — a terrific score — composed for one of them.

The turnout for the show was great, even though I tried to avoid publicity this time. NBC found out about it and they wanted to come over and cover it; so did *The Los Angeles Times*. But I told them both no. We'd had 4500 people at the "Creature" show and I was concerned that we'd get that many or more this time, and we wouldn't be able to handle it. I let a couple local newspapers carry stories, and crossed my fingers that we wouldn't get hit too bad. We got about 2100 people through there to see "The Thing," which was enough. It had been originally scheduled for just two nights, but the response to announcements proved so popular it wound up going five — from Wednesday clear through Sunday.

We got a good celebrity turnout for "The Thing," among them Ann Robinson, Rick Baker, Guillermo del Toro, Frank Darabont, John Landis, Mick Garris and Rob Zombie. Tom Weaver was friendly with two of the actors from the original *Thing*, Bob Cornthwaite and

William Self, and invited them to come, and both promised they'd be there. Bob couldn't make it, unfortunately; he was a resident of the Motion Picture Home, which got hit with an intestinal virus the week of the show. The Home was quarantined and nobody could get in or out, including Bob! But William Self came, with his son, and he said he was very impressed with the show. I asked him, "How close do you think our set came to the one that you guys used?," and he said, "This is extremely close to the set that we had in *The Thing*. This is an excellent reproduction of the set." I was real thrilled to hear that, and of course passed his comment along on to the crew.

A supporting player in the movie *The Thing from Another World*, William Self stopped by the show. Here he is (on left) with me and Jake Garber.

Among the celebrities who turned out for the show was our old friend, makeup wizard Rick Baker.

Also passing through the show were our longtime friends Frankie Thomas and Jan Merlin, stars of the *Tom Corbett, Space Cadet* TV series of the 1950s. Jan was impressed with the fact that the show was "all around you"; you could look around 360 degrees and there was always something *there*. "Being in this type of thing," he told me, "you're *still* the audience, but at the same time you're also in the show. I've seen a lot of 'theater in the round' and stuff like that, but I've never before seen a presentation that I felt like I was *involved* in. It had music, it had sound effects, it had everything a movie would have — but you're *there*. You're *surrounded* by it." He said it was one of the greatest experiences of that type he'd ever had. These were compliments I'll never forget.

Doing the "Thing" show in 2002 after a 20-year hiatus really felt great. The only sad thing for Kathy and me was that we didn't have Mike or Tom's presence. But I have to say again, the new crew combined with what was left of the old crew did a fantastic job. Mike and Tom would have been so proud. I do feel that their hands and spirits were guiding us a bit.

"The Thing" was an incredible show that proved that if you have a crew like the one we had, folks who have lots of imagination and love for the genre, you can't lose. Kathy and I have been blessed through the years with the most wonderful friends that anyone could have. They also happen to be extremely talented. We may never be rich with money but we're so very rich with friends and in this old world that is what really matters. If any of our crew old or new reads this, please know that Kathy and I love you all and feel we are the luckiest people in the world in knowing you.

And to any and all readers who have never had an opportunity to see one of our Halloween shows, here's a standing invitation: If we ever put on another show, you're personally invited. Tickets and reservations are never required. There'll be no admission fee. Like all our past shows, it'll be for fun and for free. Just bring your child-like wonder and your happy heart.

We may need it for a prop.

Kathy and I, and other members of our Halloween crew, also staged some scary shows at Valencia, California's Magic Mountain amusement park in the 1970s and early '80s; they're described on pages 197-199 and 209-210. Here are some photos from those shows.

For our 1976 Magic Mountain show, we built seven mutant trees ("The Heaps") that passengers on an open-sided train would see as they passed through a dark and lonely section of the park. What these folks didn't know was that there was a guy inside each tree, and that their big branches would grab at them.

One of the Heaps attacks the train. Notice that every passenger has scooted out of reach!

Our Magic Mountain show "Alien Invasion" was an adaptation of the "War of the Worlds" presentation we'd done at home in 1975. In this shot, a Martian appears out of the spaceship and directs a disintegrating ray at one of the soldiers.

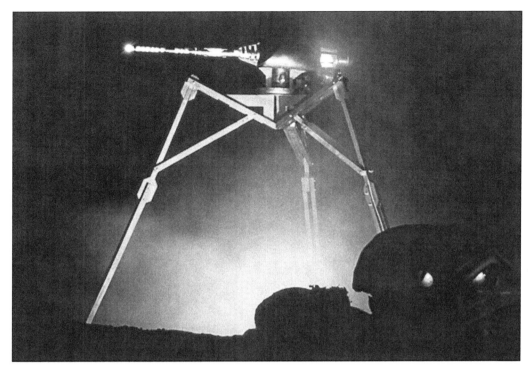

A Martian heat ray machine rises out of a pit in the earth to frighten the Magic Mountain train passengers.

The heat ray (left) "endangers" the train (right).

Another shot of the heat ray attacking the train. Notice the spaceship in the middle of the background.

Eight Goombahs (built by Tom Scherman and me) later joined the alien invasion force at Magic Mountain. At the end of the last-ever performance, we blew the hell out of them with heavy explosive charges we had put inside 'em. The train passengers who saw this last show gave us a real big round of applause.

Index

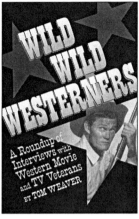

CPSIA information can be obtained at www.ICGtesting.com
Printed in the USA
BVOW052243190213

313725BV00018B/454/P